Slavery in the United States: A Narrative of the Life and Adventures of Charles Ball

Charles Ball

SLAVERY IN THE UNITED STATES:

A NARRATIVE OF THE LIFE AND ADVENTURES OF CHARLES BALL,

A BLACK MAN, WHO LIVED FORTY YEARS IN MARYLAND, SOUTH CAROLINA AND GEORGIA, AS A SLAVE, UNDER VARIOUS MASTERS, AND WAS ONE YEAR IN THE NAVY WITH COMMODORE BARNEY, DURING THE LATE WAR. CONTAINING AN ACCOUNT OF THE MANNERS AND USAGES OF THE PLANTERS AND SLAVEHOLDERS OF THE SOUTH—A DESCRIPTION OF THE CONDITION AND TREATMENT OF THE SLAVES, WITH OBSERVATIONS UPON THE STATE OF MORALS AMONGST THE COTTON PLANTERS, AND THE PERILS AND SUFFERINGS OF A FUGITIVE SLAVE, WHO TWICE ESCAPED FROM THE COTTON COUNTRY.

1837.

The

CABINET OF FREEDOM

under the supervision of

The Rev. William Jay,
Prof. Cush. of the University of New York, and
Loret. Smith, Esq.

AM I NOT A MAN AND A BROTHER

NEW YORK.

Published by John S. Taylor

1836.

INTRODUCTION

In giving a place in the CABINET OF FREEDOM to the ensuing narrative, it is deemed proper to accompany it with some remarks. The reader will be desirous to know how far it is entitled to his belief, and the editors of the Cabinet are equally desirous that he should not be misled. They have been furnished with the following certificate:

"Lewistown, Pa., July 18th, 1836.

"We, the undersigned, certify that we have read the book called 'CHARLES BALL'—that we know the black man whose narrative is given in this book, and have heard him relate the principal matters contained in the book concerning himself, long before the book was published.

"DAVID W. HOLINGS.
"W. P. ELLIOTT."*

This certificate establishes the fact, that the subject of the narrative is not a fictitious personage. Mr. Fisher, (the author) intimates in his preface, what is, indeed, sufficiently obvious from the felicity of his style, that the *language* of the book is not that of the unlettered slave, whose adventures he records. A similar intimation might with equal propriety have been given, in reference to the various profound and interesting reflections interspersed throughout the work. The author states, in a private communication, that many of the anecdotes in the book illustrative of southern society were not obtained from Ball, but from other and creditable sources; he avers, however, that all the facts which relate personally to the fugitive, were received from his own lips. How far this personal narrative is true is a question which each reader must, of course, decide for himself.

It is possible, and not improbable, that vanity may have induced the hero to exaggerate his exploits, and that ignorance and forgetfulness may in some instances, have rendered his tale discordant. The hardships he encountered in his various attempts to escape from bondage, are indeed extreme, but are not for that reason incredible, since it is difficult to estimate the amount of human suffering that can be voluntarily endured for an adequate object. The account of his voyage from Savannah to Philadelphia, strange as it is, derives strong confirmation from the following still more extraordinary account taken from a New York journal.

"The captain of a vessel from North Carolina, called on the police for advisement respecting a slave he had unconsciously brought away in his vessel, under the following curious circumstances. Three or four days after he had got to sea he began to be haunted every hour with tones of distress, seemingly proceeding from a human voice in the very lowest part of the vessel. A particular scrutiny was finally instituted, and it was concluded, that the creature, whatever and whoever it might be, must be confined down in the run, under the cabin floor, and on boring a hole with an auger, and demanding 'Who's there?' a feeble voice responded, 'Poor negro, massa!' It was clear enough then, that some run-away negro had hid himself there, before they sailed, trusting to Providence for his ultimate escape. Having discovered him, however, it was impossible to give him relief, for the captain had stowed even the cabin so completely full of cotton as but just to leave room for a small table for himself and the mate to eat on, and as for unloading at sea, that was pretty much out of the question. Accordingly there he had to lie, stretched at full length, for a tedious interval of *thirteen* days, till the vessel arrived in port and unloaded, receiving his food and drink through the auger hole.

"The fellow's story is, now he is released, that being determined to get away from slavery, he supplied himself with eggs, and biscuit, and some jugs of water, which latter he was just on the point of depositing in his lurking place, when he discovered the captain at a distance coming on board, and had to hurry down as fast as possible and leave them. That he lived on nothing but his eggs and biscuit till discovered by the captain; not even getting a drop of water, except what he had the good fortune to catch in his hand one day, when a vessel of water in the cabin was upset during a squall, and some of it ran down through the cracks of the floor over him." — *Commercial Advertiser*, 1822.

With regard to the pictures given in this work of the internal Slave-trade, and of the economy of a cotton plantation, it may be observed, that they are perfectly consistent, not only with the various other representations which have from time to time been made by unimpeachable witnesses, but also with the irresponsible despotism which is vested by law and custom, in southern masters. That despotism within the confines of a plantation, is more absolute and irresistible than any that was ever wielded by a Roman emperor. The power of the latter, when no longer supportable, was terminated by revolt or personal violence, and often with impunity. But to the, despotism of the master, there is scarcely any conceivable limit, and from its cruelty there is no refuge. His plantation is his empire, his labourers are his subjects, and revolt and violence, instead of abridging his power, are followed by inevitable and horrible punishment. The laws of the land do not, indeed, authorize the master to take life, but they do not forbid him to wear it out by excessive toil.

Public opinion sometimes exercises a more controlling influence than law, and it may perhaps be supposed, that it throws its shield before the helpless slave. But it should be recollected; that public opinion at the south is the opinion of the masters themselves, and that they are individually amenable to it, chiefly in regard to their intercourse with each other as citizens, and not in regard to the authority they exercise over their "property." In his negro quarters, or his cotton field, the planter is withdrawn from the gaze of his neighbours who have neither the right, nor the disposition, to scrutinize his conduct. He is there an unquestioned despot, and his vassals have no press to proclaim their wrongs, no tribunal to petition for a redress of grievances, and are prohibited from entering a Court of Justice as suitors, or even as witnesses against any individual whose complexion is not coloured like their own. Hence it follows, that the master is virtually the arbiter of life and death. All history and all our knowledge of human nature unite in bearing testimony to the hardening and corrupting influence of irresponsible power on its possessor. Some, indeed, are shielded against this influence by natural benevolence, or religious principle; and it is creditable to Ball's candour, that he mentions instances of kindness on the part of the masters—but such instances must necessarily, from the very constitution of our nature, be exceptions to the general rule. The cruelty and detestable injustice of the slave code in all ages, and in all countries, conclusively establishes the general effect of slavery in paralyzing the moral sense.

Some readers may be disposed to doubt Ball's veracity on account of the atrocious cruelties he relates. Such a doubt evinces a very imperfect acquaintance with southern feelings and manners. The cruelties recorded in the narrative, were practised by a few individuals, but if assembled multitudes, in the slave-states can publicly unite in perpetrating still greater atrocities, then surely the story told by Ball is not incredible.

The following deeds of horror recounted by the public journals, render tame and insignificant the acts of cruelty detailed in the work before us.

"Tuscaloosa, Alabama.

"HORRID OCCURRENCE.—Some time, during the last week, one of those outrageous transactions, and we really think disgraceful to the character of civilized man, took place near the north-east boundary line of Perry, adjoining Bibb and Autauga counties. The circumstances, we are informed by a gentleman from that county, are—that a Mr. McNeilly having lost some clothing, or other property of no great value, the slave of a neighbouring planter was charged with the theft. McNeilly, in company with his brother, found the negro driving his master's wagon—they seized him, and either did, or were about to chastise him, when the negro stabbed McNeilly so that he died in an hour afterwards. The negro was taken before a justice of the peace, who, after serious deliberation, waived his authority, perhaps through fear, as the crowd of persons from the above counties had collected to the number of seventy or eighty men, near Mr. People's (the justice) house. He acted as president of the mob, and put the vote, when it was decided he should be immediately executed by beingiBURNT TO DEATH. The sable culprit was led to a tree and tied to it, and a large quantity of pine knots collected and placed round him, and the fatal torch applied to the pile, even against the remonstrances of several gentlemen who were present, and the miserable being was, in a short time, burnt to ashes.

"This is the SECOND negro who has been THUS put to death without judge or jury in that county."

On the 28th of April, 1836, a negro was burnt alive at St. Louis, by a numerous mob. The Alton Telegraph gives the following particulars.

"All was silent as death, while the executioners were piling wood around the victim. He said not a word, probably feeling that the flames had seized upon him. He then uttered an awful howl, attempting to sing and pray, then hung his head and suffered in silence, excepting in the following instance:— After the flames had surrounded their prey, and when his clothes were in a blaze all over him, his eyes burnt out of his head, and his mouth seemingly parched to a cinder, some one in the crowd, more compassionate than the rest, proposed to put an end to his misery by shooting him, when it was replied, 'that would be of no use since he was already out of pain.' 'No, no,' said the wretch, 'I am not,—I am suffering as much as ever—shoot me, shoot me!' 'No, no,' said one of the fiends who was standing about the sacrifice they were roasting, 'he shall not be shot, I would sooner slacken the fire, if that would increase his misery!' and the man who said this, was, we understand, an officer of justice!"

"We understand," says the New Orleans Post of June 7th, 1836, "that a negro man was lately condemned by the mob, to be BURNED OVER A SLOW FIRE, which was put into execution at Grand Gulf, for murdering a black woman and her master, Mr. Green, a respectable citizen of that place, who attempted to save her from the clutches of this monster."

"We have been informed," says the Arkansas Gazette of the 29th October, 1836, "that the slave *William*, who murdered his master (*Huskey*) some weeks since, and several negroes, was taken by a party, a few days since, from the Sheriff of Hot Springs and BURNED ALIVE! yes, tied up to to limb of a tree, a fire built under him, and consumed in slow and lingering torture!"

It has been already observed, that the master is virtually the arbiter of life and death. How far the state, of public opinion at the south confirms or contradicts this assertion, may be seen from the annexed report of a suit brought to recover the value of a murdered slave. If he who takes the life of another's slave is permitted to go at large without molestation, after making compensation for the property destroyed, who shall presume to punish the owner for doing what he will with his own?

From the Nashville (Tennessee) Banner, June, 1834.

"INTERESTING TRIAL.—During the session of the circuit-court for Davison county, which adjourned a few days since, a case was tried of more than usual interest to the public, It was that of Meeks against Philips, for the value of a slave who had been killed by Philips, whilst in the employment of Meeks as his overseer. The following abstract of the evidence was furnished us by a disinterested member of the bar, who was not engaged as counsel for either side of the cause.

" 'It appeared in evidence that the negro had disobeyed Philips' orders, in going away one night, without his permission, for which, in accordance with his duty, he undertook to chastise him. The boy proved somewhat refractory, and probably offered resistance, though there was no direct evidence of the fact. From Philip's admissions, which must be taken for, as well as against him, it seems he had a scuffle with the boy, during which, the boy inflicted a blow upon him, which produced great pain. Philips, with assistance, finally subdued him. While endeavouring to swing him to the limb of a tree, he resisted by pulling back; whereupon Philips, who is a large and strong man, gave him several blows upon his head with the butt of a loaded horsewhip. Having tied him to the limb the rope gave way, and the boy fell to the ground, when Philips gave him several violent kicks in the side, and again swung him to the tree. He then called for a cow-hide, which was accordingly brought, arid the chastisement was commenced anew. The suffering wretch implored for mercy in vain. Phili s would whip him awhile, and then rest only to renew his strokes and wreak his vengeance, for he repeatedly avowed his intention of whipping him to death!—saying, he had as good a negro to put in his room, or remunerate his master for the loss of him. The sufferer, writhing under the stinging tortures of the lash, continued to implore for mercy, while those who were present interposed, and pleaded, too, in his behalf; but there was no relenting arm, until life was nearly extinct, and feeling had taken its departure. He was cut loose bleeding and weak, overcome with extreme exhaustion and debility, and died in a few minutes after.' The jury, of course, found for the plaintiff."

PREFACE.

IN the following pages, the reader will find embodied the principal incidents that have occurred in the life of a slave, in the United States of America. The narrative is taken from the mouth of the adventurer himself; and if the copy does not retain the identical words of the original, the sense and import, at least, are faithfully preserved.

Many of his opinions have been cautiously omitted, or carefully suppressed, as being of no value to the reader; and his sentiments upon the subject of slavery, have not been embodied in this work. The design of the writer, who is no more than the recorder of the facts detailed to him by another, has been to render the narrative as simple, and the style of the story as plain, as the laws of the language would permit. To introduce the reader, as it were, to a view of the cotton fields, and exhibit, not to his imagination, but to his very eyes, the mode of life to which the slaves on the southern plantations must conform, has been the primary object of the compiler.

The book has been written without fear or prejudice, and no opinions have been consulted in its composition. The sole view of the writer has been to make the citizens of the United States acquainted with each other, and to give a faithful portrait of the manners, usages, and customs of the southern people, so far as those manners, usages, and customs have fallen under the observations of a common negro slave, endued by nature with a tolerable portion of intellectual capacity. The more reliance is to be placed upon his relations of those things that he saw in the southern country, when it is recollected that he had been born and brought up in a part of the state of Maryland, in which, of all others, the spirit of the "old aristocracy," as it has not unaptly been called, retained much of its pristine vigour in his youth; and where he had an early opportunity of seeing many of the most respectable, best educated, and most highly enlightened families of both Maryland and Virginia, a constant succession of kind offices, friendly visits, and family alliances, having at that day united the most distinguished inhabitants of the two sides of the Potomac, in the social relations of one people.

It might naturally be expected, that a man who had passed through so many scenes of adversity, and had suffered so many wrongs at the hands of his fellow-man, would feel much of the bitterness of heart that is engendered by a remembrance of unatoned injuries; but every sentiment of this kind has been carefully excluded from the following pages, in which the reader will find nothing but an unadorned detail of acts, and the impressions those acts produced on the mind of him upon whom they operated.

CHAPTER I.

THE system of slavery, as practised in the United States, has been, and is now, but little understood by the people who live north of the Potomac and the Ohio; for, although individual cases of extreme cruelty and oppression occasionally occur in Maryland, yet the general treatment of the black people, is far more lenient and mild in that state, than it is farther south. This, I presume, is mainly to be attributed to the vicinity of the free state of Pennsylvania; but, in no small degree, to the influence of the population of the cities of Baltimore and Washington, over the families of the planters of the surrounding counties. For experience has taught me, that both masters and mistresses, who, if not observed by strangers, would treat their slaves with the utmost rigour, are so far operated upon, by a sense of shame or pride, as to provide them tolerably with both food and clothing, when they know their conduct is subject to the observation of persons, whose good opinion they wish to preserve. A large number of the most respectable and wealthy people in both Washington and Baltimore, being altogether opposed to the practice of slavery, hold a constant control over the actions of their friends, the farmers, and thus prevent much misery; but in the south, the case is widely different. There, every man, and every woman too, except prevented by poverty, is a slave-holder; and the entire white population is leagued together by a common bond of the most sordid interest, in the torture and oppression of the poor descendants of Africa. If the negro is wronged, there is no one to whom he can complain— if suffering for want of the coarsest food, he dare not steal—if flogged till the flesh falls from his bones, he must not murmur—and if compelled to perform his daily toil in an iron collar, no expression of resentment must escape his lips.

People of the northern states, who make excursions to the south, visit the principal cities and towns, travel the most frequented highways, or even sojourn for a time at the residences of the large planters, and partake of their hospitality and amusements, know nothing of the condition of the southern slaves. To acquire this knowledge, the traveller must take up his abode for a season, in the lodge of the overseer, pass a summer in the remote cotton fields, or spend a year within view of the rice swamps. By attending for one month, the court which the overseer of a large estate holds every evening in the cotton-gin yard, and witnessing the execution of his decrees, a Turk or a Russian would find the tribunals of his country far outdone.

It seems to be a law of nature, that slavery is equally destructive to the master and the slave; for, whilst it stupifies the latter with fear, and reduces him below the condition of man, it brutalizes the former, by the practice of continual tyranny; and makes him the prey of all the vices which render human nature loathsome.

In the following simple narrative of an unlearned man, I have endeavoured, faithfully and truly, to present to the reader, some of the most material accidents which occurred to myself, in a period of thirty years of slavery in the free Republic of the United States; as well as many circumstances, which I observed in the condition and conduct of other persons during that period.

It has been supposed, by many, that the state of the southern slaves is constantly becoming better; and that the treatment which they receive at the hands of their masters, is progressively milder and more humane; but the contrary of all this is unquestionably the truth; for, under the bad culture which is practised in the south, the land is constantly becoming poorer, and the means of getting food, more and more difficult. So long as the land is new and rich, and produces corn and sweet potatoes abundantly, the black people seldom suffer greatly for food; but, when the ground is all cleared, and planted in rice or cotton, corn and potatoes become scarce; *and when corn has to be bought on a cotton plantation, the people must expect to make acquaintance with hunger.*

My grandfather was brought from Africa, and sold as a slave in Calvert county, in Maryland, about the year 1730. I never understood the name of the ship in which he was imported, nor the name of the planter who bought him on his arrival, but at the time I knew him, he was a slave in a family called Mauel, who resided near Leonardtown. My father was a slave in a family named Hantz, living near the same place. My mother was the slave of a tobacco planter, an old man, who died, according to the best of my recollection, when I was about four years old, leaving his property in such a situation that it became necessary, as I suppose, to sell a part of it to pay his debts. Soon after his death, several of his slaves, and with others myself, were sold at public vendue. My mother had several children, my brothers and sisters, and we were all sold on the same day to different purchasers. Our new master took us away, and I never saw my mother, nor any of my brothers and sisters afterwards. This was, I presume, about the year 1785. I learned subsequently, from my father, that my mother was sold to a Georgia trader, who soon after

2

that carried her away from Maryland. Her other children were sold to slave-dealers from Carolina, and were also taken away, so that I was left alone in Calvert county, with my father, whose owner lived only a few miles from my new master's residence. At the time I was sold I was quite naked, having never had any clothes in my life; but my new master had brought with him a child's frock or wrapper, belonging to one of his own children; and after he had purchased me, he dressed me in this garment, took me before him on his horse, and started home; but my poor mother, when she saw me leaving her for the last time, ran after me, took me down from the horse, clasped me in her arms, and wept loudly and bitterly over me. My master seemed to pity her, and endeavoured to soothe her distress by telling her that he would be a good master to me, and that I should not want any thing. She then, still holding me in her arms, walked along the road beside the horse as he moved slowly, and earnestly and imploringly besought my master to buy her and the rest of her children, and not permit them to be carried away by the negro buyers; but whilst thus entreating him to save her and her family, the slave-driver, who had first bought her, came running in pursuit of her with a raw hide in his hand. When he overtook us he told her he was her master now, and ordered her to give that little negro to its owner, and come back with him.

My mother then turned to him and cried, "Oh, master, do not take me from my child!" Without making any reply, he gave her two or three heavy blows on the shoulders with his raw hide, snatched me from her arms, handed me to my master, and seizing her by one arm, dragged her back towards the place of sale. My master then quickened the pace of his horse; and as we advanced, the cries of my poor parent became more and more indistinct— at length they died away in the distance, and I never again heard the voice of my poor mother. Young as I was, the horrors of that day sank deeply into my heart, and even at this time, though half a century has elapsed, the terrors of the scene return with painful vividness upon my memory. Frightened at the sight of the cruelties inflicted upon my poor mother, I forgot my own sorrows at parting from her and clung to my new master, as an angel and a saviour, when compared with the hardened fiend into whose power she had fallen. She had been a kind and good mother to me; had warmed in her bosom in the cold nights of winter; and had often divided the scanty pittance of food allowed her by her mistress, between my brothers, and sisters, and me, and gone supperless to bed herself. Whatever victuals she could obtain beyond the coarse food, salt fish, and corn-bread, allowed to slaves on the Patuxent and Potomac rivers, she carefully distributed among her children, and treated us with all the tenderness which her own miserable condition would permit. I have no doubt that she was chained and driven to Carolina, and toiled out the residue of a forlorn and famished existence in the rice swamps, or indigo fields of the south.

My father never recovered from the effects of the shock which this sudden and overwhelming ruin of his family gave him. He had formerly been of a gay social temper, and when he came to see us on a Saturday night, he always brought us some little present, such as the means of a poor slave would allow—apples, melons, sweet potatoes, or, if he could procure nothing else, a little parched corn, which tasted better in our cabin, because he had brought it.

He spent the greater part of the time, which his master permitted him to pass with us, in relating such stories as he had learned from his companions, or in singing the rude songs common amongst the slaves of Maryland and Virginia. After this time I never heard him laugh heartily, or sing a song. He became gloomy and morose in his temper, to all but me; and sp nt nearly all his leisure time with my grandfather, who claimed kindred with some royal family in Africa, and had been a great warrior in his native country. The master of my father was a hard penurious man, and so exceedingly avaricious, that he scarcely allowed himself the common conveniences of life. A stranger to sensibility, he was incapable of tracing the change in the temper and deportment of my father, to its true cause; but attributed it to a sullen discontent with his condition as a slave, and a desire to abandon his service, and seek his liberty by escaping to some of the free states. To prevent the perpetration of this suspected crime of *running away from slavery*, the old man resolved to sell my father to a southern slave-dealer, and accordingly applied to one of those men, who was at that time in Calvert, to become the purchaser. The price was agreed on, but, as my father was a very strong, active, and resolute man, it was deemed unsafe for the Georgian to attempt to seize him, even with the aid of others, in the day-time, when he was at work, as it was known he carried upon his person a large knife. It was therefore determined to secure him by stratagem, and for this purpose, a farmer in the neighbourhood, who was made privy to the plan, alleged that he had lost a pig, which must have been stolen by some one, and that he suspected my father to be the thief. A constable was employed to arrest him, but as he was afraid to undertake the business alone, he called on his way, at the house of the master of my grandfather, to procure assistance from the overseer of the plantation. When he arrived at the house, the overseer was at the barn, and thither he repaired to make his application. At the end of the barn was the coach-house, and as the day was cool, to avoid the wind which was high, the two walked to the side of the coach-house to talk over the matter, and settle their plan of operations. It so happened, that my grandfather, whose business it was to keep the coach in good condition, was at work at this time, rubbing the plated handles of the doors, and brightening the other metallic parts of the vehicle. Hearing the voice of the overseer without, he suspended his work, and listening attentively, became a party to their councils. They agreed that they would delay the execution of their project until the next day, as it was then late. The supposed they would have no difficulty in apprehending their intended victim, as, knowing himself innocent of the theft, he would readily consent to go with the constable to a justice of the peace, to have the charge examined. That night, however, about midnight, my grandfather silently repaired to the cabin of my father, a distance of about three miles, aroused him from his sleep, made him acquainted with the extent of his danger, gave him a bottle of cider and a small bag of parched corn, and then praying to the God of his native country to protect his son, enjoined him to fly from the destruction which awaited him. In the morning, the Georgian could not find his newly purchased slave, who was never seen or heard of in Maryland from that day. He probably had prudence enough to conceal himself in the day, and travel only at night; by this means making his way slowly up the country, between the Patapsco and Patuxent, until he was able to strike across to the north, and reach Pennsylvania.

After the flight of my father, my grandfather was the only person left in Maryland, with whom I could claim kindred. He was at that time an old man, as he himself said, nearly eighty years of age, and he manifested towards me all the fondness which a person so far advanced in life could be expected to feel for a child. As he was too feeble to perform much hard labour, his master did not require him either to live or to work with the common field hands, who were employed the greater part of the year in cultivating tobacco, and preparing it for market, that being the staple crop of all the lower part of the western shore of Maryland at that time. Indeed, old Ben, as my grandfather was called, had always expressed great contempt for his fellow slaves, they being as he said, a mean and vulgar race, quite beneath his rank, and the dignity of his former station. He had, during all the time that I knew him, a small cabin of his own, with

5

about half an acre of ground attached to it, which he cultivated on his own account and from which he drew a large portion of his subsistence. He entertained strange and peculiar notions of religion, and prayed every night, though he said he ought to pray oftener; but that his God would excuse him for the non-performance of this duty in consideration of his being a slave, and compelled to devote his whole time to the service of his master. He never went to church or meeting and held, that the religion of this country was altogether false, and indeed, no religion at all; being the mere invention of priests and crafty men, who hoped thereby to profit through the ignorance and credulity of the multitude. In support of this opinion, he maintained that there could only be one true standard of faith, which was the case in his country, where all the people worshipped together in the same assembly, and believed in the same doctrines which had been of old time delivered by the true God to a holy man, who was taken up into heaven for that purpose, and after he had received the divine communication, had returned to earth, and spent a hundred years in preaching and imparting the truth which had been revealed to him, to mankind. This inspired man resided in some country, at a great distance from that of my grandfather, but had come there, across a part of the sea, in company with an angel; and instructed the people in the mysteries of the true faith, which had ever since been preserved in its utmost purity, by the descendants of those who received it, through a period of more than ten thousand years. My grandfather said, that the tenets of this religion were so plain and self-evident, that any one could understand them, without any other instruction, than the reading of a small book, a copy of which was kept in every family, and which contained all the rules both of faith and practice, necessary for any one to know or exercise. No one was permitted to expound or explain this book, as it was known to be the oracle of the true God, and it was held impious for any person to give a construction to his words, different from that which was so palpably and manifestly expressed on the face of the book.

This book was likewise written in such plain and intelligible language, that only one meaning could possibly be given to any one part of it; and was withal so compendious and brief, that people could, with very little labour, commit the whole of its precepts to memory. The priests had, at several times, attempted to publish commentaries and glossaries upon this book; but as often as this had been attempted, the perpetrators had been tried, found guilty of conspiring to corrupt the public morals, and then banished from the country. People who were disposed to worship publicly, convened together in summer, under the boughs of a large tree, and the eldest person present read the inspired book from beginning to end, which could be done in two hours, at most. Sometimes a priest was employed to read the book, but he was never, by any means, allowed to add any observations of his own, as it would have been considered absurd as well as very wicked for a mere man to attempt to add to, alter, amend, or in any manner give a colouring to the revealed word of God. In winter, when it rained constantly, the worshippers met under the roof of a house covered with the leaves of a certain tree, which grew in great abundance on the margins of all the streams.

The law imposed no penalties on those who did not profess to believe the contents of the sacred book; but those who did not live according to its rules were deemed had subjects, and were compelled to become soldiers, as being fit only for a life of bloodshed and cruelty.

The book inculcated no particular form of belief and left men free to profess what faith they pleased but its principles of morality were extremely rigid and uncompromising. Love of country, charity, and social affection, were the chief points of duty enjoined by it. Lying and drunkenness were strictly prohibited, and those guilty of these vices were severely punished. Cruelty was placed in the same rank of crimes; but the mode of punishment was left entirely to the civil law-giver. The book required neither fastings, penances, nor pilgrimages; but tenderness to wives and children, was one of its most positive injunctions.

CHAPTER II.

The name of the man who purchased me at the vendue, and became my master, was John Cox; but he was generally called Jack Cox. He was a man of kindly feelings towards his family, and treated his slaves, of whom he had several besides me, with humanity. He permitted my grandfather to visit me as often as he pleased, and allowed him sometimes to carry me to his own cabin, which stood in a lonely place, at the head of a deep hollow, almost surrounded by a thicket of cedar trees, which had grown up in a worn out and abandoned tobacco field. My master gave me better clothes than the little slaves of my age generally received in Calvert, and often told me that he intended to make me his waiter, and that if I behaved well I should become his overseer in time. These stations of waiter and overseer appeared to me to be the highest points of honour and greatness in the whole world, and had not circumstances frustrated my master's plans, as well as my own views, I should probably have been living at this time in a cabin on the corner of some tobacco plantation.

Fortune had decreed otherwise. When I was about twelve years old, my master, Jack Cox, died of a disease which had long confined him to the house. I was sorry for the death of my master, who had always been kind to me; and I soon discovered that I had good cause to regret his departure from this world. He had several children at the time of his death, who were all young; the oldest being about my own age. The father of my late master, who was still living, became administrator of his estate, and took possession of his property, and amongst the rest, of myself. This old gentleman treated me with the greatest severity, and compelled me to work very hard on his plantation for several years, until I suppose I must have been near or quite twenty years of age. As I was always very obedient, and ready to execute all his orders, I did not receive much whipping, but suffered greatly for want of sufficient and proper food. My master allowed his slaves a peck of corn, each, per week, throughout the year and this we had to grind into meal in a hand mill for ourselves. We had a tolerable supply of meat for a short time, about the month of December, when he killed his hogs. After that season we had meat once a week, unless bacon became scarce, which very often happened, in which case we had no meat at all. However, as we fortunately lived near both the Patuxent river and the Chesapeake Bay, we had abundance of fish in the spring, and as long as the fishing season continued. After that period, each slave received, in addition to his allowance of corn, one salt herring every day.

My master gave me one pair of shoes, one pair of stockings, one hat, one jacket of coarse cloth, two coarse shirts, and two pair of trousers yearly. He allowed me no other clothes. In the winter time I often suffered very much from the cold; as I had to drive the team of oxen which hauled the tobacco to market, and frequently did not get home until late at night, the distance being considerable, and my cattle travelling very slow.

One Saturday evening, when I came home from the corn field, my master told me that he had hired me out for a year at the city of Washington, and that I would have to live at the navy-yard.

On the new-year's-day following, which happened about two weeks afterwards, my master set forward for Washington, on horseback, and ordered me to accompany him on foot. It was night when we arrived at the navy-yard, and every thing appeared very strange to me.

I was told by a gentleman who had epaulets on his shoulders, that I must go on board a large ship, which lay in the river. He at the same time told a boy to show me the way. This ship proved to be the Congress frigate, and I was told that I had been brought there to cook for the people belonging to her. In the course of a few days the duties of my station became quite familiar to me; and in the enjoyment of a profusion of excellent provisions, I felt very happy. I strove by all means to please the officers and gentlemen who came on board, and in this I soon found my account. One gave me a half-worn coat, another an old shirt, and a third, a cast off waistcoat and pantaloons. Some presented me with small sums of money, and in this way I soon found myself well clothed, and with more than a dollar in my pocket. My duties, though constant, were not burthensome, and I was permitted to spend Sunday afternoon in my own way. I generally went up into the city to see the new and splendid buildings; often walked as far as Georgetown, and made many new acquaintances amongst the slaves, and frequently saw large numbers of people of my colour chained together in long trains, and driven off towards the south. At that time the Slave-trade was not regarded with so much indignation and disgust, as it is now. It was a rare thing to hear of a person of colour running away, and escaping altogether from his master: my father being the only one within my knowledge, who had, before this time, obtained his liberty in this manner, in Calvert county; and, as before stated, I never heard what became of him after his flight.

I remained on board the Congress, and about the navy-yard, two years, and was quite satisfied with my lot, until about three months before the expiration of this period, when it so happened that a schooner, loaded with iron and other materials for the use of the yard, arrived from Philadelphia. She came and lay close by the Congress, to discharge her cargo, and amongst her crew I observed a black man, with whom, in the course of a day or two, I became acquainted. He told me he was free, and lived in Philadelphia, where he kept a house of entertainment for sailors, which he said was attended to in his absence by his wife.

His description of Philadelphia, and of the liberty enjoyed there by the black people, so charmed my imagination that I determined to devise some plan of escaping from the Congress, and making my way to the north. I communicated my designs to my new friend, who promised to give me his aid. We agreed that the night before the schooner should sail, I was to be concealed in the hold, amongst a parcel of loose tobacco, which he said the captain had undertaken to carry to Philadelphia. The sailing of the schooner was delayed longer than we expected; and, finally, her captain purchased a cargo of flour in Georgetown, and sailed for the West Indies. Whilst I was anxiously awaiting some other opportunity of making my way to Philadelphia, (the idea of crossing the country to the western part of Pennsylvania never entered my mind,) new-year's-day came, and with it came my old master from Calvert, accompanied by a gentleman named Gibson, to whom he said he had sold me, and to whom he delivered me over in the navy-yard. We all three set out that same evening for Calvert, and reached the residence of my new master the next day. Here I was informed that I had become the subject of a law-suit. My new master claimed me under his purchase from old Mr. Cox; and another gentleman of the neighbourhood, named Levin Ballard, had bought me of the children of my former master, Jack Cox. This suit continued in the courts of Calvert county more than two years; but was finally decided in favour of him who had bought me of the children.

I went home with my master, Mr. Gibson, who was a farmer, and with whom I lived three years. Soon after I came to live with Mr. Gibson, I married a girl of colour named Judah, the slave of a gentleman by the name of Symmes, who resided in the same neighbourhood. I was at the house of Mr. Symmes every week; and became as well acquainted with him and his family, as I was with my master.

Mr. Symmes also married a wife about the time I did. The lady whom he married lived near Philadelphia, and when she first came to Maryland, she refused to be served by a black chambermaid, but employed a white girl, the daughter of a poor man, who lived near. The lady was reported to be very wealthy, and brought a large trunk full of plate, and other valuable articles. This trunk was so heavy that I could scarcely carry it, and it impressed my mind with the idea of great riches in the owner, at that time. After some time Mrs. Symmes dismissed her white chambermaid, and placed my wife in that situation, which I regarded as a fortunate circumstance, as it insured her good food, and at least one good suit of clothes.

The Symmes' family was one of the most ancient in Maryland, and had been a long time resident in Calvert county. The grounds had been laid out, and all the improvements projected about the family abode, in a style of much magnificence, according to the custom of the old aristocracy of Maryland and Virginia.

Appendant to the domicile, and at no great distance from the house, was a family vault, built of brick, in which reposed the occupants of the estate, who had lived there for many previous generations. This vault had not been opened or entered for fifteen years previous to the time of which I speak; but it so happened, that at this period, a young man, a distant relation of the family, died, having requested on his death-bed, that he might be buried in this family resting place. When I came on Saturday evening to see my wife and child, Mr. Symmes desired me, as I was older than any of his black men, to take an iron pick and go and open the vault, which I accordingly did, by cutting away the mortar, and removing a few bricks from one side of the building; but I could not remove more than three or four bricks before I was obliged, by the horrid effluvia which issued at the aperture, to retire. It was the most deadly and sickening scent that I have ever smelled and I could not return to complete the work until after the sun had risen the next day, when I pulled down so much of one of the side walls, as to permit persons to walk in upright. I then went in alone, and examined this house of the dead, and surely no picture could more strongly and vividly depict the emptiness of all earthly vanity, and the nothingness of human pride. Dispersed over the floor lay the fragments of more than twenty human skeletons, each in the place where it had been deposited by the idle tenderness of surviving friends. In some cases nothing remained but the hair and the larger bones, whilst in several the form of the coffin was yet visible, with all the bones resting in their proper places. One coffin, the sides of which were yet standing, the lid only having decayed and partly fallen in, so as to disclose the contents of this narrow cell, presented a peculiarly moving spectacle. Upon the centre of the lid was a large silver plate, and the head and foot were adorned with silver stars. The nails which had united the parts of the coffin had also silver heads. Within lay the skeletons of a mother and her infant child, in slumbers only to be broken by the peal of the last trumpet. The bones of the infant lay upon the breast of the mother, where the hands of affection had shrouded them. The ribs of the parent had fallen down, and rested on the back bone. Many gold rings were about the bones of the fingers. Brilliant ear-rings lay beneath where the ears had been; and a glittering gold chain encircled the ghastly and haggard vertebrae of a once beautiful neck. The shroud and flesh had disappeared, but the hair of the mother appeared strong and fresh. Even the silken locks of the infant were still preserved. Behold the end of youth and beauty, and of all that is lovely in life! The coffin was so much decayed that it could not be removed. A thick and dismal vapour hung embodied from the roof and walls of this charnal house, in appearance somewhat like a mass of dark cobwebs; but which was impalpable to the touch, and when stirred by the hand vanished away. On the second day we deposited with his kindred, the corpse of the young man, and at night I again carefully closed up the breach which I had made in the walls of this dwelling-place of the dead.

CHAPTER III.

Some short time after my wife became chambermaid to her mistress, it was my misfortune to change masters once more. Levin Ballard, who, as before stated, had purchased me of the children of my former master, Jack Cox, was successful in his law suit with Mr. Gibson, the object of which was to determine the right of property in me; and one day, whilst I was at work in the corn-field, Mr. Ballard came and told me I was his property; asking me at the same time if I was willing to go with him. I told him I was not willing to go; but that if I belonged to him I knew I must. We then went to the house, and Mr. Gibson not being at home, Mrs. Gibson told me I must go with Mr. Ballard.

I accordingly went with him, determining to serve him obediently and faithfully. I remained in his service almost three years, and as he lived near the residence of my wife's master, my former mode of life was not materially changed, by this change of home.

Mrs. Symmes spent much of her time in exchanging visits with the families of the other large planters, both in Calvert, and the neighbouring counties; and through my wife, I became acquainted with the private family history of many of the principal persons in Maryland.

There was a great proprietor, who resided in another county, who owned several hundred slaves; and who permitted them to beg of travellers on the high-way. This same gentleman had several daughters, and according to the custom of the time, kept what they called open house: that is, his house was free to all persons of genteel appearance, who chose to visit it. The young ladies were supposed to be the greatest fortunes in the country, were reputed beautiful, and consequently were greatly admired.

Two gentlemen, who were lovers of these girls, desirous of amusing their mistresses, invited a young man, whose standing in society they supposed to be beneath theirs, to go with them to the manor, as it was called. When there, they endeavoured to make him an object of ridicule, in presence of the ladies; but he so well acquitted himself, and manifested such superior wit and talents, that one of the young ladies fell in love with him, and soon after, wrote him a letter, which led to their marriage. His two pretended friends were never afterwards countenanced by the family, as gentlemen of honour; but the fortunate husband avenged himself of his heartless companions, by inviting them to his wedding, and exposing them to the observation of the vast assemblage of fashionable people, who always attended a marriage, in the family of a great planter.

The two gentlemen, who had been thus made to fall into the pit that they had dug for another, were so much chagrined at the issue of the adventure, that one, soon left Maryland; and the other became a common drunkard, and died a few years afterwards.

My change of masters, realised all the evil apprehensions which I had entertained. I found Mr. Ballard sullen and crabbed in his temper, and always prone to find fault with my conduct—no matter how hard I had laboured, or how careful I was to fulfil all his orders, and obey his most unreasonable commands. Yet, it so happened, that he never beat me, for which I was altogether indebted to the good character, for inus try, sobriety, and humility, which I had established in the neighbourhood. I think he was ashamed to abuse me, lest he should suffer in the good opinion of the public; for he often fell into the most violent fits of anger against me, and overwhelmed me with coarse and abusive language. He did not give me clothes enough to keep me warm in winter, and compelled me to work in the woods, when there was deep snow on the ground, by which I suffered very much. I had determined at last to speak to him to sell me to some person in the neighbourbood, so that I might still be near my wife and children—but a different fate awaited me.

My master kept a store at a small village on the bank of the Patuxent river, called B— —, although he resided at some distance on a farm. One morning he rose early, and ordered me to take a yoke of oxen and go to the village, to bring home a cart which was there, saying he would follow me. He arrived at the village soon after I did, and took his breakfast with his store-keeper. He then told me to come into the house and get my breakfast. Whilst I was eating in the kitchen, I observed him talking earnestly, but lowly, to a stranger near the kitchen door. I soon after went out, and hitched my oxen to the cart, and was about to drive off, when several men came round about me, and amongst them the stranger whom I had seen speaking with my master. This man came up to me, and, seizing me by the collar, shook me violently, saying I was his property, and must go with him to Georgia. At the sound of these words, the thoughts of

14

my wife and children rushed across my mind, and my heart died away within me. I saw and knew that my case was hopeless, and that resistance was vain, as there were near twenty persons present, all of whom were ready to assist the man by whom I was kidnapped. I felt incapable of weeping or speaking, and in my despair I laughed loudly. My purchaser ordered me to cross my hands behind, which were quickly bound with a strong cord; and he then told me that we must set out that very day for the south. I asked if I could not be allowed to go to see my wife and children, or if this could not be permitted, if they might not have leave to come to see me; but was told that I would be able to get another wife in Georgia.

My new master, whose name I did not hear, took me that same day across the Patuxent, where I joined fifty-one other slaves, whom he had bought in Maryland. Thirty-two of these were men, and nineteen were women. The women were merely tied together with a rope, about the size of a bed cord, which was tied like a halter round the neck of each; but the men, of whom I was the stoutest and strongest, were very differently caparisoned. A strong iron collar was closely fitted by means of a padlock round each of our necks. A chain of iron, about a hundred feet in length, was passed through the hasp of each padlock, except at the two ends, where the hasps of the padlocks passed through a link of the chain. In addition to this, we were handcuffed in pairs, with iron staples and bolts, with a short chain, about a foot long, uniting the handcuffs and their wearers in pairs. In this manner we were chained alternately by the right and left hand; and the poor man, to whom I was thus ironed, wept like all infant when the blacksmith, with his heavy hammer, fastened the ends of the bolts that kept the staples from slipping from our arms. For my own part, I felt indifferent to my fate. It appeared to me that the worst had come, that could come, and that no change of fortune could harm me.

After we were all chained and handcuffed together, we sat down upon the ground; and here reflecting upon the sad reverse of fortune that had so suddenly overtaken me, and the dreadful suffering which awaited me, I became weary of life, and bitterly execrated the day I was born. It seemed that I was destined by fate to drink the cup of sorrow to the very dregs, and that I should find no respite from misery but in the grave. I longed to die, and escape from the hands of my tormentors; but even the wretched privilege of destroying myself was denied me; for I could not shake off my chains, nor move a yard without the consent of my master. Reflecting in silence upon my forlorn condition, I at length concluded that as things could not become worse—and as the life of man is but a continued round of changes, they must, of necessity, take a turn in my favour at some future day. I found relief in this vague and indefinite hope, and when we received orders to go on board the scow, which was to transport us over the Patuxent, I marched down to the water with a firmness of purpose of which I did not believe myself capable, a few minutes before.

We were soon on the south side of the river, and taking up our line of march, we travelled about five miles that evening, and stopped for the night at one of those miserable public houses, so frequent in the lower parts of Maryland and Virginia, called *"ordinaries."*

Our master ordered a pot of mush to be made for our supper; after despatching which, we all lay down on the naked floor to steep in our handcuffs and chains. The women, my fellow-slaves, lay on one side of the room; and the men who were chained with me, occupied the other. I slept but little this night, which I passed in thinking of my wife and little children, whom I could not hope ever to see again. I also thought of my grandfather, and of the long nights I had passed with him, listening to his narratives of the scenes through which he had passed in Africa. I at length fell asleep, but was distressed by painful dreams. My wife and children appeared to be weeping and lamenting my calamity; and beseeching and imploring my master on their knees, not to carry me away from them. My little boy came and begged me not to go and leave him, and endeavoured, as I thought, with his little hands to break the fetters that bound me. I awoke in agony and cursed my existence. I could not pray, for the measure of my woes seemed to be full, and I felt as if there was no mercy in heaven, nor compassion on earth, for a man who was born a slave. Day at length came, and with the dawn, we resumed our journey towards the Potomac. As we passed along the road, I saw the slaves at work in the corn and tobacco-fields. I knew they toiled hard and lacked food but they were not, like me, dragged in chains from their wives, children, and friends. Compared with me, they were the happiest of mortals. I almost envied them their blessed lot.

Before night we crossed the Potomac, at Hoe's Ferry, and bade farewell to Maryland. At night we stopped at the house of a poor gentleman, at least he appeared to wish my master to consider him a gentleman; and he had no difficulty in establishing his claim to poverty. He lived at the side of the road, in a framed house, which had never been plastered within—the weather-boards being the only wall. He had about fifty acres of land enclosed by a fence, the remains of a farm which had once covered two or three hundred acres; but the cedar bushes had encroached upon all sides, until the cultivation had been confined to its present limits. The land was the very picture of sterility, and there was neither barn nor stable on the place. The owner was ragged, and his wife and children were in a similar plight. It was with difficulty that we obtained a bushel of corn, which our master ordered us to parch at a fire made in the yard, and to eat for our supper. Even this miserable family possessed two slaves, half-starved, half-naked wretches, whose appearance bespoke them familiar with hunger, and victims of the lash; but yet there was one pang which they had not known,—they had not been chained and driven from their parents, or children, into hopeless exile.

We left this place early in the morning, and directed our course toward the south-west; our master riding beside us, and hastening our march, sometimes by words of encouragement, and sometimes by threats of punishment. The women took their place in the rear of our line. We halted about nine o'clock for breakfast, and received as much cornbread as we could eat, together with a plate of broiled herrings, and about three pounds of pork amongst us. Before we left this place, I was removed from near the middle of the chain, and placed at the front end of it; so that I now became the leader of the file, and held this post of honour until our irons were taken from us, near the town of Columbia in South Carolina. We continued our route this day along the high road between the Potomac and Rappahannock: and I several times saw each of those rivers before night. Our master gave us no dinner to day, but we halted a short time before sundown, and got as much corn mush, and sour milk, as we could eat for supper. It was now the beginning of the month of May, and the weather, in the fine climate of Virginia, was very mild and pleasant; so that our master was not obliged to provide us with fire at night.

From this time, to the end of our journey southward, we all slept, promiscuously, men and women, on the floors of such houses as we chanced to stop at. We had no clothes except those we wore, and a few blankets; the larger portion of our gang being in rags at the time we crossed the Potomac. Two of the women were pregnant; the one far advanced— and she already complained of inability to keep pace with our march; but her complaints were disregarded. We crossed the Rappahannock at Port Royal, and afterwards passed through the village of Bowling Green; a place with which I became better acquainted in after times; but which now presented the quiet so common to all the small towns in Virginia, and indeed in all the southern states. Time did not reconcile me to my chains, but it made me familiar with them; and in a few days the horrible sensations attendant upon my cruel separation from my wife and children, in some measure subsided; and I began to reflect upon my present hopeless and desperate situation, with some degree of calmness; hoping that I might be able to devise some means of escaping from the hands of my new master, who seemed to place particular value on me, as I could perceive from his conversation with such persons as we happened to meet at our resting places. I heard him tell a tavern-keeper where we halted, that if he had me in Georgia, he could get five hundred dollars for me; but he had bought me for his brother, and he believed he would not sell me; but in this he afterwards changed his opinion. I examined every part of our long chain, to see if there might not be some place in it at which it could be severed; but found it so completely secured, that with any means in my power, its separation was impossible. From this time I endeavoured to beguile my sorrows, by examining the state of the country through which we were travelling, and observing the condition of my fellow-slaves, on the plantations along the high-road upon which we sojourned.

We all had as much corn bread as we could eat. This was procured by our owner at the small dram shops, or *ordinaries*, at which we usually tarried all night. In addition to this, we generally received a salt herring though not *every* day. On Sunday, our master bought as much bacon, as, when divided amongst us, gave about a quarter of a pound to each person in our gang.

In Calvert county, where I was born, the practice amongst slave-holders, was to allow each slave one peck of corn weekly, which was measured out every Monday morning; at the same time each one receiving seven salt herrings. This formed the week's provision, and the master who did not give it, was called a *hard master*, whilst those who allowed their people any thing more, were deemed kind and indulgent. It often happened, that the stock of salt herrings laid up by a master in the spring, was not sufficient to enable him to continue this rate of distribution through the year; and when the fish failed, nothing more than the corn was dealt out. On the other hand, some planters, who had large stocks of cattle; and many cows, kept the sour milk, after all the cream had been skimmed from it, and made a daily distribution of this amongst the working slaves. Some who had large apple orchards, gave their slaves a pint of cider each per day, through the autumn. It sometimes happened, too, in the lower counties of Maryland, that there was an allowance of pork, made to the slaves one day in each week; though on some estates this did not take place more than once in a month. This allowance of meat was disposed of in such a manner as to permit each slave to get a slice; very often amounting to half a pound. The slaves were also permitted to work for themselves at night, and on Sunday. If they chose to fish, they had the privilege of selling whatever they caught. Some expert fishermen caught and sold as many fish and oysters, as enabled them to buy coffee, sugar, and other luxuries for their wives, besides keeping themselves and their families in Sunday clothes; for, the masters in Maryland only allowed the men one wool hat, one pair of shoes, two shirts, two pair of trousers— one pair of tow cloth, and one of woollen—and one woollen jacket in the year. The women were furnished in proportion. All other clothes they had to provide for themselves. Children not able to work in the field, were not provided with clothes at all, by their masters. It is, however, honourable to the Maryland slave-holders, that they never permit women to go naked in the fields, or about the house; and if the men are industrious and *employ themselves well on Sundays and holydays,* they can always keep themselves in comfortable clothes.

In Virginia, it appeared to me that the slaves were more rigorously treated than they were in my native place. It is easy to tell a man of colour who is poorly fed, from one who is well supplied with food, by his personal appearance. A half-starved negro is a miserable looking creature. His skin becomes dry, and appears to be sprinkled over with whitish husks, or scales; the glossiness of his face vanishes, his hair loses its colour, becomes dry, and when stricken with a rod, the dust flies from it. These signs of bad treatment I perceived to be very common in Virginia; many young girls who would have been beautiful, if they had been allowed enough to eat, had lost all their prettiness through mere starvation; their fine glossy hair had become of a reddish colour, and stood out round their heads like long brown wool.

CHAPTER IV.

Our master at first expressed a determination to pass through the city of Richmond; but for some reason, which he did not make known to us, he changed his mind, and drove us up the country, crossing the Matepony, North Anna and South Anna rivers. For several days we traversed a region, which had been deserted by the occupants—being no longer worth culture—and immense thickets of young red cedars, now occupied the fields, in digging of which, thousands of wretched slaves had worn out their lives in the service of merciless masters.

In some places these cedar thickets, as they are called, continued for three or four miles together, without a house to enliven the scene, and with scarcely an original forest tree to give variety to the landscape. One day, in the midst of a wilderness of cedars, we came in view of a stately and venerable looking brick edifice, which, on nearer inspection, I discovered to be a church. On approaching it, our driver ordered us to halt, and dismounting from his horse, tied him to a young cedar tree, and sat himself down upon a flat tomb-stone, near the west end of the church, ordering us, at the same time, to sit down among the grass and rest ourselves. The grave yard in which we were now encamped, occupied about two acres of ground, which was surrounded by a square brick wall, much dilapidated, and in many places broken down nearly to the ground. The gates were decayed and gone, but the gate-ways were yet distinct. The whole enclosure was thickly strewed with graves, many of which were surmounted by beautiful marble slabs; others were designated by plain head and foot stones; whilst far the larger number only betrayed the resting places of their sleeping tenant, by the simple mounds of clay, which still maintained their elevation above the level of the surrounding earth. From the appearance of this burial place, I suppose no one had been interred there for thirty years. Several hollies, planted by the hands of friendship, grew amongst the hillocks, and numerous flowering shrubs and bushes, now in bloom, gave fragrance to the air of the place. The cedars which covered the surrounding plain, with a forest impervious to the eye, had respected this lonely dwelling of the dead, and not one was to be seen within the walls.

Though it was now the meridian of day in spring, the stillness of midnight pervaded the environs of this deserted and forsaken temple; the pulpit, pews, and gallery of which were still standing, as I could perceive through the broken door-way, and maintained a freshness and newness of appearance, little according with the time-worn aspect of the exterior scenery.

It was manifest that this earthly dwelling of the Most High, now so desolate and ruinous, was once the resort of a congregation of people, gay, fashionable, and proud; who had disappeared from the land, leaving only this fallen edifice, and these grassy tombs, as the mementos of their existence. They had passed away, even as did the wandering red men, who roamed through the lofty oak forests which once shaded the ground where we now lay. As I sat musing upon the desolation that surrounded me, my mind turned to the cause which had converted a former rich and populous country, into the solitude of a deserted wilderness.

The ground over which we had travelled, since we crossed the Potomac, had generally been a strong reddish clay, with an admixture of sand, and was of the same quality with the soil of the counties of Chester, Montgomery, and Bucks, in Pennsylvania. It had originally been highly fertile and productive, and had it been properly treated, would doubtlessly have continued to yield abundant and prolific crops; but the gentlemen who became the early proprietors of this fine region, supplied themselves with slaves from Africa, cleared large plantations of many thousands of acres—cultivated tobacco—and became suddenly wealthy; built spacious houses and numerous churches, such as this; but, regardless of their true interest, they valued their lands less than their slaves, exhausted the kindly soil by unremitting crops of tobacco, declined in their circumstances, and finally grew poor, upon the very fields that had formerly made their possessors rich; abandoned one portion after another, as not worth planting any longer, and, pinched by necessity, at last sold their slaves to Georgian planters, to procure a subsistence; and when all was gone, took refuge in the wilds of Kentucky, again to act the same melancholy drama, leaving their native land to desolation and poverty. The churches then followed the fate of their builders. The revolutionary war deprived the parsons of their legal support, and they fled from the altar which no longer maintained them. Virginia has become poor by the folly and wickedness of slavery, and dearly has she paid for the anguish and sufferings she has inflicted upon our injured, degraded, and fallen race.

After remaining about two hours in this place, we again resumed our march; and wretched as I was I felt relieved when we departed from this abode of the spirit of ruin.

We continued our course up the country westward, for two or three days, moving at a slow pace, and at length turning south, crossed James river, at a place about thirty miles above Richmond, as I understood at the time. We continued our journey from day to day, in a course and by roads which appeared to me to bear generally about south-west, for more than four weeks, in which time we entered South Carolina, and in this state, near Camden, I first saw a field of cotton in bloom.

I had endeavoured through the whole journey, from the time we crossed the Rappahannock river, to make such observations upon the country, the roads we travelled, and the towns we passed through, as would enable me, at some future period, to find my way back to Maryland. I was particularly careful to note the names of the towns and villages through which we passed, and to fix on my memory, not only the names of all the rivers, but also the position and bearing of the ferries over those streams.

After leaving James river, I assumed an air of cheerfulness and even gaiety—I often told stories to my master of the manners and customs of the Maryland planters, and asked him if the same usages prevailed in Georgia, whither we were destined. By repeatedly naming the rivers that we came to, and in the order which we had reached them, I was able at my arrival in Georgia, to repeat the name of every considerable stream from the Potomac to the Savannah, and to tell at what ferries we had crossed them. I afterwards found this knowledge of great service to me; indeed, without it I should never have been able to extricate myself from slavery.

After leaving James river, our road led us southwest, through that region of country, which, in Virginia and the Carolinas, they call the upper country. It lies between the head of the tides, in the great rivers, and the lower ranges of the Alleghany Mountains. I had, at that time, never seen a country cultivated by the labour of freemen, and consequently, was not able to institute any comparison between the southern plantations, and the farms in Pennsylvania, the fields of which are ploughed and reaped by the hands of their owners; but my recollection of the general aspect of upper Virginia and Carolina is still vivid. When contrasted with the exhausted and depopulated portion of Virginia, lying below the head of the tide, much of which I had seen, the lands traversed by us in the month of May and early part of June, were indeed fertile and beautiful; but when compared with what the same plantations would have been, in the hands of such farmers as I have seen in Pennsylvania, divided into farms of the proper size, the cause of the general poverty and weakness of the slave-holding states is at once seen. The plantations are large in the south, often including a thousand acres or more; the population is consequently thin, as only one white family, beside the overseer, ever resides on one plantation.

As I advanced southward, even in Virginia. I perceived that the state of cultivation became progressively worse. Here, as in Maryland, the practice of the best farmers who cultivate grain, of planting the land every alternate year in corn, and sowing it in wheat or rye in the autumn of the same year in which the corn is planted, and whilst the corn is yet standing in the field, so as to get a crop from the same ground every year, without allowing it time to rest or recover, exhausts the finest soil in a few years, and in one or two generations reduces the proprietors to poverty. Some, who are supposed to be very superior farmers, only plant the land in corn once in three years; sowing it in wheat or rye as in the former case; however, without any covering of clover or other grass to protect it from the rays of the sun. The culture of tobacco prevails over a large portion of Virginia, especially south of James river, to the exclusion of almost every other crop, except corn. This destructive crop ruins the best land in a short time; and in all the lower parts of Maryland and Virginia the traveller will see large old family mansions, of weather-beaten and neglected appearance, standing in the middle of vast fields of many hundred acres, the fences of which have rotted away, and have been replaced by a wattled work in place of a fence, composed of short cedar stakes driven into the ground, about two feet apart, and standing about three feet above the earth, the intervals being filled up by branches cut from the cedar trees, and worked into the stakes horizontally, after the manner of splits in a basket.

Many of these fields have been abandoned altogether, and, are overgrown by cedars, which spring up in infinite numbers almost as soon as a field ceases to be ploughed, and furnish materials for fencing such parts of the ancient plantation as are still kept enclosed. In many places the enclosed fields are only partially cultivated, all the hills and poorest parts being given up to the cedars and chinquopin bushes. These estates, the seats of families that were once powerful, wealthy, and proud, are universally destitute of the appearance of a barn, such as is known among the farmers of Pennsylvania. The out houses, stables, gardens, and offices, have fallen to decay, and the dwelling-house is occupied by the descendants of those who erected it, still pertinaciously adhering to the halls of their ancestry, with a half dozen or ten slaves, the remains of the two or three hundred who toiled upon these grounds in former days. The residue of the stock has been distributed in marriage portions to the daughters of the family gone to a distance — have been removed to the west by emigrating sons, or have been sold to the southern traders, from time to time, to procure money to support the dignity of the house, as the land grew poorer, and the tobacco crop shorter, from year to year.

Industry, enterprise, and ambition, have fled from these abodes, and sought refuge from sterility and barrenness in the vales of Kentucky, or the plains of Alabama; whilst the present occupants, vain of their ancestral monuments, and proud of an obscure name, contend with all the ills that poverty brings upon fallen greatness, and pass their lives in a contest between mimic state and actual penury — too ignorant of agriculture to know how to restore fertility to a once prolific and still substantial soil, and too spiritless to sell their effects and search a new home under other skies. The sedge grass every where takes possession of the worn out fields, until it is supplanted by the chinquopin and the cedar. This grass grows in thick set bunches or stools, and no land is too poor for it. It rises to the height of two or three feet, and grows, in many places, in great profusion — is utterly worthless, either for hay or pasturage, but affords shelter to numerous rabbits, and countless flocks of partridges, and, at a short distance, has a beautiful appearance, as its elastic blue tops wave in the breeze.

In Maryland and Virginia, although the slaves are treated with so much rigour, and oftentimes with so much cruelty, I have seen instances of the greatest tenderness of feeling on the part of their owners. I myself had three masters in Maryland, and I cannot say now, even after having resided so many years in a state where slavery is not tolerated, that either of them (except the last, who sold me to the Georgians, and was an unfeeling man,) used me worse than they had a moral right to do, regarding me merely as an article of property, and not entitled to any rights as a man, political or civil. My mistresses, in Maryland, were all good women; and the mistress of my wife, in whose kitchen I spent my Sundays and many of my nights, for several years, was a lady of most benevolent and kindly feelings. She was a true friend to me, and I shall always venerate her memory.

It is now my opinion, after all I have seen, that there are no better-hearted women in the world, than the ladies of the ancient families, as they are called, in old Virginia, or the country below the mountains and the same observations will apply to the ladies of Maryland. The stock of slaves has belonged to the family for several generations, and there is a kind of family pride, in being the proprietors of so many human beings, which, in many instances, borders on affection for people of colour.

If the proprietors of the soil in Maryland and Virginia, were skilful cultivators—had their lands in good condition—and kept no more slaves on each estate than would be sufficient to work the soil in a proper manner, and keep up the repairs of the place—the condition of the coloured people would not be, by any means, a comparatively unhappy one. I am convinced, that in nine cases in ten, the hardships and sufferings of the coloured population of lower Virginia, is attributable to the poverty and distress of its owners. In many instances, an estate scarcely yields enough to feed and clothe the slaves in a comfortable manner, without allowing any thing for the support of the master and family but it is obvious, that the family must first be supported, and the slaves must be content with the surplus— and this, on a poor, old, worn out tobacco plantation, is often very small, and wholly inadequate to the comfortable sustenance of the hands, as they are called. There, in many places, nothing is allowed to the poor negro, but his peck of corn per week, without the sauce of a salt herring, or even a little salt itself.

Wretched as may be the state of the negroes, in the quarter, that of the master and his wife and daughters, is, in many instances, not much more enviable in the old apartments of the *great house*. The sons and daughters of the family are gentlemen and ladies by birthright—and were the former to be seen at the plough, or the latter at the churn, or the wash tub, the honour of the family would be stained, and the dignity of the house degraded. People must and will be employed about something, and if they cannot be usefully occupied, they will most surely engage in some pursuit wholly unprofitable. So it happens in Virginia—the young men spend their time in riding about the country, whilst they ought to be ploughing or harrowing in the cornfield; and the young women are engaged in reading silly books, or visiting their neighbours' houses, instead of attending to the dairy, or manufacturing cloth for themselves and their brothers. During all this, the father is too often defending himself against attorneys, or making such terms as he can with the sheriff, for debts, in which he has been involved by the vicious idleness of his children, and his own want of virtue and courage, to break through the evil tyranny of old customs, and compel his offspring to learn, in early life, to procure their subsistence by honest and honourable industry. In this state of things there is not enough for all. Pride forbids the sale of the slaves, as long as it is possible to avoid it, and their meagre allowance of corn is stinted rather than it shall be said, the master was obliged to sell them. Somebody must suffer, and "self-preservation is the first law of nature," says the proverb— hunger must invade either the great house or the quarter, and it is but reasonable to suppose, that so unwelcome an intruder would be expelled, to the last moment, from the former. In this conflict of pride and folly, against industry and wisdom, the slave-holders have been unhappily engaged for more than fifty years.

They are attempting to perform impossibilities— to draw the means of supporting a life of idleness, luxury, and splendour, from a once generous, but long since worn out and exhausted soil—a soil, which, carefully used, would at this day have richly repaid the toils of the husbandman, by a noble abundance of all the comforts of life; but which, tortured into barrenness by the double curse of slavery and tobacco, stands—and until its proprietors are regenerated, and learn the difference between a land of slaves and a nation of freemen— must continue to stand, *a monument of the poverty and punishment which Providence has decreed as the reward of idleness and tyranny.* The general features of slavery are the same everywhere; but the utmost rigour of the system is only to be met with on the cotton plantations of Carolina and Georgia, or in the rice fields which skirt the deep swamps and morasses of the southern rivers. In the tobacco fields of Maryland and Virginia, great cruelties are practised— not so frequently by the owners, as by the overseers of the slaves; but yet, the tasks are not so excessive as in the cotton region, nor is the press of labour so incessant throughout the year. It is true, that from the period when the tobacco plants are set in the field, there is no resting time until it is housed; but it is planted out about the first of May, and must be cut and taken out of the field before the frost comes. After it is hung and dried, the labour of stripping and preparing it for the hogshead in leaf, or of manufacturing it into twist, is comparatively a work of leisure and ease. Besides, on almost every plantation the hands are able to complete the work of preparing the tobacco by January, and sometimes earlier; so that the winter months form some sort of respite from the toils of the year. The people are obliged, it is true, to occupy themselves in cutting wood for the house, making rails and repairing fences, and in clearing new land, to raise the tobacco plants for the next year; but as there is usually time enough, and to spare, for the completion of all this work, before the season arrives for setting the plants in the field, the men are seldom flogged much, unless they are very lazy or negligent, and the women are allowed to remain in the house, in very cold, snowy, or rainy weather. I who am intimately acquainted with the slavery, both of Maryland and Virginia, and know that there is no material difference between the two, aver, that a description of one is a description of both; and that the coloured people here have many advantages over those of the cotton region. There are seldom more than one hundred, of all ages and conditions, kept on one tobacco plantation; though there are sometimes many more; but this is not frequent; whilst on the cotton estates, I have seen four or five hundred, working together in the same vast field. In Maryland, the owners of the estates, generally, reside at home throughout the year; and the mistress of the mansion is seldom absent more than a few weeks in the winter, when she visits Baltimore or Washington,— the same is the case in Virginia. Her constant residence on the estate makes her acquainted, personally, with all the slaves, and she frequently interests herself in their welfare, often interceding with the master, her husband, to prevent the overseer from beating them unmercifully.

The young ladies of the family also, if there be any, after they have left school, are generally at home until they are married. Each of them universally claims a young black girl as her own, and takes her under her protection. This enables the girl to extend the protection and friendship of her *young mistress* to her father, mother, brothers and sisters. The sons of the family likewise have their favourites among the black boys, and have many disputes with the *overseer* if he abuses them. All these advantages accrue to the black people, from the circumstance of the master and his family living at home. In Maryland I never knew a mistress, or a young mistress, who would not listen to the complaints of the slaves. It is true, we were always obliged to approach the door of the mansion, in the most humble and supplicating manner, with our hats in our hands, and the most subdued and beseeching language in our mouths—but, in return, we generally received words of kindness, and very often a redress of our grievances; though I have known very great ladies, who would never grant any request from the *plantation hands*, but always referred them and their petitions to their master, under a pretence that they could not meddle with things that did not belong to the house. The mistresses of the great families, generally gave mild language to the slaves; though they sometimes sent for the overseer and had them severely flogged; but I have never heard any mistress in either Maryland or Virginia, indulge in the low, vulgar and profane vituperations, of which I was myself the object in Georgia, for several years, whenever I came into the presence of my mistress. Flogging—though often severe and excruciating in Maryland, is not practised with the order, regularity, and system, to which it is reduced in the south. On the Potomac, if a slave gives offence, he is generally chastised on the spot, in the field where he is at work, as the overseer always carries a whip— sometimes a twisted cow-hide, sometimes a kind of horsewhip, and very often a simple hickory switch or gad, cut in the adjoining woods. For stealing meat, or other provisions, or for any of the *higher* offences, the slaves are stripped, tied up by the hands—sometimes by the thumbs—and whipped at the quarter— but, many times, on a large tobacco plantation, there is not more than one of these regular whippings in a week—though on others, where the master happens to be a bad man, or a drunkard, the back of the unhappy Maryland slave, is seamed with scars from his neck to his hips.

It was my fortune, whilst I was a slave in Maryland, always to have comparatively mild masters; and as I uniformly endeavoured to do whatever was held to be the duty of a good slave, according to the customs of the country, I was never tied up to be flogged there, and never received a blow from my master, after I was fifteen years old. I was never under the control of an overseer in Maryland; or, it is very likely that I should not have been able to give this account of myself.

It is the custom of all the tobacco planters, in Maryland and Virginia, to plant a certain portion of their land in corn every year; so much as they suppose will be sufficient to produce bread, as they term it, for the negroes. By bread, is understood, a peck of corn per week, for each of their slaves.

After my return from the navy-yard, at Washington, I was generally employed in the culture of tobacco; but my attention was necessarily divided between the tobacco and the corn. The corn crop is, however, only a matter of secondary consideration, as no grain, of any kind, is grown for sale, by the planters; and if they raised as much, in my time, as supplied the wants of the *people*, and the horses of the stable, it was considered good farming. The sale of the tobacco was regarded as the only means of obtaining money, or any commodity which did not grow on the plantation.

It is unfortunate for the slaves, that in a tobacco or cotton growing country, no attention whatever is paid to the rearing of sheep — consequently, there is no wool to make winter clothes for the *people*, and oftentimes they suffer, excessively, from the cold; whereas, if their masters kept a good flock of sheep to supply them with wool, they could easily spin and weave in their cabins, a sufficiency of cloth to clothe them comfortably.

As many persons may be unacquainted with the process of cultivating tobacco, a short account of the growth of this plant, may not be uninteresting. The operation is to be commenced in the month of February, by clearing a piece of new land, and burning the timber cut from it, on the ground, so as to form a coat of ashes over the whole space, if possible. This ground is then to be dug up with a hoe, and the sticks and roots are to be carefully removed from it. In this bed, the tobacco seeds are sown about the beginning of March, not in hills, or in rows, but by broad cast, as in sowing turnips. The seeds do not spring soon, but generally the young plant appears early in April. If the weather, at the time the tobacco comes up, as it is called, is yet frosty, a covering of pine tops, or red cedar branches, is thickly spread over the whole patch, which consists of from one to four or five acres, according to the dimensions of the plantation to be provided with plants. As soon as the weather becomes fine, and the young tobacco begins to grow, the covering of the branches is removed, and the bed is exposed to the rays of the sun. From this time, the patch must be carefully attended, and kept clear of all grass and weeds. In the months of March and April the *people* are busily employed in ploughing the fields in which the tobacco is to be planted in May. Immediately after the corn is planted, every one, man, woman, and child, able to work with a hoe, or carry a tobacco plant, is engaged in working up the whole plantation, already ploughed a second time, into hills about four feet apart, laid out in regular rows across the field, by the course of the furrows. These hills are formed into squares or diamonds, at equal distance, both ways, and into these are transplanted the tobacco plants from the beds in which the seeds were sown. This transplantation must be done when the earth is wet with rain, and it is best to do it, if possible, just before, or at the time the rain falls, as cabbages are transplanted in a kitchen garden; but as the planting a field of one or two hundred acres, with tobacco, is not the work of an hour, as soon as it is deemed certain that there will be a sufficient fall of rain, to answer the purpose of planting out tobacco, all hands are called to the tobacco field, and no matter how fast it may rain, or how violent the storm may be, the removal of the plants from the bed, and fixing them in the hills where they are to grow in the field, goes on, until the crop is planted out, or the rain ceases, and the sun begins to shine. Nothing but the darkness of night, and the short respite, required by the scanty meal of the slaves, produce any cessation in the labour of tobacco planting, until the work is done, or the rain ceases, and the clouds disappear. Some plants die under the operation of removal, and their places are to be supplied from those left in the bed, at the fall of the next rain.

Sometimes the tobacco worm appears amongst the plants, before their removal from the bed, and from the moment this loathsome reptile is seen, the plants are to be carefully examined every day, for the purpose of destroying any worms that may be found. It is, however, not until the plants have been set in the field, and have begun to grow and flourish, that the worms come forth in their fall strength. If unmolested, they would totally destroy the largest field of tobacco in the months of June and July. At this season of the year, every slave that is able to kill a tobacco worm, is kept in the field, from morning until night. Those who are able to work with hoes, are engaged in weeding the tobacco, and at the same time destroying all the worms they find. The children do nothing but search for, and destroy the worms. All this labour and vigilance, however, would not suffice to keep the worms under, were it not for the aid of turkeys and ducks. On some large estates, they raise from one to two hundred turkeys, and as many ducks—not for the purpose of sale; but for the destruction of tobacco worms. The ducks, live in the tobacco field, day and night, except when they go to water; and as they are great gormandizers, they take from the plants and destroy an infinite number of worms. They are fond of them as an article of food, and require no watching to keep them in their place; but it is otherwise with the turkeys. These require very peculiar treatment. They must be kept all night in a large coop, spacious enough to contain the whole flock, with poles for them to roost on. As soon as it is light in the morning, the coop is opened, the flock turned out, and driven to the tobacco field.

Two hundred turkeys should be followed by four or five active lads, or young men, to keep them together, and at their duty. One turkey will destroy as many worms, as five men could do in the same period of time; but it seems that tobacco worm are not the natural food of turkeys; and they are prone to break out of the field, and escape to the woods or pastures in search of grasshoppers, which they greatly prefer to tobacco worms, for breakfast. However, if kept amongst the tobacco, they commit terrible ravages amongst the worms, and will eat until they are filled up to the throat. When they cease eating worms, they are to be driven back to the coop, and shut up, where they must have plenty of water, and a peck of corn to a hundred turkeys. If they get no corn, and are forced to live on tobacco worms only, they droop, become sickly, and would doubtlessly die. In the evening, they are again driven to the field, and treated again in the same manner as in the morning.

The tobacco worm, is of a bright green colour, with a series of rings or circles round its body. I have seen them as large as a man's longest finger. I was never able to discover in what manner they originate. They certainly do not change into a butterfly as some other worms do; and I could never perceive that they deposite eggs anywhere. I am of opinion that there is something in the very nature of the tobacco plant, which produces these nauseous reptiles, for they are too large, when at full growth, to be ranked with insects.

In the month of August, the tobacco crop is laid by, as it is termed; which means that they cease working in the fields, for the purpose of destroying the weeds and grass; the plants having now become so large, as not to be injured by the under vegetation. Still, however, the worms continue their ravages, and it is necessary to employ all hands in destroying them. In this month, also, the tobacco is to be topped, if it has not been done before. When the plants have reached the height of two or three feet, according to the goodness of the soil, and the vigour of the growth, the top is to be cut off, to prevent it from going to seed. This topping, causes all the powers of the plant, which would be exhausted in the formation of flowers and seeds, to expand in leaves fit for use. After the tobacco is fully grown, which in some plants happens early in August, it is to be carefully watched, to see when it is ripe, or fit for cutting. The state of the plant is known by its colour, and by certain pale spots which appear on the leaves. It does not all arrive at maturity at the same time: and although some plants ripen early in August, others are not ripe before the middle of September. When the plants are cut down, they are laid on the ground for a short time, then taken up, and the stalks split open to facilitate the drying of the leaves. In this condition it is removed to the drying house, and there hung up under sheds, until it is fully dry. From thence it is removed into the tobacco house, and laid up in bulk, ready for stripping and manufacturing.

CHAPTER V.

It is time to resume the narrative of my journey southward. At the period of which I now write, tobacco was universally cultivated in those parts of Virginia through which I travelled; and that, with the corn crops, constituted nearly the whole objects of agricultural labour.

The quantity of wheat and rye, which I saw on my journey, was very small. A little oats was growing on the estates of some gentlemen, who were fond of breeding fine horses. I did not perceive any material difference in the condition of the country, as I passed south, until after crossing the Roanoke river. Near this stream we passed a very large estate, on which, there appeared to me, to be nearly a thousand acres of tobacco growing. Our master was informed, by a gentleman whom we met here, that this property belonged to Mr. Randolph, a member of Congress, and one of the largest planters in Virginia. The land appeared to me not to be any better than the tobacco lands in Maryland, though a little more sandy. The mansion house was low, and of ordinary appearance. The fields were badly fenced; and the whole place was in poor condition. We passed close by a gang of near a hundred hands—men and women, at work with hoes, in a tobacco field. I had not, in all Virginia, seen any slaves more destitute of clothes. Many of the men, and some of the young women, were without shirts; and several young lads had only a few rags about their loins. Their skins looked dry and husky, which proved that they were not well fed. They were followed by an overseer who carried in his hand a kind of whip which I had never before seen; though I afterward became familiar with this terrible weapon. South of the Roanoke, the land became more sandy, and pine timber generally prevailed—in many places, to the exclusion of all other trees. In North Carolina, the same course of culture is pursued, as that which I have noted in Virginia; and the same, disastrous consequences result from it; though, as the country has not been settled so long as the northern part of Virginia and Maryland, so great a portion of the land has not been worn out and abandoned in the former, as in the latter. Here, also, the red cedar is seldom seen; as the pitch-pine takes possession of all waste and deserted fields. In this state the houses are not so well built as they are further north; there are fewer carriages, and the number of good horses, judging from those I saw on the road, must be much less. The inhabitants of the country are plainer in their dress, and they have fewer people of fashion, than are to be met in Virginia. The plantations here were not so large as those I saw on the north of the Roanoke; but larger tracts of country are covered with wood, than any I had heretofore seen. The condition of the slaves is not worse here, than it is in Virginia; nor is there any wheat in Carolina, worth speaking of.

As we approached the Yadkin river, the tobacco disappeared from the fields, and the cotton plant took its place, as an article of general culture. We passed the Yadkin by a ferry, on Sunday morning; and on the Wednesday following, in the evening, our master told us we were in the state of South Carolina. We staid this night in a small town called Lancaster; and I shall never forget the sensations which I experienced this evening, on finding myself in chains, in the state of South Carolina. From my earliest recollections, the name of South Carolina had been little less terrible to me than that of the bottomless pit. In Maryland, it had always been the practice of masters and mistresses, who wished to terrify their slaves, to threaten to sell them to South Carolina; where, it was represented, that their condition would be a hundred fold worse than it was in Maryland. I had regarded such a sale of myself, as the greatest of evils that could befall me, and had striven to demean myself in such manner, to my owners, as to preclude them from all excuse for transporting me to so horrid a place. At length I found myself, without having committed any crime, or even the slightest transgression, in the place and condition, of which I had, through life, entertained the greatest dread. I slept but little this night, and for the first time felt weary of life. It appeared to me that the cup of my misery was full— that there was no hope of release from my present chains, unless it might be to exchange them for the long lash of the ov rseers of the cotton plantations; in each of whose hands I observed such a whip as I saw in possession of Mr. Randolph's slave driver in Virginia. I seriously meditated on self-destruction, and had I been at liberty to get a rope, I believe I should have hanged myself at Lancaster. It appeared to me that such an act, done by a man in my situation, could not be a violation of the precepts of religion, nor of the laws of God.

I had now no hope of ever again seeing my wife and children, or of revisiting the scenes of my youth. I apprehended that I should, if I lived, suffer the most excruciating pangs that extreme and long continued hunger could inflict; for I had often heard, that in South Carolina, the slaves were compelled in times of scarcity, to live on cotton seeds.

From the dreadful apprehensions of future evil, which harrassed and harrowed my mind that night, I do not marvel, that the slaves who are driven to the south often destroy themselves. Self-destruction is much more frequent among the slaves in the cotton region than is generally supposed. When a negro kills himself, the master is unwilling to let it be known, lest the deed should be attributed to his own cruelty. A certain degree of disgrace falls upon the master whose slave has committed suicide—and the same man, who would stand by, and see his overseer give his slave a hundred lashes, with the long whip, on his bare back, without manifesting the least pity for the sufferings of the poor tortured wretch, will express very profound regret if the same slave terminates his own life, to avoid a repetition of the horrid flogging. Suicide amongst the slaves is regarded as a matter of dangerous example, and one which it is the business and the interest of all proprietors to discountenance and prevent. All the arguments which can be devised against it are used to deter the negroes from the perpetration of it; and such as take this dreadful means of freeing themselves from their miseries, are always branded in reputation after death, as the worst of criminals; and their bodies are not allowed the small portion of Christian rites which are awarded to the corpses of other slaves.

Surely if any thing can justify a man in taking his life into his own hands, and terminating his existence, no one can attach blame to the slaves on many of the cotton plantations of the south, when they cut short their breath, and the agonies of the present being, by a single stroke. What is life worth, amidst hunger, nakedness and excessive toil, under the continually uplifted lash?

It was long after midnight before I fell asleep; but the most pleasant dreams succeeded to these sorrowful forebodings. I thought I had, by some means, escaped from my master, and through infinite and unparalleled dangers and sufferings, had made my way back to Maryland; and was again in the cabin of my wife, with two of my little children on my lap; whilst their mother was busy in preparing for me a supper of fried fish, such as she often dressed, when I was at home, and had taken to her the fish I had caught in the Patuxent river. Every object was so vividly impressed upon my imagination in this dream, that when I awoke, a firm conviction settled upon my mind, that by some means, at present incomprehensible to me, I should yet again embrace my wife, and caress my children in their humble dwelling. Early in the morning, our master called us up; and distributed to each of the party, a cake made of corn meal, and a small piece of bacon. On our journey, we had only eaten twice a day, and had not received breakfast until about nine o'clock; but he said this morning meal was given to welcome us to South Carolina. He then addressed us all, and told us we might now give up all hope of ever returning to the places of our nativity; as it would be impossible for us to pass through the states of North Carolina and Virginia, without being taken up and sent back. He further advised us to make ourselves contented, as he would take us to Georgia, a far better country than any we had seen; and where we would be able to live in the greatest abundance. About sunrise we took up our march on the road to Columbia, as we were told. Hitherto our master had not offered to sell any of us, and had even refused to stop to talk to any one on the subject of our sale, although he had several times been addressed on this point, before we reached Lancaster; but soon after we departed from this village, we were overtaken on the road by a man on horseback, who accosted our driver by asking him if his *niggers* were for sale. The latter replied, that he believed he would not sell any yet, as he was on his way to Georgia, and cotton being now much in demand, he expected to obtain high prices for us from persons who were going to settle in the new purchase. He, however, contrary to his custom, ordered us to stop, and told the stranger he might look at us, and that he would find us as fine a lot of hands, as were ever imported into the country—that we were all prime property, and he had no doubt would command his own prices in Georgia.

The stranger, who was a thin, weather-beaten, sun-burned figure, then said, he wanted a couple of breeding-wenches, and would give as much for them as they would bring in Georgia—that he had lately heard from Augusta, and that *niggers* were not higher there than in Columbia and, as he had been in Columbia the week before, he knew what *niggers* were worth. He then walked along our line, as we stood chained together, and looked at the whole of us—then turning to the women, asked the prices of the two pregnant ones. Our master replied, that these were two of the best breeding-wenches in all Maryland—that one was twenty-two, and the other only nineteen—that the first was already the mother of seven children, and the other of four—that he had himself seen the children at the time he bought their mothers—and that such wenches would be cheap at a thousand dollars each; but as they were not able to keep up with the gang, he would take twelve hundred dollars for the two. The purchaser said this was too much, but that he would give nine hundred dollars for the pair. This price was promptly refused; but our master, after some consideration, said he was willing to sell a bargain in these wenches, and would take eleven hundred dollars for them, which was objected to on the other side; and many faults and failings were pointed out in the merchandise. After much bargaining, and many gross jests on the part of the stranger, he offered a thousand dollars for the two; and said he would give no more. He then mounted his horse, and moved off; but after he had gone about one hundred yards, he was called back; and our master said, if he would go with him to the next blacksmith's shop on the road to Columbia, and pay for taking the irons off the rest of us, he might have the two women.

This proposal was agreed to, and as it was now about nine o'clock, we were ordered to hasten on to the next house, where, we were told, we must stop for breakfast. At this place we were informed that it was ten miles to the next smith's shop, and our new acquaintance was obliged by the terms of his contract, to accompany us thither. We received, for breakfast, about a pint of boiled rice to each person, and after this was despatched, we again took to the road, eager to reach the blacksmith's shop, at which we expected to be relieved of the iron rings and chains, which had so long galled and worried us. About two o'clock, we arrived at the longed-for residence of the smith; but, on inquiry, our master was informed that he was not at home, and would not return before evening. Here a controversy arose, whether we should all remain here until the smith returned, or the stranger should go on with us to the next smithery, which was said to be only five miles distant. This was a point not easily settled, between two such spirits as our master and the stranger; both of whom had been overseers in their time, and both of whom had risen to the rank of proprietors of slaves.

The matter had already produced angry words, and much vaunting on the part of the stranger;— "that a freeman of South Carolina was not to be imposed upon; that by the constitution of the state, his rights were sacred, and he was not to be deprived of his liberty, at the arbitrary will of a man just from amongst the Yankees, and who had brought with him to the south, as many Yankee tricks as he had *niggers*, and he believed many more." He then swore, that "all the niggers in the drove were Yankee *niggers* "

"When I *overseed* for Colonel Polk," said he, "on his rice plantation, he had two Yankee *niggers* that he brought from Maryland, and they were running away every day. I gave them a hundred lashes more than a dozen times; but they never quit running away, till I chained them together, with iron collars round their necks, and chained them to spades, and made them do nothing but dig ditches to drain the rice swamps. They could not run away then, unless they went together, and carried their chains and spades with them. I kept them in this way two years, and better *niggers* I never had. One of them died one night, and the other was never good for any thing after he lost his mate. He never ran away afterwards, but he died too, after a while." He then addressed himself to the two women, whose master he had become, and told them that if ever they ran away, he would treat them in the same way. Wretched as I was myself, my heart bled for these poor creatures, who had fallen into the hands of a tiger in human form. The dispute between the two masters was still raging, when, unexpectedly, the blacksmith rode up to his house, on a thin, bony-looking horse, and, dismounting, asked his wife what these gentlemen were making such a *frolick* about. I did not hear her answer, but both the disputants turned and addressed themselves to the smith—the one to know what price he would demand, to take the irons off all these *niggers*, and the other to know how long it would take him to perform the work. It is here proper for me to observe, that there are many phrases of language in common use in Carolina and Georgia, which are applied in a way that would not be understood by persons from one of the northern states. For instance, when several persons are quarrelling, brawling, making a great noise, or even fighting, they say, "*the gentlemen are frolicking!*" I heard many other terms equally strange, whilst I resided in the southern country, amongst such white people as I became acquainted with; though my acquaintance was confined, in a great measure, to overseers, and such people as did not associate with the rich planters and great families.

The smith at length agreed to take the irons from the whole of us for two dollars and fifty cents, and immediately set about it, with the air of indifference that he would have manifested in tearing a pair of old shoes from the hoofs of a wagon-horse. It was four weeks and five days, from the time my irons had been riveted upon me, until they were removed, and great as had been my sufferings whilst chained to my fellow-slaves, I cannot say that I felt any pleasure in being released from my long confinement; for I knew that my liberation was only preparatory to my final, and, as I feared, perpetual subjugation to the power of some such monster, as the one then before me, who was preparing to drive away the two unfortunate women whom he had purchased, and whose life's-blood he had acquired the power of shedding at pleasure, for the sum of a thousand dollars. After we were released from our chains, our master sold the whole lot of irons, which we had borne, from Maryland, to the blacksmith, for seven dollars.

The smith then procured a bottle of rum, and treated his two new acquaintances to a part of its contents — wishing them both good luck with their *niggers*. After these civilities were over, the two women were ordered to follow their new master, who shaped his course across the country, by a road leading westward. At parting from us, they both wept aloud, and wrung their hands in despair. We all went to them, and bade them a last farewell. Their road led into a wood, which they soon entered, and I never saw them, nor heard of them again.

These women had both been driven from Calvert county, as well as myself, and the fate of the younger of the two, was peculiarly severe.

She had been brought up as the waiting-maid of a young lady, the daughter of a gentleman, whose wife and family often visited the mistress of my own wife. I had frequently seen this woman when she was a young girl, in attendance upon her young mistress, and riding in the same carriage with her. The father of the young lady died, and soon after, she married a gentleman who resided a few miles off. The husband received a considerable fortune with his bride, and amongst other things, her waiting-maid, who was reputed a great beauty among people of colour. He had been addicted to the fashionable sports of the country, before marriage, such as horse-racing, fox-hunting, &c. and I had heard the black people say he drank too freely; but it was supposed that he would correct all these irregularities after marriage, more especially as his wife was a great belle, and withal very handsome. The reverse, however, turned out to be the fact. Instead of growing better, he became worse; and in the course of a few years, was known all over the country, as a drunkard and a gambler. His wife, it was said, died of grief, and soon after her death, his effects were seized by his creditors, and sold by the sheriff. The former waiting-maid, now the mother of several children, was purchased by our present master, for three hundred dollars, at the sheriff's sale, and this poor wretch, whose employment in early life had been to take care of her young mistress, and attend her in her chamber, and at her toilet, after being torn from her husband and her children, had now gone to toil out a horrible existence beneath the scorching sun of a South Carolina cotton field, under the dominion of a master, as void of the manners of a gentleman, as he was of the language of humanity.

It was now late in the afternoon; but, as we had made little progress to-day, and were now divested of the burden of our chains, as well as freed from the two women, who had hitherto much retarded our march, our master ordered us to hasten on our way, as we had ten miles to go that evening. I had been so long oppressed by the weight of my chains, and the iron collar about my neck, that for some time after I commenced walking at my natural liberty, I felt a kind of giddiness, or lightness of the head. Most of my companions complained of the same sensation, and we did not recover our proper feelings, until after we had slept one night. It was after dark when we arrived at our lodging-place, which proved to be the house of a small cotton-planter, who, it appeared, kept a sort of a house of entertainment for travellers, contrary to what I afterwards discovered to be the usual custom of cotton-planters. This man and my master had known each other before, and seemed to be well acquainted. He was the first person that we had met since leaving Maryland, who was known to my master, and as they kept up a very free conversation, through the course of the evening, and the house in which they were, was only separated from the kitchen, in which we were lodged, by a space of a few feet, I had an opportunity of hearing much that was highly interesting to me. The landlord, after supper, came with our master to look at us, and to see us receive our allowance of boiled rice from the hands of a couple of black women, who had prepared it in a large iron kettle. Whilst viewing us, the former asked the latter, what he intended to do with his drove; but no reply was made to this inquiry—and as our master had, through our whole journey, maintained a studied silence on this subject, I felt a great curiosity to know what disposition he intended to make of the whole gang, and of myself in particular. On their return to the house, I advanced to a small window in the kitchen, which brought me within a few yards of the place where they sat, and from which I was able to hear all they said, although they spoke in a low tone of voice. I here learned, that so many of us as could be sold for a good price, were to be disposed of in Columbia, on our arrival at that place, and that the residue would be driven to Augusta and sold there.

The landlord assured my master that at this time slaves were much in demand, both in Columbia and Augusta; that purchasers were numerous and prices good; and that the best plan of effecting good sales would be to put up each *nigger*, separately, at auction, after giving a few days' notice, by an advertisement, in the neighbouring country. Cotton, he said, had not been higher for many years, and as a great many persons, especially young men, were moving off to the new purchase in Georgia, prime hands were in high demand, for the purpose of clearing the land in the new country—that the boys and girls, under twenty, would bring almost any price at present, in Columbia, for the purpose of picking the growing crop of cotton, which promised to be very heavy; and as most persons had planted more than their hands would be able to pick, young *niggers*, who would soon learn to pick cotton, were prime articles in the market. As to those more advanced in life, he seemed to think the prospect of selling them at an unusual price, not so good, as they could not so readily become expert cotton-pickers— he said further, that from some cause, which he could not comprehend, the price of rice had not been so good this year as usual; and that he had found it cheaper to purchase rice to feed his own *niggers* than to provide them with corn, which had to be brought from the upper country. He therefore, advised my master, not to drive us towards the rice plantation of the low country. My master said he would follow his advice, at least so far as to sell a portion of us in Carolina, but seemed to be of opinion that his prime hands would bring him more money in Georgia, and named me, in particular, as one who would be worth, at least, a thousand dollars, to a man who was about making a settlement, and clearing a plantation in the new purchase, I therefore concluded, that, in the course of events, I was likely to become the property of a Georgian, which turned out in the end, to be the case, though not so soon as I at this time apprehended. I slept but little this night, feeling a restlessness when no longer in chains; and pondering over the future lot of my life, which appeared fraught only with evil and misfortune. Day at length dawned, and with its first light we were ordered to betake ourselves to the road, which, we were told, would lead us to Columbia, the place of intended sale of some, if not all of us. For several days past, I had observed that in the country through which we travelled, little attention was paid to the cultivation of any thing but cotton. Now this plant was almost the sole possessor of the fields. It covered the plantations adjacent to the road, as far as I could see, both before and behind me, and looked not unlike buckwheat before it blossoms. I saw some small fields of corn, and lots of sweet potatoes, amongst which the young vines of the water-melon were frequently visible. The improvements on the plantations were not good. There were no barns, but only stables and sheds, to put the cotton under, as it was brought from the field. Hay seemed to be unknown in the country, for I saw neither hay-stacks nor meadows; and the few fields that were lying fallow, had but small numbers of cattle in them, and these were thin and meagre. We had met with no flocks of sheep of late, and the hogs that we saw on the road-side, were in bad condition. The horses and mules that I saw at work in the cotton-fields, were poor and badly harnessed, and the half-naked condition of the negroes, who drove them, or followed with the hoe, together with their wan complexions, proved to me that they had too much work, or not enough food. We passed a cotton-gin this morning, the first that I ever saw; but they were not at work with it. We also met a party of ladies and gentlemen on a journey of pleasure, riding in two very handsome carriages, drawn by sleek and spirited horses, very different in appearance from the moving skeletons that I had noticed drawing the ploughs in the fields. The black drivers of the coaches were neatly clad in gay-coloured clothes, and contrasted well with their half-naked brethren, a gang of whom were hoeing cotton by the road-side, near them, attended by an overseer in a white linen shirt and pantaloons, with one of the long negro whips in his hand.

I observed that these poor people did not raise their heads, to look either at the fine coaches and horses then passing, or at us; but kept their faces steadily bent towards the cotton-plants, from among which they were removing the weeds. I almost shuddered at the sight, knowing, that I myself was doomed to a state of servitude, equally cruel and debasing, unless, by some unforeseen occurrence, I might fail into the hands of a master of less inhumanity of temper than the one who had possession of the miserable creatures before me.

CHAPTER VI.

It was manifest, that I was now in a country, where the life of a black man was no more regarded than that of an ox, except as far as the man was worth the more money in the market. On all the plantations that we passed, there was a want of live stock of every description, except slaves, and they wore deplorably abundant.

The fields were destitute of every thing that deserved the name of grass, and not a spear of clover was anywhere visible. The few cattle that existed, were browsing on the boughs of the trees, in the woods. Every thing betrayed a scarcity of the means of supplying the slaves, who cultivated the vast cotton-fields, with a sufficiency of food. We travelled this day more than thirty miles, and crossed the Catawba river in the afternoon, on the bottoms of which I saw, for the first time, fields of rice, growing in swamps, covered with water. Causeways were raised through the low-lands in which the rice grew, and on these, the road was formed on which we travelled. These rice-fields, or rather swamps, had, in my eyes, a beautiful appearance. The rice was nearly two feet in height above the water, and of a vivid green colour, covering a large space, of at least a hundred acres. Had it not been for the water, which appeared stagnant and sickly, and swarmed with frogs and thousands of snakes, it would have been as fine a sight as one need wish to took upon. After leaving the low grounds along the river, we again entered plantations of cotton, which lined the roads on both sides, relieved, here and there, by corn-fields, and potato-patches. We stopped for the night at a small tavern, and our master said we were within a day's journey of Columbia.

We here, again, received boiled rice for supper, without salt, or any kind of seasoning; a pint was allotted to each person, which we greedily devoured, having had no dinner to-day, save an allowance of corn-cakes, with the fat of about five pounds of bacon, extracted by frying, in which we dipped our bread. I slept soundly after this day's march, the fatigues of the body having, for once, overcome the agitations of the mind. The next day, which was, if my recollection is accurate, the ninth of June, was the last of our journey before our company separated; and we were on the road before the stars had disappeared from the sky. Our breakfast, this morning, consisted of bacon soup, a dish composed of corn meal, boiled in water, with a small piece of bacon to give the soup a taste of meat. For dinner we had boiled Indian peas, with a small allowance of bacon. This was the first time that we had received two rations of meat in the same day, on the whole journey, and some of our party were much surprised at the kindness of our master; but I had no doubt that his object was to make us look fat and hearty, to enable him to obtain better prices for us at Columbia.

At supper this night, we had corn mush, in large wooden trays, with melted lard to dip the mush in before eating it. We might have reached Columbia this day if we had continued our march, but we stopped, at least an hour before sun-set, about three miles from town, at the house of a man who supported the double character of planter, and keeper of a house of entertainment; for I learned from his slaves that their master considered it disreputable to be called a tavern-keeper, and would not put up a sign, although he received pay of such persons as lodged with him. His house was a frame building, weather-boarded with pine boards, but had no plastering within. The furniture corresponded with the house which contained it, and was both scanty and mean, consisting of pine tables and wooden chairs, with bottoms made of corn husks. The house was only one story high, and all the rooms, six or seven in number, parlour, bed-rooms, and kitchen, were on the first floor. As the weather was warm and the windows open, I had an opportunity of looking into the sleeping rooms of the family, as I walked round the house, which I was permitted freely to do. The beds and their furniture answered well to the chairs and tables; yet in the large front room I observed on an old fashioned side-board, a great quantity of glass ware, of various descriptions, with two or three dozen silver spoons, a silver tea urn, and several knives and forks with silver handles. In the corner of this room stood a bed with gaudy red curtains, with figures of lions, elephants, naked negroes, and other representations of African scenery.

The master of the house was not at home when we arrived, but came in from the field shortly afterwards. He met my master with the cordiality of an old friend, though he had never seen him before, said he was happy to see him at his house, and that the greatest pleasure he enjoyed was derived from the entertainment of such gentlemen as thought proper to visit his house; that he was always glad to see strangers, and more especially gentlemen who were adding so much to the wealth and population of Carolina, as those merchants who imported servants from the north. He then observed that he had never seen a finer lot of property pass his house than we were, and that any gentleman who brought such a stock of hands into the country was a public benefactor, and entitled to the respect and gratitude of every friend of the south. He assured my master that he was happy to see him at his house, and that if he thought proper to remain a few days with him, it would be his chief business to introduce him to the gentlemen of the neighbourhood, who would all be glad to become acquainted with a merchant of his respectability. In the state of Maryland, my master had been called a *negro buyer, or Georgia trader*, sometimes a *negro driver*; but here, I found that he was elevated to the rank of merchant, and a merchant of the first order too; for it was very clear that in the opinion of the landlord, no branch of trade was more honourable than the traffic in us poor slaves. Our master observed that he had a mind to remain here a short time, and try what kind of market Columbia would present, for the sale of his lot of servants; and that he would make this house his home, until he had ascertained what could be done in town, and what demand there was in the neighbourhood for servants. We were not called *slaves* by these men, who talked of selling us, and of the price we would bring, with as little compunction of conscience as they would have talked of the sale of so many mules.

It is the custom throughout all the slave-holding states amongst people of fashion, never to speak of their negroes as slaves, but always as servants; but I had never before met with the keeper of a public house, in the country, who had arrived at this degree of refinement. I had been accustomed to hear this order of men, and indeed the greater number of white people, speak of the people of colour as *niggers*. We remained at this place more than two weeks; I presume because my master found it cheaper to keep us here than in town, or perhaps, because he supposed we might recover from the hardships of our journey more speedily in the country.

As it was here that my real acquaintance with South Carolina commenced, I have noted, with more particularity the incidents that occurred, than I otherwise should have done. This family was composed of the husband, wife, three daughters, all young women, and two sons, one of whom appeared to be about twenty, and the other, perhaps seventeen years old. They had nine slaves in all, one very old man, quite crooked with years and labour—two men of middle age—one lad, perhaps sixteen—one woman, with three children, the oldest about seven,—and a young girl of twelve or fourteen. The farm, or plantation, they lived on, contained about one hundred and fifty acres of cleared land, sandy, and the greater part of it poor, as was proved by the stinted growth of the cotton.

At the time of our arrival at this house, I saw no persons about it, except the four ladies—the mother and her three daughters—the husband being in the field, as noticed above. According to the orders of my master, I had taken the saddle from his horse and put him in a stable; and it was not until after the first salutations of the new landlord to my master were over, that he seemed to think of asking him whether he had come on foot, on horse-back, or in a coach. He at length, however, turned suddenly and asked him with an air of surprise, where he had left his horses and carriage. My master said he had no carriage, that he travelled on horseback, and that his horse was in the stable. The landlord then apologized for the trouble he must have had, in having his horse put away himself; and said that at this season of the year, the planters were so hurried by their crops, and found so much difficulty in keeping down the grass, that, they were generally obliged to keep all their servants in the field; that for his part, he had been compelled to put his coachman, and even the waiting-maids of his daughters into the cotton fields, and that at this time, his family were without servants, a circumstance that had never happened before! "For my part," said he, "I have always prided myself on bringing up my family well, and can say, that although I do not live in so fine a house as some of the other planters of Carolina, yet my children are as great ladies and gentlemen as any in the state. Not one of them has ever had to do a day's work yet, and as long as I live, never shall. I sent two of my daughters to Charleston last summer, and they were there three months; and I intend to send the youngest there this summer. They have all learned to dance here in Columbia, where I sent them two quarters to a Frenchman, and he made me pay pretty well for it. They went to the same dancing school with the daughters of Wade Hampton and Colonel Fitzhugh. I am determined that they shall never marry any but gentlemen of the first character, and I know they will always follow my advice in matters of this kind. They are prudent and sensible girls, and are not going to do as Major Pollack's daughter did this spring, who ran away with a Georgia cracker who brought a drove of cattle for sale from the Indian country, and who had not a *nigger* in the world. He staid with me sometime, and wished to have something to say to my second daughter, but the thing would not do."

Here he stopped short in his narrative, and seeming to muse a moment, said to his guest, "I presume, as you travel alone, you have no family." "No," replied my master, "I am a single man." "I thought so by your appearance," said the loquacious landlord, "and I shall be glad to introduce you to my family this evening. My sons are two as fine fellows as there are in all Carolina. My oldest boy is lieutenant in the militia, and in the same company that marched with Gen. Marion in the war. He was on the point of fighting a duel last winter, with young M'Corkle in Columbia; but the matter was settled between them. You will see him this evening, when he returns from the coit-party. A coit-party of young bucks meets once every week about two miles from this, and as I wish my sons to keep the best company, they both attend it. There is to be a cock-fight there this afternoon, and my youngest son, Edmund, has the finest cock in this country. He is of the true game blood, — the real Dominica game breed; and I sent to Charleston for his gaffs. There is a bet of ten dollars a side between my son's cock, and one belonging to young Blainey, the son of Major Blainey. Young Blainey is a hot-headed young blood, and has been concerned in three duels, though I believe he never fought but one; but I know Edmund will not take a word from him, and it will be well if he and his cock do not both get well licked."

Here the conversation was arrested by the sound of horses' feet on the road, and in the next instant, two young men rode up at a gallop, mounted on lean looking horses; one of the riders carrying a pole on his shoulder, with a game cock in a net bag, tied to one end of it. On perceiving them the landlord exclaimed with an oath, "There's two lads of spirit! stranger, — and if you will allow me the liberty of asking you your name, I will introduce you to them." At the suggestion of his name, my master seemed to hesitate a little, but after a moment's pause, said, "They call me M'Giffin, sir." "My name is Hulig, sir," replied the landlord, "and I am very happy to be acquainted with you, Mr. M'Giffin," at the same time shaking him by the hand, and introducing his two sons, who were by this time at the door.

This was the first time I had ever heard the name of my master, although I had been with him five weeks. I had never seen him before the day on which he seized and bound me in Maryland, and as he took me away immediately, I did not hear his name at the time. The people who assisted to fetter me, either from accident or design, omitted to name him, and after we commenced our journey, he had maintained so much distant reserve and austerity of manner towards us all, that no one ventured to ask him his name. We had called him nothing but "master," and the various persons at whose houses we had stopped on our way, knew as little of his name as we did. We had frequently been asked the name of our master, and perhaps had not always obtained credence, when we said we did not know it.

Throughout the whole journey, until after we were released from our irons, he had forbidden us to converse together beyond a few words in relation to our temporary condition and wants; and as he was with us all day, and never slept out of hearing of us at night, he rigidly enforced his edict of silence. I presume that the reason of this prohibition of all conversation, was to prevent us from devising plans of escape; but he had imposed as rigid a silence on himself as was enforced upon us; and after having passed from Maryland to South Carolina, in his company, I knew no more of my master, than, that he knew how to keep his secrets, guard his slaves, and make a close bargain. I had never heard him speak of his home or family; and therefore had concluded that he was an unmarried man, and an adventurer, who felt no more attachment for one place than another, and whose residence was not very well settled; but, from the large sums of money which he must have been able to command and carry with him to the north, to enable him to purchase so large a number of slaves, I had no doubt that he was a man of consequence and consideration in the place from whence he came.

In Maryland, I had always observed that men, who were the owners of large stocks of negroes, were not averse to having publicity given to their names; and that the possession of this species of property even there, gave its owner more vanity and egotism, than fell to the lot of the holders of any other kind of estate; and in truth, my subsequent experience proved, that without the possession of slaves, no man could ever arrive at, or hope to rise to any honourable station in society;—yet, my master seemed to take no pride in having at his disposal the lives of so many human beings. He never spoke to us in words of either pity or hatred; and never spoke of us, except to order us to be fed or watered, as he would have directed the same offices to be performed for so many horses, or to inquire where the best prices could be obtained for us. He regarded us only as objects of traffic and the materials of his commerce; and although he had lived several years in Carolina and Georgia, and had there exercised the profession of an overseer, he regarded the southern planters as no less the subjects of trade and speculation, than the slaves he sold to them; as will appear in the sequel. It was to this man that the landlord introduced his two sons, and upon whom he was endeavouring to impose a belief, that he was the head of a family which took rank with those of the first planters of the district. The ladies of the household, though I had seen them in the kitchen when I walked round the house, had not yet presented themselves to my master, nor indeed were they in a condition to be seen anywhere but in the apartment they occupied at the time. The young gentlemen gave a very gasconading account of the coit-party and cock-fight, from which they had just returned, and according to their version of the affair, it might have been an assemblage of at least half the military officers of the state; for all the persons of whom they spoke, were captains, majors, and colonels. The eldest said, he had won two bowls of punch at coits; and the youngest; whose cock had been victor in the battle, on which ten dollars were staked, vaunted much of the qualities of his bird; and supported his veracity by numerous oaths, and reiterated appeals to his brother for the truth of his assertions. Both these young men were so much intoxicated, that they with difficulty maintained an erect posture in walking.

By this time the sun was going down, and I observed two female slaves, a woman and girl, approaching the house on the side of the kitchen from the cotton field. They were coming home to prepare supper for the family; the ladies whom I had seen in the kitchen not having been there for the purpose of performing the duties appropriate to that station, but having sought it as a place of refuge from the sight of my master, who had approached the front of their dwelling silently, and so suddenly as not to permit them to gain the foot of the stairway in the large front room, without being seen by him, to whose view they by no means wished to expose themselves before they had visited their toilets. About dark the supper was ready in the large room, and, as it had two fronts, one of which looked into the yard where my companions and I had been permitted to seat ourselves, and had an opportunity of seeing, by the light of the candle, all that was done within, and of hearing all that was said. The ladies, four in number, had entered the room before the gentlemen; and when the latter came in my master was introduced, by the landlord to his wife and daughters, by the name and title of *Colonel M'Giffin*, which, at that time, impressed me with a belief that he was really an officer, and that he had disclosed this circumstance without my knowledge; but I afterwards perceived that in the south it is deemed respectful to address a stranger by the title of Colonel, or Major, or General, if his appearance will warrant the association of so high a rank with his name. My master had declared his intention of becoming the inmate of this family for some time, and no pains seemed to be spared on their part to impress upon his mind the high opinion that they entertained of the dignity of the owner of fifty slaves; the possession of so large a number of human creatures being, in Carolina, a certificate of character, which entitles its bearer to enter whatever society he may choose to select, without any thing more being known of his birth, his life, or reputation. The man who owns fifty servants must needs be a gentleman amongst the higher ranks, and the owner of half a hundred *niggers* is a sort of nobleman amongst the low, the ignorant, and the vulgar. The mother and three daughters, whose appearance, when I saw them in the kitchen, would have warranted the conclusion that they had just risen from bed, without having time to adjust their dress, were now gaily, if not neatly attired; and the two female slaves, who had come from the field at sundown to cook the supper, now waited at the table. The landlord talked much of his crops, his plantation and slaves, and of the distinguished families who exchanged visits with his own; but my master took very little part in the conversation of the evening, and appeared disposed to maintain the air of mystery which had hitherto invested his character.

After it was quite dark, the slaves came in from the cotton-field, and taking little notice of us, went into the kitchen, and each taking thence a pint of corn, proceeded to a little mill, which was nailed to a post in the yard, and there commenced the operation of grinding meal for their suppers, which were afterwards to be prepared by baking the meal into cakes at the fire. The woman who was the mother of the three small children, was permitted to grind her allowance of corn first, and after her came the old man, and the others in succession. After the corn was converted into meal, each one kneaded it up with cold water into a thick dough, and raking away the ashes from a small space on the kitchen hearth, placed the dough, rolled up in green leaves, in the hollow, and covering it with hot embers, left it to be baked into bread, which was done in about half an hour. These loaves constituted the only supper of the slaves belonging to this family; for I observed that the two women who had waited at the table, after the supper of the white people was disposed of, also came with their corn to the mill on the post, and ground their allowance like the others. They had not been permitted to taste even the fragments of the meal that they had cooked for their masters and mistresses. It was eleven o'clock before these people had finished their supper of cakes, and several of them, especially the younger of the two lads, were so overpowered with toil and sleep, that they had to be roused from their slumbers when their cakes were done, to devour them.

We had for our supper to-night, a pint of boiled rice to each person, and a small quantity of stale and very rancid butter, from the bottom of an old keg, or firkin, which contained about two pounds, the remnant of that which once filled it. We boiled the rice ourselves, in a large iron kettle; and, as our master now informed us that we were to remain here some time, many of us determined to avail ourselves of this season of respite from our toils, to wash our clothes, and free our persons from the vermin which had appeared amongst our party several weeks before, and now begun to be extremely tormenting. As we were not allowed any soap, we were obliged to resort to the use of a very fine and unctuous kind of clay, resembling fullers' earth, but of a yellow colour, which was found on the margin of a small swamp near the house. This was the first time that I had ever heard of clay being used for the purpose of washing clothes; but I often availed myself of this resource afterwards, whilst I was a slave in the south. We wet our clothes, then rubbed this clay all over the garments, and by scouring it out in warm water with our hands, the cloth, whether of woollen, cotton, or linen texture, was left entirely clean. We subjected our persons to the same process, and in this way freed our camp from the host of enemies that had been generated in the course of our journey.

This washing consumed the whole of the first day of our residence on the plantation of Mr. Hulig. We all lay the first night in a shed, or summer kitchen, standing behind the house, and a few yards from it, a place in which the slaves of the plantation washed their clothes, and passed their Sundays in warm weather, when they did not work; but as this place was quite too small to accommodate our party, or indeed to contain us, without crowding us together in such a manner as to endanger our health, we were removed, the morning after our arrival, to an old decayed frame building, about one hundred yards from the house, which had been erected, as I learned, for a cotton-gin, but into which its possessor, for want of means I presume, had never introduced the machinery of the gin. This building was near forty feet square; was without any other floor than the earth, and had neither doors nor windows, to close the openings which had been left for the admission of those who entered it. We were told that in this place the cotton of the plantation was deposited in the picking season, as it was brought from the field, until it could be removed to a neighbouring plantation, where there was a gin to divest it of its seeds.

Here we took our temporary abode—men and women promiscuously. Our provisions, whilst we remained here, were regularly distributed to us; and the daily allowance to each person, consisted of a pint of corn, a pint of rice, and about three or four pounds of butter, such as we had received on the night of our arrival, divided amongst us, in small pieces from the point of a table knife. The rice we boiled in the iron kettle,—we ground our corn at the little mill on the post in the kitchen, and converted the meal into bread, in the manner we had been accustomed to at home— sometimes on the hearth, and sometimes before the fire, on a hoe. The butter was given us as an extraordinary ration, to strengthen and recruit us after our long march, and give us a healthy and expert appearance at the time of our future sale.

We had no beds of any kind to sleep on, but each one was provided with a blanket, which had been the companion of our travels. We were left entirely at liberty to go out or in when we pleased, and no watch was kept over us either by night or day.

Our master had removed us so far from our native country, that he supposed it impossible for any of us ever to escape from him, and surmount all the obstacles that lay between us and our former homes. He went away immediately after we were established in our new lodgings, and remained absent until the second evening about sundown, when he returned, came into our shed, sat down on a block of wood in the midst of us, and asked if any one had been sick; if we had got our clothes clean; and if we had been supplied with an allowance of rice, corn, and butter. After satisfying himself upon these points, he told us that we were now at liberty to run away if we chose to do so; but if we made the attempt we should most certainly be re-taken, and subjected to the most terrible punishment. "I never flog," said he, "My practice is to *cat-haul*; and if you run away, and I catch you again—as I surely shall do—and give you one cat-hauling, you will never run away again, nor attempt it." I did not then understand the import of cat-hauling, but in after times, became well acquainted with its signification.

We remained in this place nearly two weeks, during which time our allowance of food was not varied, and was regularly given to us. We were not required to do any work; and I had liberty and leisure to walk about the plantation, and make such observations as I could upon the new state of things around me. Gentlemen and ladies came every day to look at us, with a view of becoming our purchasers; and we were examined with minute care as to our ages, former occupations, and capacity of performing labour. Our persons were inspected, and more especially the hands were scrutinized, to see if all the fingers were perfect, and capable of the quick motions necessary in picking cotton. Our master only visited us once a day, and sometimes he remained absent two days; so that he seldom met any of those who came to see us; but, whenever it so happened that he did meet them, he laid aside his silence and became very talkative, and even animated in his conversation, extolling our good qualities, and averring that he had purchased some of us of one colonel, and others of another general in Virginia; that he could by no means have procured us, had it not been that, in some instances, our masters had ruined themselves, and were obliged to sell us to save their families from ruin; and in others, that our owners were dead, their estates deeply in debt, and we had been sold at public sale; by which means he had become possessed of us. He said our habits were unexceptionable, our characters good, and that there was not one amongst us all who had ever been known to run away, or steal any thing from our former masters. I observed that running away, and stealing from his master, were regarded as the highest crimes of which a slave could be guilty; but I heard no questions asked concerning our propensity to steal from other people besides our masters, and I afterwards learned, that this was not always regarded as a very high crime by the owner of a slave, provided he would perpetrate the theft, so adroitly as not to be detected in it.

We were severally asked by our visiters, if we would be willing to live with them, if they would purchase us, to which we generally replied in the affirmative; but our owner declined all the offers that were made for us, upon the ground that we were too poor—looked too bad to be sold at present—and that in our condition he could not expect to get a fair value for us.

One evening, when our master was with us, a thin, sallow-looking man rode up to the house, and alighting from his horse, came to us, and told him that he had come to buy a boy; that he wished to get a good field hand, and would pay a good price for him. I never saw a human countenance that expressed more of the evil passions of the heart than did that of this man, and his conversation corresponded with his physiognomy. Every sentence of his language was accompanied with an oath of the most vulgar profanity, and his eyes appeared to me to be the index of a soul as cruel as his visage was disgusting and repulsive.

After looking at us for some time, this wretch singled *me* out as the object of his choice, and coming up to me, asked me how I would like him for a master. In my heart I detested him; but a slave is often afraid to speak the truth, and divulge all he feels; so with myself in this instance, as it was doubtful whether I might not fall into his hands, and be subject to the violence of his temper, I told him that if he was a good master, as every gentleman ought to be, I should be willing to live with him. He appeared satisfied with my answer, and turning to my master, said he would give a high price for me. "I can," said he, "by going to Charleston, buy as many Guinea negroes as I please for two hundred dollars each, but as I like this fellow, I will give you four hundred for him." This offer struck terror into my very heart, for I knew it was as much as was generally given for the best and ablest slaves, and I expected that it would immediately be accepted as my price, and that I should be at once consigned to the hands of this man, of whom I had formed so abhorrent an opinion. To my surprise and satisfaction, however, my master made no reply to the proposition; but stood for a moment, with one hand raised to his face and his fore-finger on his nose, and then turning suddenly to me said, "Charles, go into the house; I shall not sell you to-day." It was my business to obey the order of departure, and as I went beyond the sound of their voices, I could not understand the purport of the conversation which followed between these two traffickers in human blood; but after a parley of about a quarter of an hour, the hated stranger started abruptly away, and going to the road, mounted his horse, and rode off at a gallop, banishing himself and my fears together.

I did not see my master again this evening, and when I came out of our barracks in the morning, although it was scarcely daylight, I saw him standing near one corner of the building, with his head inclined towards the wall, evidently listening to catch any sounds within. He ordered me to go and feed his horse, and have him saddled for him by sunrise. About an hour afterwards he came to the stable in his riding dress; and told me that he should remove us all to Columbia in a few days. He then rode away, and did not return until the third day afterwards.

CHAPTER VII.

IT was now about the middle of June, the weather excessively warm, and from eleven o'clock, A. M. until late in the afternoon, the sand about our residence was so hot, that we could not stand on it with our bare feet in one posture, more than one, or two minutes. The whole country, so far as I could see, appeared to be a dead plain, without the least variety of either hill or dale. The pine was so far the predominating timber of the forest, that at a little distance the entire woods appeared to be composed of this tree.

I had become weary of being confined to the immediate vicinity of our lodgings, and determined to venture out into the fields of the plantation, and see the manner of cultivating cotton. Accordingly, after I had made my morning meal upon corn cakes, I sallied out in the direction which I had seen the slaves of the plantation take at the time they left the house at daylight, and following a path through a small field of corn, which was so tall as to prevent me from seeing beyond it, I soon arrived at the field in which the people were at work with hoes amongst the cotton, which was about two feet and a half high, and had formed such long branches, that they could no longer plough in it without breaking it. Expecting to pass the remainder of my life in this kind of labour, I felt anxious to know the evils, if any, attending it, and more especially the manner in which the slaves wore treated or, the cotton estates.

The people now before me, were all diligently and laboriously weeding and hilling the cotton with hoes, and when I approached them, they scarcely took time to speak to me, but continued their labour as if I had not been present. As there did not appear to be any overseer with them, I thought I would go amongst them, and enter into conversation with them; but upon addressing myself to one of the men, and telling him, if it was not disagreeable to him, I should be glad to become acquainted with him, he said he should be glad to be acquainted with me, but master Tom did not allow him to talk much to people when he was at work. I asked him where his master Tom was; but before he had time to reply, some one called—"Mind your work there, you rascals." Looking in the direction of the sound, I saw master Tom, sitting under the shade of a sassafras tree, at the distance of about a hundred yards from us. Deeming it unsafe to continue in the field without the permission of its lord, I approached the sassafras tree, with my hat in my hand, and in a very humble manner, asked leave to help the people work awhile, as I was tired of staying about the house and doing nothing. He said he did not care; I might go and work with th m awhile, but, I must take care not to talk too much, and keep his hands from their work.

Now, having authority on my side, I returned, and taking a hoe from the hands of a small girl, told her to pull up weeds, and I would take her row for her. When we arrived at the end of the rows which we were then hilling, master Tom, who still held his post under the sassafras tree, called his people to come to breakfast. Although I had already broken my fast, I went with the rest for the purpose of seeing what their breakfast was composed of. At the tree I saw a keg which contained about five gallons, with water in it; and a gourd lying by it; near this was a basket made of splits, large enough to hold more than a peck. It contained the breakfast of the people, covered by some green leaves of the magnolia, or great bay tree of the south. When the leaves were removed, I found that the supply of provisions consisted of one cake of corn meal, weighing about half a pound, for each person. This bread had no sort of seasoning, not even salt, and constituted the only breakfast of these poor people, who had been toiling from early dawn until about eight o'clock. There was no cake for me, and master Tom did not say any thing to me on the state of my stomach; but the young girl, whose hoe I had, taken in the field, offered me a part of her cake, which I refused. After the breakfast was despatched, we again returned to our work; but the master ordered the girl, whose hoe I had, to go and get another hoe which lay at some distance in the field, and take her row again. I continued in the field until dinner, which took place about one o'clock, and was the same, in all respects, as the breakfast had been.

Master Tom was the younger of the two brothers who returned from the cook-fight on the evening of our arrival at this place,—he left the field about ten o'clock, and was succeeded by his elder brother, as overseer for the remainder of the day. After this change of superintendents, my companions became more loquacious, and in the course of an hour or two, I had become familiar with the condition of my fellow-labourers who told me that the elder of their young masters was much less tyrannical than his younger brother; and that whilst the former remained in the field they would be at liberty to talk as much as they pleased, provided they did not neglect their work. One of the men who appeared to be about forty years of age, and who was the foreman of the field, told me that he had been born in South Carolina, and had always lived there, though he had only belonged to his present master about ten years. I asked him if his master allowed him no meat, nor any kind of provisions except bread; to which he replied that they never had any meat except at Christmas, when each hand on the place received about three pounds of pork; that from September, when the sweet potatoes were at the maturity of their growth, they had an allowance of potatoes as long as the crop held out, which was generally until about March; but that for the rest of the year, they had nothing but a peck of corn a week, with such weeds and other vegetables as they could gather from the fields for greens—that their master did not allow them any salt, and that the only means they had of procuring this luxury, was, by work ng on Sundays for the neigbouring planters, who paid them in money at the rate of fifty cents per day, with which they purchased salt and some other articles of convenience.

This man told me that his master furnished him with two shirts of tow linen, and two pair of trousers, one of woollen and the other of linen cloth, one woollen jacket, and one blanket every year. That he received the woollen clothes at Christmas, and the linen at Easter; and all the other clothes, if he had any, he was obliged to provide for himself by working on Sunday. He said, that for several years past, he had not been able to provide any clothes for himself; as he had a wife, with several small children, on an adjoining plantation, whose master gave only, one suit of clothes in the year to the mother, and none of any kind to the children, which had compelled him to lay out all his savings in providing clothes for his family, and such little necessaries as were called for by his wife, from time to time. He had not had a shoe on his foot for several years, but in winter made a kind of moccasin for himself of the bark of a tree, which he said was abundant in the swamps, and could be so manufactured as to make good ropes, and tolerable moccasins, sufficient at least, to defend the feet from the frost though not to keep them dry.

The old man whom I have alluded to before, was in the field with the others, though he was not able to keep up his row. He had no clothes on him except the remains of an old shirt, which hung in tatters from his neck and arms; the two young girls had nothing on them but petticoats, made of coarse tow cloth, and the woman who was the mother of the children, wore the remains of a tow linen shift, the front part of which was entirely gone; but a piece of old cotton bagging tied round her loins, served the purposes of an apron. The younger of the two boys was entirely naked.

The man who was foreman of the field, was a person of good sense for the condition of life in which fortune had placed him, and spoke to me freely of his hard lot. I observed that under his shirt, which was very ragged; he wore a piece of fine linen cloth, apparently part of an old shirt, wrapped closely round his back, and confined in front by strings, tied down his breast. I asked him why be wore that piece of gentleman's linen under his shirt, and shall give his reply in his own words as well as I can recollect them, at a distance of near thirty years.

"I have always been a hard working man, and have suffered a great deal from hunger in my time. It is not possible for a man to work hard every day for several months, and get nothing but a peck of corn a week to eat, and not feel hungry. When a man is hungry, you know, (if you have ever been hungry,) he must eat whatever he can get. I have not tasted meat since last Christmas, and we have had to work uncommonly hard this summer. Master has a flock of sheep, that run in the woods, and they come every night to sleep in the lane near the house. Two weeks ago last Saturday, when we quit work at night, I was very hungry, and as we went to the house we passed along the lane where the sheep lay. There were nearly fifty of them, and some were very fat. The temptation was more than I could bear. I caught one of them, cut its head off with the hoe that I carried on my shoulder, and threw it under the fence. About midnight, when all was still about the house, I went out with a knife, took the sheep into the woods, and dressed it by the light of the moon. The carcass I took home, and after cutting it up, placed it in the great kettle over a good fire, intending to boil it and divide it, when cooked, between my fellow-slaves (whom I knew to be as hungry as I was) and myself. Unfortunately for me, master Tom, who had been out amongst his friends that day, had not returned at bed-time; and about one o'clock in the morning, at the time when I had a blazing fire under the kettle, I heard the sound of the feet of a horse coming along the lane. The kitchen walls were open so that the light of my fire could not be concealed, and in a moment I heard the horse blowing at the front of the house. Conscious of my danger, I stripped my shirt from my back, and pushed it into the boiling kettle, so as wholly to conceal the flesh of the sheep. I had scarcely completed this act of precaution, when master Tom burst into the kitchen, and with a terrible oath, asked me what I was doing so late at night, with a great fire in the kitchen. I replied, 'I am going to wash my shirt, master, and am boiling it to get it clean.' 'Washing your shirt at this time of night!' said he, 'I will let you know that you are not to sit up all night and be lazy and good for nothing all day. There shall be no boiling of shirts here on Sunday morning,' and thrusting his cane into the kettle, he raised my shirt out and threw it on the kitchen floor.

"He did not at first observe the mutton, which rose to the surface of the water as soon as the shirt was removed; but, after giving the shirt a kick towards the door, he again turned his face to the fire, and seeing a leg standing several inches out of the pot, he demanded of me what I had in there and where I had got this meat? Finding that I was detected, and that the whole matter must be discovered, I said,—'Master, I am hungry, and am cooking my supper.' 'What is it you have in here?' 'A sheep,' said I, and as the words were uttered, he knocked me down with his cane, and after beating me severely, ordered me to cross my hands until he bound me fast with a rope that hung in the kitchen, and answered the double purpose of a clothes' line, and a cord to tie us with when we were to be whipped. He put out the fire under the kettle, drew me into the yard, tied me fast to the mill-post, and leaving me there for the night, went and called one of the negro boys to put his horse in the stable, and went to his bed. The cord was bound so tightly round my wrists, that before morning, the blood had burst out under my finger nails; but I suppose my master slept soundly for all that. I was afraid to call any one to come and release me from my torment, lest a still more terrible punishment might overtake me.

"I was permitted to remain in this situation until long after sunrise the next morning, which being Sunday, was quiet and still; my fellow-slaves being permitted to take their rest after the severe toil of the past week, and my old master and two young ones having no occasion to rise to call the hands to the field, did not think of interrupting their morning slumbers, to release me from my painful confinement. However, when the sun was risen about an hour, I heard the noise of persons moving in the great house, and soon after, a loud and boisterous conversation, which I well knew portended no good to me. At length they all three came into the yard where I lay, lashed to the post, and approaching me, my old master asked me if I had any accomplices in stealing the sheep. I told them none—that it was entirely my own act—and that none of my fellow-slaves had any hand in it. This was the truth; but if any of my companions had been concerned with me, I should not have betrayed them; for such an act of treachery could not have alleviated the dreadful punishment which I knew awaited me, and would only have involved them in the same misery.

"They called me a thief, loaded me with oaths and imprecations, and each one proposed the punishment which he deemed the most appropriate to the enormity of the crime that I had committed. Master Tom was of opinion, that I should be lashed to the post at the foot of which I lay, and that each of my fellow slaves should be compelled to give me a dozen lashes in turn, with a roasted and greased hickory *gad*, until I had received, in the whole, two hundred and fifty lashes on my bare back, and that he would stand by, with the whip in his hand, and *compel* them not to spare me; but after a short debate this was given up, as it would probably render me unable to work in the field again for several weeks. My master Ned was in favour of giving me a dozen lashes every morning for a month, with the whip; but my old master said, this would be attended with too much trouble, and besides, it would keep me from my work, at least half an hour every morning, and proposed, in his turn, that I should not be whipped at all, but that the carcass of the sheep should be taken from the kettle in its half-boiled condition, and hung up in the kitchen loft without salt; and that I should be compelled to subsist on this putrid mutton without any other food, until it should be consumed. This suggestion met the approbation of my young masters, and would have been adopted, had not mistress at this moment come into the yard, and hearing the intended punishment, loudly objected to it, because the mutton would, in a day or two, create such an offensive stench, that she and my young mistresses would not be able to remain in the house. My mistress swore dreadfully, and cursed me for an ungrateful sheep thief, who, after all her kindness in giving me soup and warm bread when I was sick last winter, was always stealing every thing I could get hold of. She then said to my master, that such villany ought not to be passed over in a slight manner, and that as crimes, such as this, concerned the whole country, my punishment ought to be public for the purpose of example; and advised him to have me whipped that same afternoon, at five o'clock; first giving notice to the planters of the neighbourhood to come and see the spectacle, and to bring with them their slaves, that they might be witnesses to the consequences of stealing sheep.

"They then returned to the house to breakfast; but as the pain in my hands and arms produced by the ligatures of the cord with which I was bound, was greater than I could bear, I now felt exceedingly sick, and lost all knowledge of my situation. They told me I fainted; and when I recovered my faculties, I found myself lying in the shade of the house, with my hands free, and all the white persons in my master's family, standing around me. As soon as I was able to stand, the rope was tied round my neck, and the other end again fastened to the mill post. My mistress said I had only pretended to faint; and master Tom said, I would have something worth fainting for before night. He was faithful to his promise; but, for the present, I was suffered to sit on the grass in the shade of the house.

"As soon as breakfast was over, my two young masters had their horses saddled, and set out to give notice to their friends of what had happened, and to invite them to come and see me punished for the crime I had committed. My mistress gave me no breakfast, and when I begged one of the black boys whom I saw looking at me through the pales, to bring me some water in a gourd to drink, she ordered him to bring it from a puddle in the lane. My mistress had always been very cruel to all her black people.

"I remained in this situation until about eleven o'clock, when one of my young mistresses came to me and gave me a piece of jonny-cake about the size of my hand, perhaps larger than my hand, telling me at the same time, that my fellow-slaves had been permitted to re-boil the mutton that I had left in the kettle, and make their breakfast of it, but that her mother would not allow her to give me any part of it. It was well for them that I had parboiled it with my shirt, and so defiled it, that it was unfit for the table of my master, otherwise, no portion of it would have fallen to the black people—as it was, they had as much meat as they could consume in two days, for which I had to suffer.

"About twelve o'clock, one of my young masters returned, and soon afterwards the other came home. I heard them tell my old master that they had been round to give notice of my offence to the neighbouring planters, and that several of them would attend to see me flogged, and would bring with them some of their slaves, who m be able to report to their companions what had been done to me for stealing.

"It was late in the afternoon before any of the gentlemen came; but, before five o'clock, there were more than twenty white people, and at least fifty black ones present, the latter of whom had been compelled, by their masters, to come and see me punished. Amongst others, an overseer from a neighbouring estate attended, and to him was awarded the office of executioner. I was stripped of my shirt, and the waist-band of my trousers was drawn closely round me, below my hips, so as to expose the whole of my back, in its entire length.

"It seems that it had been determined to beat me with thongs of raw cow-hide, for the overseer had two of these in his hands, each about four feet long; but one of the gentlemen present said this might bruise my back so badly, that I could not work for some time; perhaps not for a week or two; and as I could not be spared from the field without great disadvantage to my master's crop, he suggested a different plan, by which, in his opinion, the greatest degree of pain could be inflicted on me, with the least danger of rendering me unable to work. As he was a large planter, and had more than fifty slaves, all were disposed to be guided by his counsels, and my master said he would submit the matter entirely to him as a man of judgment and experience in such cases. He then desired my master to have a dozen pods of red pepper boiled in half a gallon of water, and desired the overseer to lay aside his thongs of raw hide, and put a new cracker of silk, to the lash of his negro whip. Whilst these preparations were being made, each of my thumbs was lashed closely to the end of a stick about three feet long, and a chair being placed beside the mill post, I was compelled to raise my hands and place the stick, to which my thumbs were bound, over the top of the post, which is about eighteen inches square; the chair was then taken from under me, and I was left hanging by the thumbs, with my face towards the post, and my feet about a foot from the ground. My two great toes were then tied together, and drawn down the post as far as my joints could be stretched; the cord was passed round the post two or three times and securely fastened. In this posture I had no power of motion, except in my neck, and could only move that at the expense of beating my face against the side of the post.

"The pepper tea was now brought, and poured into a basin to cool, and the overseer was desired to give me a dozen, lashes just above the waist-band; and not to cover a space of more than four inches on my back, from the waist-band upwards. He obeyed the injunction faithfully, but slowly, and each crack of the whip was followed by a sensation as painful as if a red hot iron had been drawn across my back. When the twelve strokes had been given, the operation was suspended, and a black man, one of the slaves present, was compelled to wash the gashes in my skin, with the scalding pepper tea, which was yet so hot that he could not hold his hand in it. This doubly-burning liquid was thrown into my raw and bleeding wounds, and produced a tormenting smart, beyond the description of language. After a delay of ten minutes, by the watch, I received another dozen lashes, on the part of my back which was immediately above the bleeding and burning gashes of the former whipping; and again the biting, stinging, pepper tea was applied to my lacerated and trembling muscles. This operation was continued at regular intervals, until I had received ninety-six lashes, and my back was cut and scalded from end to end. Every stroke of the whip had drawn blood; many of the gashes were three inches long; my back burned as if it had been covered by a coat of hot embers, mixed with living coals; and I felt my flesh quiver like that of animals that I slaughtered by the butcher and are flayed whilst yet half alive. My face was bruised, and my nose bled profusely, for in the madness of my agony, I had not been able to refrain from beating my head violently against the post.

"Vainly did I beg and implore for mercy. I was kept bound to the post with my whole weight hanging upon my thumbs, an hour and a half, but it appeared to me that I had entered upon eternity, and that my sufferings would never end. At length, however, my feet were unbound, and afterwards my hands; but when released from the cords, I was so far exhausted as not to be able to stand, and my thumbs were stiff and motionless. I was carried into the kitchen, and laid on a blanket, where my ss came to see me; and after looking at my lacerated back, and telling me that my wounds were only skin deep, said I had come off well, after what I had done, and that I ought to be thankful that it was not worse with me. She then bade me not to groan so loud, nor make so much noise, and left me to myself. I lay in this condition until it was quite dark, by which time the burning of my back had much abated, and was succeeded by an aching soreness, which rendered me unable to turn over, or bend my spine in the slightest manner. My mistress again visited me, and brought with her about half a pound of fat bacon, which she made one of the black women roast before the fire on a fork, until the oil ran freely from it, and then rub it warm over my back. This was repeated until I was greased from the neck to the hips, effectually. An old blanket was then thrown over me, and I was left to pass the night alone. Such was the terror stricken into my fellow-slaves, by the example made of me, that, although they loved and pitied me, not one of them dared to approach me during this night.

"My strength was gone, and I at length fell asleep, from which I did not awake until the horn was blown the next morning, to call the people to the corn crib, to receive their weekly allowance of a peck of corn. I did not rise, nor attempt to join the other people, and shortly afterwards my master entered the kitchen, and in a soft and gentle tone of voice, asked me if I was dead. I answered him that I was not dead, and making some effort, found I was able to get upon my feet. My master had become frightened when he missed me at the corn crib, and being suddenly seized with an apprehension that I was dead, his heart had become softened, not with compassion for my sufferings, but with the fear of losing his best field hand; but when he saw me stand before him erect, and upright, the recollection of the lost sheep revived in his mind, and with it, all his feelings of revenge against the author of its death.

"'So you are not dead yet, you thieving rascal,' said he; and cursing me with many bitter oaths, ordered me to go along to the crib and get my corn, and go to work with the rest of the hands. I was forced to obey, and taking my basket of corn from the door of the crib, placed it in the kitchen loft, and went to the field with the other people.

"Weak and exhausted as I was, I was compelled to do the work of an able hand, but was not permitted to taste the mutton, which was all given to the others, who were carefully guarded whilst they were eating, lest they should give me some of it."

This man's back was not yet well. Many of the gashes made by the lash were yet sore, and those that were healed had left long white stripes across his body. He had no notion of leaving the service of his tyrannical master, and his spirit was so broken and subdued, that he was ready to suffer and to bear all his hardships; not, indeed, without complaining, but without attempting to resist his oppressors, or to escape from their power. I saw him often whilst I remained at this place, and ventured to tell him once that if I had a master who would abuse me as his had abused him, I would run away. "Where could I run, or in what place could I conceal myself?" said he. "I have known many slaves who ran away, but they were always caught, and treated worse afterwards than they had been before. I have heard that there is a place called Philadelphia, where the black people are all free, but I do not know which way it lies, nor what road I should take to go there; and if I knew the way, how could I hope to get there? would not the patrol be sure to catch me?

I pitied this unfortunate creature, and was at the same time fearful, that, in a short time, I should be equally the object of pity myself. How well my fears were justified the sequel of my narrative will show.

CHAPTER VIII.

We had been stationed in the old cotton-gin house, about twenty days, had recovered from the fatigues of our journey, and were greatly improved our strength and appearance, when our master returned one evening, after an absence of two days, and told us that we must go to Columbia the next day; and must, for this purpose, have our breakfast ready by sunrise. On the following morning he called us at daylight, and we made all despatch in preparing our morning repast, the last that we were to take in our present residence.

As our equipments consisted of the few clothes we had on our persons, and a solitary blanket to each individual, our baggage was easily adjusted, and we were on the road before the sun was up half an hour; and in less than an hour we were in Columbia, drawn up in a long line in the street opposite the court-house.

The town, which was small and mean looking, was full of people, and I believe that more than a thousand gentlemen came to look at us within the course of this day. We were kept in the street about an hour, and were then taken into the jail-yard and permitted to sit down; but were not shut up in the jail. The court was sitting in Columbia at this time, and either this circumstance, or the intelligence of our arrival in the country, or both, had drawn together a very great crowd of people.

We were supplied with victuals by the jailer, and had a small allowance of salt pork for dinner. We slept in the jail at night, and as none of us had been sold on the day of our arrival in Columbia, and we had not heard any of the persons who came to look at us make proposals to our master for our purchase, I supposed it might be his intention to drive us still farther south before he offered us for sale; but I discovered my error on the second day, which was Tuesday. This day the crowd in town was much greater than it had been on Monday; and, about ten o'clock, our master came into the yard, in company with the jailer, and after looking at us some time, the latter addressed us in a short speech, which continued perhaps five minutes. In this harangue he told us we had come to live in the finest country in the world; that South Carolina was the richest and best part of the United States; and that he was going to sell us to gentlemen who would make us all very happy, and would require us to do no hard work; but only raise cotton and pick it. He then ordered a handsome young lad, about eighteen years of age, to follow him into the street, where we observed a great concourse of persons collected. Here the jailer made another harangue to the multitude, in which he assured them that he was just about to sell the most valuable lot of slaves that had ever been offered in Columbia. That we were all young; in excellent health, of good habits, having been all purchased in Virginia, from the estates of tobacco planters; and that there was not one in the whole lot who had lost the use of a single finger, or was blind of an eye.

He then cried the poor lad for sale, and the first bid he received was two hundred dollars. Others quickly succeeded, and the boy, who was a remarkably handsome youth, was striken off in a few minutes to a young man who appeared not much older than himself, at three hundred and fifty dollars. The purchaser paid down his price to our master on a table in the jail, and the lad, after bidding us farewell, followed his new master with tears running down his cheeks.

He next sold a young girl, about fifteen or sixteen years old, for two hundred and fifty dollars, to a lady who attended the sales in her carriage, and made her bids out of the window. In this manner the sales were continued for about two hours and a half; when they were adjourned until three o'clock. In the afternoon they were again resumed, and kept open until about five o'clock, when they were closed for the day. As my companions were sold, they were taken from amongst us, and we saw them no more.

The next morning, before day, I was awakened from my sleep by the sound of several heavy fires of cannon which were discharged, as it seemed to me, within a few yards of the place where I lay. These were succeeded by fifes and drums, and all the noise with which I had formerly heard the fourth of July ushered in, at the navy-yard in Washington.

Since I had left Maryland I had carefully kept the reckoning of the days of the week; but had not been careful to note the dates of the month; yet as soon as daylight appeared, and the door of our apartment was opened, I inquired and learned, that this was, as I had supposed it to be, the day of universal rejoicing.

I understood that the court did not sit this day, but a great crowd of people gathered, and remained around the jail, all the morning; many of whom were intoxicated, and sang and shouted in honour of free government, and the rights of man. About eleven o'clock, a long table was spread under a row of trees which grew in the street, not far from the jail, and which appeared to me, to be of the kind called in Pennsylvania, the pride of China. At this table, several hundred persons sat down to dinner, soon after noon; and continued to eat, and drink, and sing songs in honour of liberty, for more than two hours. At the end of the dinner, a gentleman rose and stood upon his chair, near one end of the table, and begged the company to hear him for a few minutes. He informed them that he was a candidate for some office—but what office it was I do not recollect—and said, that as it was an acknowledged principle of our free government, that all men were born free and equal, he presumed it would not be deemed an act of arrogance in him, to call upon them for their votes, at the coming election.

This first speaker was succeeded by another, who addressed his audience in nearly the same language; and after he had concluded, the company broke up. I heard a black man that belonged to the jailer, or, who was at least in his service, say that there had been a great meeting that morning in the court house, at which several gentlemen had made speeches.

When I lived at the navy-yard, the officers sometimes permitted me to go up town with them, on the fourth of July, and listen to the fine speeches that were made there, on such occasions.

About five o'clock, the jailer came and stood at the front door of the jail, and proclaimed, in a very loud voice, that a sale of most valuable slaves would immediately take place; that he had sold many fine hands yesterday, but they were only the refuse and most worthless part of the whole lot;—that those who wished to get great bargains and prime property, had better attend now; as it was certain that such negroes had never been offered for sale in Columbia before.

In a few minutes the whole assembly, that had composed the dinner party, and hundreds of others, were convened around the jail door, and the jailer again proceeded with his auction. Several of the stoutest men, and handsomest women in the whole company, had been reserved for this day; and I perceived that the very best of us, were kept back for the last. We went off at rather better prices than had been obtained on the former day; and I perceived much eagerness amongst the bidders, many of whom were not sober. Within less than three hours, only three of us remained in the jail; and we were ordered to come and stand at the door, in front of the crier who made a most extravagant eulogium upon our good qualities, and capacity to perform labour. He said, "These three fellows are as strong as horses, and as patient as mules; one of them can do as much work as two common men, and they are perfectly honest. Mr. M'Giffin says, he was assured by their former masters, that they were never known to steal, or run away. They must bring good prices, gentlemen, or they will not be sold. Their master is determined, that if they do not bring six hundred dollars, he will not sell them, but will take them to Georgia next summer, and sell them to some of the new settlers. These boys can do any thing. This one," referring to me, "can cut five cords of wood in a day, and put it up. He is a rough carpenter, and a first rate field hand." "This one," laying his hand on the shoulder of one of my companions, "is a blacksmith; and can lay a ploughshare; put new steel upon an axe; or mend a broken chain." The other, he recommended as a good shoemaker; and well acquainted with the process of tanning leather.

We were all nearly of the same age; and very stout, healthy, robust young men, in full possession of our corporal powers; and if we had been shut up in a room, with ten of the strongest of those who had assembled to purchase us, and our liberty had depended on tying them fast to each other, I have no doubt that we should have been free, if ropes had been provided for us.

After a few minutes of hesitancy amongst the purchasers, and a closer examination of our persons than had been made in the jail-yard, an elderly gentleman said he would take the carpenter; and the blacksmith, and shoemaker, were immediately taken by others, at the required price.

It was now sundown. The heat of the day had been very oppressive, and I was glad to be released from the confined air of the jail; and the hot atmosphere, in which so many hundreds were breathing. My new master asked me my name, and ordered me to follow him.

We proceeded to a tavern, where a great number of persons were assembled, at a short distance from the jail. My master entered the house, and joined in the conversation of the party, in which the utmost hilarity prevailed. They were drinking toasts in honour of liberty and independence, over glasses of toddy; a liquor composed of a mixture of rum, water, sugar, and nutmeg.

It was ten o'clock at night before my master and his companions had finished their toasts and toddy; and all this time, I had been standing before the door, or sitting on a log of wood, that lay in front of the house. At one time, I took a seat on a bench, at the side of the house; but was soon driven from this position by a gentleman, in military clothes, with a large gilt epaulet on each shoulder, and a profusion of glittering buttons on his coat; who passing near me in the dark, and happening to cast his eye on me, demanded of me, in an imperious tone, how I dared to sit on that seat. I told him I was a stranger, and did not know that it was wrong to sit there. He then ordered me with an oath, to begone from there; and said, if he caught me on that bench again, he would cut my head off. "Did you not see white people sit upon that bench, you saucy rascal?" said he. I assured him I had not seen any white gentleman sit on the bench, as it was near night when I came to the house; that I had not intended to be saucy, or misbehave myself; and that I hoped he would not be angry with me, as my master had left me at the door, and had not told me where I was to sit.

I remained on the log until the termination of the festival, in honour of liberty and equality; when my master came to the door, and observed in my hearing, to some of his friends, that they had celebrated the day in a handsome manner.

No person, except the military gentleman, had spoken to me, since I came to the house, in the evening with my master, who seemed to have forgotten me; for he remained at the door, warmly engaged in conversation, on various political subjects, a full hour after he rose from the toast party. At length, however, I heard him say—"I bought a negro this evening,—I wonder where he is." Rising immediately from the log on which I had been so long seated, I presented myself before him, and said, "Here, master." He then ordered me to go to the kitchen of the inn, and go to sleep; but said nothing to me about supper. I retired to the kitchen, where I found a large number of servants, who belonged to the house and amongst them two young girls, who had been purchased by a gentleman, who lived near Augusta; and who, they told me, intended to set out for his plantation the next morning, and take them with him.

These girls had been sold out of our company on the first day; and had been living in the tavern kitchen since that time. They appeared quite contented, and evinced no repugnance to setting out the next morning for their master's plantation. They were of that order of people who never look beyond the present day; and so long as they had plenty of victuals, in this kitchen, they did not trouble themselves with reflections upon the cotton field.

One of the servants gave me some cold meat, and a piece of wheaten bread; which was the first I had tasted since I left Maryland, and indeed, it was the last that I tasted, until I reached Maryland again.

I here met with a man, who was born and brought up in the Northern Neck of Virginia, on the banks of the Potomac, and within a few miles of my native place. We soon formed an acquaintance; and sat up nearly all night. He was the chief hostler in the stable of this tavern; and told me, that he had often thought of attempting to escape, and return to Virginia. He said he had little doubt of being able to reach the Potomac; but having no knowledge of the country, beyond that river, he was afraid that he should not be able to make his way to Philadelphia; which he regarded as the only place in which he could be safe, from the pursuit of his master. I was myself then young, and my knowledge of the country, north of Baltimore, was very vague and undefined. I, however, told him, that I had heard, that if a black man could reach any part of Pennsylvania, he would be beyond the reach of his pursuers. He said he could not justly complain of want of food; but the services required of him were so unreasonable, and the punishment frequently inflicted upon him, so severe, that he was determined to set out for the north, as soon as the corn was so far ripe, as to be fit to be roasted. He felt confident, that by lying in the woods, and unfrequented places all day, and travelling only by night, he could escape the vigilance of all pursuit; and gain the Northern Neck, before the corn would be gathered from the fields. He had no fear of wanting food, as be could live well on roasting ears, as long as the corn was in the milk; and afterwards, on parched corn, as long as the grain remained in the field, I advised him, as well as I could, as to the best means of reaching the state of Pennsylvania; but was not able to give him any very definite instructions.

This man possessed a very sound understanding; and having been five years in Carolina, was well acquainted with the country. He gave me such an account of the sufferings of the slaves, on the cotton

and indigo plantations—of whom I now regarded myself as one—
that I was unable to sleep any this night. From the resolute manner
in which he spoke of his intended elopement, and the regularity with
which he had connected the various combinations of the enterprise, I
have no doubt that he undertook that which he intended to perform.
Whether he was successful or not, in the enterprise, I cannot say; as I
never saw him, nor heard of him, after the next morning.

This man certainly communicated to me the outlines of the plan,
which I afterwards put in execution; and by which I gained my
liberty, at the expense of sufferings, which none can appreciate,
except those who have borne all that the stoutest human constitution
can bear, of cold and hunger, toil and pain. The conversation of this
slave, aroused in my breast so many recollections of the past, and
fears of the future, that I did not lie down; but sat on an old chair
until daylight.

From the people of the kitchen I again received some cold victuals
for my breakfast, but I did not see my master until about nine
o'clock; the toddy of the last evening, causing him to sleep late this
morning. At length, a female slave gave me notice that my master
wished to see me in the dining room, whither I repaired, without a
moment's delay. When I entered the room, he was sitting near the
window, smoking a pipe, with a very long handle—I believe more
than two feet in length.

He asked no questions, but addressing me by the title of "boy,"
ordered me to go with the hostler of the inn, and get his horse and
chaise ready. As soon as this order could be executed, I informed
him that his chaise was at the door, and we immediately commenced
our journey to the plantation of my master, which, he told me, lay at
the distance of twenty miles from Columbia. He said I must keep up
with him; and, as he drove at the rate of five or six miles an hour, I
was obliged to run, nearly half the time; but I was then young, and
could easily travel fifty or sixty miles in a day. It was with great
anxiety that I looked for the place, which was in future to be my
home; but this did not prevent me from making such observations
upon the state of the country through which we travelled, as the
rapidity of our march permitted.

This whole region had originally been one vast wilderness of pine
forest, except the low grounds and river bottoms, here called
swamps; in which all the varieties of trees, shrubs, vines, and plants,

peculiar to such places, in southern latitudes, vegetated in unrestrained luxuriance. Nor is pine the only timber that grows on the uplands, in this part of Carolina; although it is the predominant tree, and in some places, prevails to the exclusion of every other— oak, hickory, sassafras, and many others are found.

Here, also, I first observed groves of the most beautiful of all the trees of the wood—the great Southern Magnolia, or Green Bay. No adequate conception can be formed of the appearance, or the fragrance, of this most magnificent tree, by any one who has not seen it, or scented the air when tainted by the perfume of its flowers. It rises in a right line to the height of seventy or eighty feet; the stem is of a delicate taper form, and casts off numerous branches, in nearly right angles with itself; the extremities of which, decline gently towards the ground, and become shorter and shorter in the ascent, until at the apex of the tree, they are scarcely a foot in length; whilst below they are many times found twenty feet long. The immense cones formed by these trees are as perfect as those diminutive forms which nature exhibits in the bur of the pine tree. The leaf of the magnolia is smooth, of an oblong taper form, about six inches in length, and half as broad. Its colour is the deepest and purest green. The foliage of the Bay tree is as impervious as a brick wall to the rays of the sun, and its coolness, in the heat of a summer day, affords one of the greatest luxuries of a cotton plantation. It blooms in May, and bears great numbers of broad, expanded white flowers, the odour of which is exceedingly grateful, and so abundant, that I have no doubt, that a grove of these trees, in full bloom, may be smelled at a distance of fifteen or twenty miles. I have heard it asserted in the south, that their scent has been perceived by persons fifty, or sixty miles from them.

This tree is one of nature's most splendid, and in the climate where she has placed it, one of her most agreeable productions. It is peculiar to the southern temperate latitudes, and cannot bear the rigours of a northern winter; though I have heard that groves of the Bay are found on Fishing Creek, in Western Virginia, not far from Wheeling, and near the Ohio river. Could this tree be naturalized in Pennsylvania, it would form an ornament to her towns, cities, and country seats, at once the most tasteful and the most delicious. A forest of these trees, in the month of May, resembles a wood, enveloped in an untimely fall of snow at midsummer, glowing in the rays of a morning sun.

We passed this day through cotton fields and pine woods, alternately; but the scene, was sometimes enlivened by the appearance of lots of corn, and sweet potatoes, which, I observed, were generally planted near the houses. I afterwards learned that this custom of planting the corn and potatoes near the house of the planter, is general over all Carolina. The object is, to prevent the slaves from stealing; and thus procuring more food, than, by the laws of the plantation, they are entitled to.

In passing through a lane, I this day saw a field, which appeared to me to contain about fifty acres, in which people were at work with hoes, amongst a sort of plants that I had never seen before. I asked my master what this was, and he told me it was indigo. I shall have occasion to say more of this plant hereafter.

We at length arrived at the residence of my master, who descended from his chaise, and leaving me in charge of the horse at the gate, proceeded to the house, across a long court yard. In a few minutes two young ladies, and a young gentleman, came out of the house, and walked to the gate, near which I was with the horse. One of the ladies said, they had come to look at me, and see what kind of a boy her pa had brought home with him. The other one said I was a very smart looking boy; and this compliment flattered me greatly; they being the first kind words that had been addressed to me since I left Maryland. The young gentleman asked me if I could run fast, and if I had ever picked cotton. His manner did not impress me so much in his favour, as the address of his sister had done for her. These three young persons were the son and daughters of my master. After looking at me a short time, my young master, (for so I must now call him,) ordered me to take the harness from the horse, give him water at a well which was near, and come into the kitchen, where some boiled rice was given me for my dinner.

I was not required to go to work this first day of my abode in my new residence; but after I had eaten my rice, my young master told me I might rest myself or walk out and see the plantation, but that I must be ready to go with the overseer the next morning.

CHAPTER IX.

By the laws of the United States I am still a slave; and though I am now growing old, I might even yet be deemed of sufficient value to be worth pursuing as far as my present residence, if those to whom the law gives the right of dominion over my person and life, knew where to find me. For these reasons I have been advised, by those whom I believe to be my friends, not to disclose the true names of any of those families in which I was a slave, in Carolina or Georgia, lest this narrative should meet their eyes, and in some way lead them to a discovery of my retreat.

I was now the slave of one of the most wealthy planters in Carolina, who planted cotton, rice, indigo, corn, and potatoes; and was the master of two hundred and sixty slaves.

The description of one great cotton plantation will give a correct idea of all others; and I shall here present an outline of that of my master.

He lived about two miles from Caugaree river; which bordered his estate on one side, and in the swamps of which were his rice fields. The country hereabout is very flat; the banks of the river are low; and in wet seasons large tracts of country are flooded by the superabundant water of the river. There are no springs; and the only means of procuring water, on the plantations, is from wells, which must be sunk in general about twenty feet deep, before a constant supply of water can be obtained. My master had two of these wells on his plantation; one at the mansion house, and one at the quarter.

My master's house was of brick, (brick houses are by no means common amongst the planters, whose residences are generally built of frame work, weather boarded with pine boards, and covered with shingles of the white cedar or juniper cypress,) and contained two large parlours, and a spacious hall or entry on the ground floor. The main building was two stories high and attached to this was a smaller building, one story and a half high, with a large room, where the family generally took breakfast; with a kitchen at the farther extremity from the main building.

There was a spacious garden behind the house, containing, I believe, about five acres, well cultivated, and handsomely laid out. In this garden grew a great variety of vegetables; some of which I have never seen in the market of Philadelphia. It contained a profusion of flowers, three different shrubberies, a vast number of ornamental and small fruit trees, and several small hot houses, with glass roofs. There was a head gardener, who did nothing but attend to this garden through the year and during the summer he generally had two men and two boys to assist him. In the months of April and May this garden was one of the sweetest and most pleasant places that I ever was in. At one end of the main building was a small house, called the library, in which my master kept his books and papers, and where he spent much of his time.

At some distance from the mansion was a pigeon house, and near the kitchen was a large wooden building, called the kitchen quarter, in which the house servants slept; and where they generally took their meals. Here, also, the washing of the family was done; and all the rough or unpleasant work of the kitchen department,—such as cleaning and salting fish, putting up pork, &c., was assigned to this place.

There was no barn on this plantation, according to the acceptation of the word *barn* in Pennsylvania; but there was a wooden building, about forty feet long, called the coach-house; in one end of which the family carriage, and the chaise in which my master, rode were kept. Under the same roof was a stable, sufficiently capacious to contain ten or twelve horses. In one end of the building the corn intended for the horses was kept; and the whole of the loft, or upper story, was occupied by the fodder, or blades and tops of the corn.

About a quarter of a mile from the dwelling-house were the huts or cabins of the plantation slaves, or field hands, standing in rows, much like the Indian villages which I have seen in the country of the Cherokees. These cabins were thirty-eight in number, generally about fifteen or sixteen feet square, built of hewn logs, covered with shingles, and provided with floors of pine boards. These houses were all dry and comfortable, and were provided with chimneys, so that the people when in them, were well sheltered from the inclemencies of the weather. In this practice of keeping their slaves well sheltered at night, the southern planters are pretty uniform; for they know, that upon this circumstance, more than any other in that climate, depends the health of the slave, and consequently his value.

In these thirty-eight cabins were lodged two hundred and fifty people, of all ages, sexes, and sizes. Ten or twelve were generally employed in the garden, and about the house.

At a distance of about one hundred yards from the lines of cabins stood the house of the overseer; a small two-story log building, with a yard and garden attached to it of proportionate dimensions. This small house was the abode of a despot, more absolute, and more cruel than were any of those we read of in the Bible, who so grievously oppressed the children of Israel. In one corner of the overseer's garden stood the corn crib, also a log building, in which was stored up the corn, constituting the yearly provisions of the coloured people. In another corner of the same garden was a large vault, covered with sods, very like some ice-houses that I have seen. This was the potato-house, and in it were deposited the sweet potatoes, also intended to supply the people.

At a short distance beyond the garden of the overseer stood a large building, constituting the principal feature in the landscape of every great cotton plantation. This was the house, containing the cotton-gin, and the sheds to contain the cotton, when brought from the field in the seed; and also the bales, after being pressed and prepared for market.

As I shall be obliged to make frequent references to the cotton-gin, it may perhaps be well to describe it. Formerly there was no way of separating the cotton from the seed, but by pulling it of with the fingers—a very tedious and troublesome process— but a person from the north, by the name of Whitney, at length discovered the gin, which is a very simple though very powerful machine. It is composed of a wooden cylinder, about six or eight feet in length, surrounded at very short intervals, with small circular saws, in such a manner that as the cylinder is turned rapidly round, by a leather strap on the end, similar to a turner's lathe, the teeth of the saws, in turning over, continually cut downwards in front of the cylinder, which is placed close to a long hopper, extending the whole length of the cylinder, and so close to it that the seeds of the cotton cannot pass between them This cylinder revolves, with almost inconceivable rapidity, and great caution is necessary in working with the gin, not to touch the saws. One end of the cylinder and hopper being slightly elevated, the seeds as they are stripped of the wool, are gradually but certainly moved toward the lower end, where they drop down into a heap, after being as perfectly divested of the cotton as they could be by the most careful picking with the fingers.

The rapid evolutions of the cylinder are procured by the aid of cogs and wheels, similar to those used in small grist mills.

It is necessary to be very careful in working about a cotton-gin; more especially in removing the seeds from before the saws; for if they do but touch the hand the injury is very great. I knew a black man who had all the sinews of the inner part of his right hand torn out—some of them measuring more than a foot in length—and the flesh of his palm cut into tatters, by carelessly putting his hand too near the saws, when they were in motion, for the idle purpose of feeling the strength of the current of air created by the motions of the cylinder. A good gin will clean several thousand pounds of cotton, in the seed, in a day. To work the gin two horses are necessary; though one is often compelled to perform the labour.

There was no smoke-house, nor any other place, for curing or preserving meat, attached to the quarter; and whilst I was on this plantation no pork was ever salted for the use of the slaves.

After remaining in the kitchen some time, I went into the garden, and remained with the gardener, assisting him to work until after sundown; when my old master came to the gate, and called one of the garden boys to him. The boy soon returned, and told me I must go with him to the quarter, as his master had told him to take me to the overseer. When we arrived at the overseer's house he had not yet returned from the field; but in a few minutes we saw him coming at some distance through a cotton field, followed by a great number of black people. As he approached us, the boy that was with me handed him a small piece of paper, which he carried in his hand, and without saying a word, ran back toward the house, leaving me to become acquainted with the overseer in the best way I could. But I found this to be no difficult task; for he had no sooner glanced his eye over the piece of paper, than, turning to me, he asked me my name; and calling to a middle-aged man who was passing us at some distance, told him he must take me to live with him, and that my supper should be sent to me from his own house.

I followed my new friend to his cabin, which I found to be the habitation of himself, his wife, and five children. The only furniture in this cabin, consisted of a few blocks of wood for seats; a short bench, made of a pine board, which served as a table; and a small bed in one corner composed of a mat, made of common rushes, spread upon some corn husks, pulled and split into fine pieces, and kept together by a narrow slip of wood, confined to the floor by wooden pins. There was a common iron pot, standing beside the chimney; and several wooden spoons and dishes hung against the wall. Several blankets also hung against the wall upon wooden pins. An old box, made of pine boards, without either lock or binges, occupied one corner.

At the time I entered this humble abode the mistress was not at home. She had not yet returned from the field; having been sent, as the husband informed me, with some other people late in the evening, to do some work in a field about two miles distant. I found a child, about a year old, lying on the mat-bed, and a little girl about four years old beside it.

These children were entirely naked, and when we came to the door, the elder rose front its place and ran to its father, and clasping him round one of his knees, said, "Now we shall get good supper." The father laid his hand upon the head of his naked child, and stood silently looking in its face—which was turned upwards toward his own for a moment— and then turning to me, said, "Did you leave any children at home!" The scene before me—the question propounded—and the manner of this poor man and his child, caused my heart to swell until my breast seemed too small to contain it. My soul fled back upon the wings of fancy to my wife's lowly dwelling in Maryland; where I had been so often met on a Saturday evening, when I paid them my weekly visit, by my own little ones, who clung to my knees for protection and support, even as the poor little wretch now before me, seized upon the weary limb of its hapless and destitute father, hoping that, naked as he was, (for he too was naked, save only the tattered remains of a pair of old trousers,) he would bring, with his return at evening its customary scanty supper. I was unable to reply; but stood motionless, leaning against the walls of the cabin. My children seemed to flit by the door in the dusky twilight; and the twittering of a swallow, which that moment fluttered over my head, sounded in my ear as the infantile tittering of my own little boy; but on a moment's reflection I knew that we were separated without the hope of ever again meeting; that they no more heard the welcome tread of my feet, and could never again receive the little gifts with which, poor as I was, I was accustomed to present them. I was far from the place of my nativity, in a land of strangers, with no one to care for me beyond the care that a master bestows upon his ox; with all my future life, one long, waste, barren desert, of cheerless, hopeless, lifeless slavery; to be varied only by the pangs of hunger and the stings of the lash.

My revery was at length broken by the appearance of the mother of the family, with her three eldest children. The mother wore an old ragged shift; but the children, the eldest of whom appeared to be about twelve, and the youngest six years old, were quite naked. When she came in, the husband told her that the overseer had sent me to live with them; and she and her oldest child, who was a boy, immediately set about preparing their supper, by boiling some of the leaves of the weed called lamb's-quarter, in the pot. This, together with some cakes of cold corn bread, formed their supper. My supper was brought to me from the house of the overseer by a small girl, his daughter. It was about half a pound of bread, cut from a loaf made of corn meal. My companions gave me a part of their boiled greens, and we all sat down together to my first meal in my new habitation.

I had no other bed than the blanket which I had brought with me from Maryland; and I went to sleep in the loft of the cabin which was assigned to me as my sleeping room; and in which I continued to lodge as long as I remained on this plantation.

The next morning I was waked, at the break of day, by the sound of a horn, which was blown very loudly. Perceiving that it was growing light, I came down, and went out immediately in front of the house of the overseer, who was standing near his own gate, blowing the horn. In a few minutes the whole of the working people, from all the cabins were assembled; and as it was now light enough for me distinctly to see such objects as were about me, I at once perceived the nature of the servitude to which I was, in future, to be subject.

As I have before stated, there were altogether on this plantation, two hundred and sixty slaves; but the number was seldom stationary for a single week. Births were numerous and frequent, and deaths were not uncommon. When I joined them I believe we counted in all two hundred and sixty-three; but of these only one hundred and seventy went to the field to work. The others were children, too small to be of any service as labourers; old and blind persons, or incurably diseased. Ten or twelve were kept about the mansion-house and garden, chosen from the most handsome and sprightly of the gang.

I think about one hundred and sixty-eight assembled this morning, at the sound of the horn—two or three being sick, sent word to the overseer that they could not come.

The overseer wrote something on a piece of paper, and gave it to his little son. This I was told was a note to be sent to our master, to inform him that some of the hands were sick—it not being any part of the duty of the overseer to attend to a sick negro.

The overseer then led off to the field, with his horn in one hand and his whip in the other; we following—men, women, and children, promiscuously— and a wretched looking troop we were. There was not an entire garment amongst us.

More than half of the gang were entirely naked. Several young girls, who had arrived at puberty, wearing only the livery with which nature had ornamented them, and a great number of lads, of an equal or superior age, appeared in the same costume. There was neither bonnet, cap, nor head dress of any king amongst us, except the old straw hat that I wore; and which my wife had made for me in Maryland. This I soon laid aside to avoid the appearance of singularity; and, as owing to the severe treatment I had endured whilst travelling in chains, and being compelled to sleep on the naked floor, without undressing myself, my clothes were quite worn out, I did not make a much better figure than my companions; though still I preserved the semblance of clothing so far, that it could be seen that my shirt and trousers had once been distinct and separate garments. Not one of the others had on even the remains of two pieces of apparel. Some of the men had old shirts, and some ragged trousers, but no one wore both. Amongst the women, several wore petticoats, and many had shifts. Not one of the whole number wore both of these vestments.

We walked nearly a mile through one vast cotton field, before we arrived at the place of our intended day's labour. At last the overseer stopped at the side of the field, and calling to several of the men by name, ordered them to call their companies and turn into their rows. The work we had to do today was to hoe and weed cotton, for the last time; and the men whose names had been called, and who were, I believe, eleven in number, were designated as captains, each of whom had under his command a certain number of the other bands. The captain was the foreman of his company, and those under his command had to keep up with him. Each of the men and women

81

had to take one row; and two, and in some cases where they were very small, three of the children had one. The first captain, whose name was Simon, took the first row,— and the other captains were compelled to keep up with him. By this means the overseer had nothing to do but to keep Simon hard at work, and he was certain that all the others must work equally hard.

Simon was a stout, strong man, apparently about thirty-five years of age; and for some reason unknown to me, I was ordered to take the row next to his. The overseer with his whip in his hand walked about the field after us, to see that our work was well done. As we worked with hoes, I had no difficulty in learning how the work was to be performed.

The fields of cotton at this season of the year are very beautiful. The plants, amongst which we worked this day, were about three feet high, and in full bloom, with branches so numerous that they nearly covered the whole ground—leaving scarcely space enough between them to permit us to move about, and work with our hoes.

About seven o'clock in the morning the overseer sounded his horn; and we all repaired to the shade of some perscimmon trees, which grew in a corner of the field, to get our breakfast. I here saw a cart drawn by a yoke of oxen, driven by an old black man, nearly blind. The cart contained three barrels, filled with water, and several large baskets full of corn bread, that had been baked in the ashes. The water was for us to drink, and the bread was our breakfast. The little son of the overseer was also in the cart, and had brought with him the breakfast of his father, in a small wooden bucket.

The overseer had bread, butter, cold ham, and coffee for his breakfast. Ours was composed of a corn cake, weighing about three quarters of a pound to each person, with as much water as was desired. I at first supposed that this bread was dealt out to the people as their allowance; but on further inquiry I found this not to be the case. Simon, by whose side I was now at work, and who seemed much pleased with my agility and diligence in my duty, told me that here, as well as every where in this country, each person received a peck of corn at the crib door, every Sunday evening, and that in ordinary times, every one had to grind this corn and bake it, for him or herself, making such use of it as the owner thought proper; but that for some time past, the overseer, for the purpose of saving the time which had been lost in baking the bread, had made it the duty of an old woman, who was not capable of doing much work in the field, to stay at the quarter, and bake the bread of the whole gang. When baked, it was brought to the field in a cart, as I saw, and dealt out in loaves.

They still had to grind their own corn, after night; and as there were only three hand-mills on the plantation, he said they experienced much difficulty in converting their corn into meal. We worked in this field all day; and at the end of every hour, or hour and a quarter, we had permission to go to the cart, which was moved about the field, so as to be near us, and get water.

Our dinner was the same, in all respects, as our breakfast, except that, in addition to the bread, we had a little salt, and a radish for each person. We were not allowed to rest at either breakfast or dinner, longer than while we were eating; and we worked in the evening as long as we could distinguish the weeds from the cotton plants.

Simon informed me, that formerly, when they baked their own bread, they had left their work soon after sundown, to go home and bake for the next day, but the overseer had adopted the new policy for the purpose of keeping them at work until dark.

When we could no longer see to work, the horn was again sounded, and we returned home. I had now lived through one of the days—a succession of which make up the life of a slave—on a cotton plantation.

As we went out in the morning, I observed several women, who carried their young children in their arms to the field. These mothers laid their children at the side of the fence, or under the shade of the cotton plants, whilst they were at work; and when the rest of us went to get water, they would go to give suck to their children, requesting some one to bring them water in gourds, which they were careful to carry to the field with them. One young woman did not, like the others, leave her child at the end of the row, but had contrived a sort of rude knapsack, made of a piece of coarse linen cloth, in which she fastened her child, which was very young, upon her back; and in this way carried it all day, and performed her task at the hoe with the other people.

I pitied this woman, and as we were going home at night, I came near her, and spoke to her. Perceiving as soon as she spoke that she had not been brought up amongst the slaves of this plantation— for her language was different from theirs—I asked her why she did not do as the other women did, and leave her child at the end of the row in the shade. "Indeed," said she, "I cannot leave my child in the weeds amongst the snakes. What would be my feelings if I should leave it there, and a scorpion were to bite it? Besides, my child cries so piteously, when I leave it alone in the field, that I cannot bear to hear it. Poor thing, I wish we were both in the grave, where all sorrow is forgotten."

I asked this woman, who did not appear to be more than twenty years old, how long she had been here, and where she came from. "I have been here," said she, "almost two years, and came from the Eastern Shore. I once lived as well as any lady in Maryland. I was born a slave, in the family of a gentleman whose name was Le Compt. My master was a man of property; lived on his estate, and entertained much company. My mistress, who was very kind to me, made me her nurse, when I was about ten years old, and put me to live with her own children. I grew up amongst her daughters; not as their equal and companion, but as a favoured and indulged servant. I was always well dressed, and received a portion of all the delicacies of their table. I wanted nothing, and had not the trouble of providing even for myself. I believe there was not a happier being in the world than I was. At present none can be more wretched.

"When I was yet a child, my master had given me to his oldest daughter, who was about one year older than I was. To her, I had always looked as my future mistress; and expected that whenever she became a wife, I should follow her person, and cease to be a member of the family of her father. When I was almost seventeen, my young mistress married a gentleman of the Eastern Shore of Virginia, who had been addressing her, more than a year.

"Soon after the wedding was over, my new master removed his wife to his own residence; and took me and a black boy of my own age, that the lady's father had given her, with him. He had caused it to be reported in Maryland, that he was very wealthy; and was the owner of a plantation, with a large stock of slaves and other property. It was supposed at the time of the marriage, that my young mistress was making a very good match, and all her friends were pleased with it. When her lover came to visit her, he always rode in a handsome gig, accompanied by a black man on horseback, as his servant. This man told us in the kitchen, that his master was one of the most fashionable men in Virginia; was a man of large fortune, and that all the young ladies in the county he lived in, had their eyes upon him. These stories I repeated carefully to my young mistress; and added every persuasion that I could think of, to induce her to accept her lover, as her husband. My feelings had become deeply interested in the issue of this matter; for whilst the master was striving to win the heart of my young mistress, the servant had already conquered mine.

"It was more than a hundred miles from the residence of my old master, to that of my young one; and when we arrived at the latter place, my mistress and I soon found, that we had been equally credulous, and were equally deceived. We were taken to an old dilapidated mansion, which was quite in keeping with every thing on the estate to which it was attached. The house was almost without furniture; and there were no servants in it, except myself and my companion. The black man who had so effectually practiced upon me, belonged to one of my new master's companions,—and had a wife and three children in the neighbourhood.

"My mistress, soon discovered that her husband's companions were gamblers and horse racers; who frequently convened at her house, to concert or mature some scheme, the object of which was to cheat some one.

"My old master was a member of the church, and was very scrupulous in the observance of his moral duties. His precepts had been deeply implanted in the mind of my young mistress; and the society of these sportsmen, (as the friends of my young master denominated themselves,) became so revolting to her feelings, that after she had been married nearly a year, and had exhausted all her patience, and all her fortitude, in endeavouring to reclaim her husband from the vile associations and pursuits, by which his time and his affections were engaged, she determined at last to return to her father, for a time, and to take me with her, for the purpose of ascertaining whether this would not bring him to reflect upon the wrong he had done her, as well as himself.

"She communicated to me her designs, and we were waiting for an opportunity of carrying them into effect, when one evening, near sundown, my master came to me in the kitchen; and told me he wished me to go to the house of a gentleman who lived about a mile distant, and deliver a letter for him; without letting my mistress know any thing of the matter. I immediately set out, expecting to return in half an hour. As I left the house I saw my mistress in the garden; and I never saw her again.

"Between the house of my master, and that to which he had sent me, was a grove of young pine trees, that had grown up in a field, that had formerly been cultivated; but which had been neglected, on account of its poverty, for many years. Through this thicket, the path which I had to travel led; and when near the middle of the wood, I saw a white man step into the path, only a few yards before me, with a rope in his hand. Sometime before this, my mistress had told me, that she wished to get me back to her father's house in Maryland, because she was afraid that my master would sell me to the negro buyers; and the moment I saw the man with the rope, in my path, the words of my mistress were recollected.

"I screamed, and turned to fly towards home; but at the first step was met by the coloured man, who had attended my master, as his servant, when he visited Maryland, at the time he was courting my mistress—and who had made so deep an impression on my heart. This was the first time I had seen him, since I came to live in Virginia; and base as I knew he must be, from his former conduct to me, yet at sight of him, my former affection for a moment revived, and I rushed into his arms which were extended towards me, hoping that he would save me from the danger I so much dreaded from behind. He saw that I was frightened, and had fled to him for protection, and only said, 'Come with me.' I followed him, more by instinct than by reason, and holding to his arm, ran as fast as I could— I knew not whither. I did not observe whether we were on the path or not. I do not know how far we had run, when he stopped, and said—'We must remain here for some time.'

"In a few minutes the white man whom I had seen in the path, came up with us, and seizing me by the hands, he and my pretended protector bound them together, at my back, and to suppress my cries, tied a large handkerchief round my head, and over my mouth. It was now becoming dark, and they hurried out of the wood, and across the fields, to a small creek, the water of which fell into the Chesapeake Bay. Here was a boat; and another white man in it. They forced me on board; and the white men taking the oars, whilst the black managed the rudder, we were quickly out in the bay, and in less than an hour, I was on board a small schooner, lying at anchor; where I found eleven others, who like myself, had been dragged from their homes and their friends, to be sold to the southern traders.

"I have no doubt, that my master had sold me without the knowledge of my mistress; and that he endeavoured to persuade her, that I had run away: perhaps he was successful in this endeavour.

"I heard no more of my mistress, for whom I was very sorry, for I knew she would be greatly distressed at losing me.

"The vessel remained at anchor where we found her that night, and the next day until evening, when she made sail, and beat up the bay all night against a head wind. When she approached the western shore, she hoisted a red handkerchief at her mast head, and a boat came off from the land, large enough to carry us all, and we were removed to a house on the bank of York river, where I found about thirty men and women, all imprisoned in the cellar of a small tavern. The men were in irons, but the women were not bound with any thing. The cords and handkerchief had been taken from me, whilst on board the vessel. We remained at York river more than a week; and whilst there, twenty-five or thirty persons were brought in, and shut up with us.

"When we commenced our journey for the south, we were about sixty in number. The men were chained together, but the women were all left quite at liberty. At the end of three weeks, we reached Savannah river, opposite the town of Augusta, where we were sold out by our owner. Our present master was there, and purchased me and another woman who has been at work in the field to-day.

"Soon after I was brought home, the overseer compelled me to be married to a man I did not like. He is a native of Africa, and still retains the manners and religion of his country. He has not been with us to day, as he is sick, and under the care of the doctor. I must hasten home to get my supper, and go to rest; and glad I should be, if I were never to rise again.

"I have several times been whipped unmercifully, because I was not strong enough to do as much work with the hoe, as the other women, who have lived all their lives on this plantation, and have been accustomed from their infancy to work in the field.

"For a long time after I was brought here, I thought it would be impossible for me to live, on the coarse and scanty food, with which we are supplied. When I contrast my former happiness with my present misery, I pray for death to deliver me, from my sufferings."

I was deeply affected by the narrative of this woman, and as we had loitered on our way, it was already dark, whilst we were at some distance from the quarter; but the sound of the overseer's horn, here interrupted our conversation—at hearing which, she exclaimed, "We are too late, let us run; or we shall be whipped;" and setting off as fast as she could carry her child, she left me alone. A moment's reflection, however, convinced me that I too had better quicken my pace—I quickly passed the woman, encumbered with her infant, and arrived in the crowd of the people, some time, perhaps a minute, before her.

CHAPTER X.

AT the time I joined the company, the overseer was calling over the names of the whole, from a little book; and the first name that I heard was that of my companion whom I had just left, which was Lydia—called by him Lyd. As she did not answer, I said, "Master, Lydia, the woman that carries the baby on her back, will be here in a minute— I left her just behind." The overseer took no notice of what I said, but went on with his roll-call.

As the people answered to their names, they passed off to the cabins, except three—two women and a man; who, when their names were called, were ordered to go into the yard, in front of the overseer's house. My name was the last on the list; and when it was called I was ordered into the yard with the three others. Just as we had entered, Lydia came up out of breath, with the child in her arms; and following us into the yard, dropped on her knees before the overseer, and begged him to forgive her. "Where have you been?" said he. Poor Lydia now burst into tears, and said, "I only stopped to talk awhile to this man," pointing to me; "but, indeed, master overseer, I will never, do so again." "Lie down," was his reply. Lydia immediately fell prostrate upon the ground and in this position he compelled her to remove her old tow linen shift, the only garment she wore, so as to expose her hips, when he gave her ten lashes, with his long whip, every touch of which brought blood, and a shriek from the sufferer. He then ordered her to go and get her supper, with an injunction never to stay behind again. The other three culprits were then put upon their trial.

The first was a middle aged woman, who had, as her overseer said, left several hills of cotton in the course of the day, without cleaning and hilling them in a proper manner. She received twelve lashes. The other two were charged in general terms, with having been lazy, and of having neglected their work that day. Each of these received twelve lashes.

These people all received punishment in the same manner that it had been inflicted upon Lydia, and when they were all gone, the overseer turned to me and said—"Boy, you are a stranger here yet, but I called you in, to let you see how things are done here, and to give you a little advice. When I get a new negro under my command, I never whip at first; I always give him a few days to learn his duty, unless he is an outrageous villain, in which case I anoint him a little at the beginning. I call over the names of all the hands twice every week, on Wednesday and Saturday evenings, and settle with them according to their general conduct, for the last three days. I call the names of my captains every morning, and it is their business to see that they have all their hands in their proper places. You ought not to have staid behind to-night with Lyd; but as this is your first offence, I shall overlook it, and you may go and get your supper." I made a low bow, and thanked master overseer for his kindness to me, and left him. This night for supper, we had corn bread and cucumbers; but we had neither salt, vinegar, nor pepper, with the cucumbers.

I had never before seen people flogged in the way our overseer flogged his people. This plan of making the person who is to be whipped, lie down upon the ground, was new to me, though it is much practised in the south; and I have since seen men and women too, cut nearly in pieces by this mode, of punishment. It has one advantage over tying people up by the hands, as it prevents all accidents from sprains in the thumbs or wrists. I have known people to hurt their joints very much, by struggling when tied up by the thumbs, or wrists, to undergo a severe whipping. The method of ground whipping, as it is called, is, in my opinion, very indecent, as it compels females to expose themselves in a very shameful manner.

The whip used by the overseers on the cotton plantations, is different from all other whips, that I have ever seen. The staff is about twenty or twenty-two inches in length, with a large and heavy head, which is often loaded with a quarter or half a pound of lead, wrapped in cat-gut, and securely fastened on, so that nothing but the greatest violence can separate it from the staff. The lash is ten feet long, made of small strips of buckskin, tanned so as to be dry and hard, and plaited carefully and closely together, of the thickness, in the largest part, of a man's little finger, but quite small at each extremity. At the farthest end of this thong is attached a cracker, nine inches in length, made of strong sewing silk, twisted and knotted, until it feels as firm as the hardest twine.

This whip, in an unpractised hand, is a very awkward and inefficient weapon; but the best qualification of the overseer of a cotton plantation is the ability of using this whip with adroitness; and when wielded by an experienced arm, it is one of the keenest instruments of torture ever invented by the ingenuity of man. The cat-o'-nine tails, used in the British military service, is but a clumsy instrument beside this whip; which has superseded the cow-hide, the hickory, and every other species of lash, on the cotton plantations. The cow-hide and hickory, bruise and mangle the flesh of the sufferer; but this whip cuts, when expertly applied, almost as keen as a knife, and never bruises the flesh, nor injures the bones.

It was now Saturday night, and I wished very much for Sunday morning to come that I might see the manner of spending the Sabbath, on a great cotton plantation. I expected, that as these people had been compelled to work so hard, and fare so poorly all the week, they would be inclined to repose themselves on Sunday; and that the morning of this day would be passed in quietness, if not in sleep, by the inhabitants of our quarter. No horn was blown by the overseer, to awaken us this morning, and I slept, in my little loft, until it was quite day; but when I came down, I found our small community a scene of universal bustle and agitation.

Here it is necessary to make my readers acquainted with the rules of polity, which governed us on Sunday, (for I now speak of myself, as one of the slaves on this plantation,) and with the causes which gave rise to these rules.

All over the south, the slaves are discouraged, as much as possible, and by all possible means, from going to any place of religious worship on Sunday. This is to prevent them from associating together, from different estates, and distant parts of the country; and plotting conspiracies and insurrections. On some estates, the overseers are required to prohibit the people from going to meeting off the plantation, at any time, under the severest penalties. While preachers cannot come upon the plantations, to preach to the people, without first obtaining permission of the master, and afterwards procuring the sanction of the overseer. No slave dare leave the plantation to which he belongs, a single mile, without a written pass from the overseer, or master; but by exposing himself to the danger of being taken up and flogged. Any white man who meets a slave off the plantation without a pass, has a right to take him up, and flog him at his discretion. All these causes combined, operate powerfully to keep the slave at home. But, in addition to those principles of restraint, it is a rule on every plantation, that no overseer ever departs from, to flog every slave, male or female, that leaves the estate for a single hour, by night or by day—Sunday not excepted—without a written pass.

The overseer who should permit the people under his charge to go about the neighbourhood without a pass, would soon lose his character, and no one would employ him; nor would his reputation less certainly suffer in the estimation of the planters, were he to fall into the practice of granting passes, except on the most urgent occasions; and for purposes generally to be specified in the pass.

A cotton planter has no more idea of permitting his slaves to go at will, about the neighbourhood on Sunday, than a farmer in Pennsylvania has of letting his horses out of his field on that day. Nor would the neighbours be less inclined to complain of the annoyance, in the former, than in the latter case.

There has always been a strong repugnance, amongst the planters, against their slaves becoming members of any religious society, Not, as I believe, because they are so maliciously disposed towards their people as to wish to deprive them of the comforts of religion— provided the principles of religion did not militate against the principles of slavery— but they fear that the slaves, by attending meetings, and listening to the preachers, may imbibe with the morality they teach, the notions of equality and liberty, contained in the gospel. This, I have no doubt, is the ground of all the dissatisfaction, that the planters express, with the itinerant preachers, who have from time to time, sought opportunities of instructing the slaves in their religious duties.

The cotton planters have always, since I knew any thing of them, been most careful to prevent the slaves from learning to read; and such is the gross ignorance that prevails, that many of them could not name the four cardinal points.

At the time I first went to Carolina, there were a great many African slaves in the country, and they continued to come in for several years afterwards. I became intimately acquainted with some of these men. Many of them believed there were several gods; some of whom were good, and others evil, and they prayed as much to the latter as to the former. I knew several who must have been, from what I have since learned, Mohamedans; though at that time, I had never heard of the religion of Mohamed.

There was one man on this plantation, who prayed five times every day, always turning his face to the east, when in the performance of his devotion.

There is, in general, very little sense of religious obligation, or duty, amongst the slaves on the cotton plantations; and Christianity cannot be, with propriety, called the religion of these people. They are universally subject to the grossest and most abject superstition; and uniformly believe in witchcraft, conjuration, and the agency of evil spirits in the affairs of human life. Far the greater part of them are either natives of Africa, or the descendants of those who have always, from generation to generation, lived in the south, since their ancestors were landed on this continent; and their superstition, for it does not deserve the name of religion, is no better, nor is it less ferocious, than that which oppresses the inhabitants of the wildest regions of Negro-land.

They have not the slightest religious regard for the Sabbath-day, and their masters make no efforts to impress them with the least respect for this sacred institution. My first Sunday on this plantation was but a prelude to all that followed; and I shall here give an account of it.

At the time I rose this morning, it wanted only about fifteen or twenty minutes of sunrise; and a large number of the men, as well as some of the women, had already quitted the quarter, and gone about the business of the day. That is, they had gone to work for wages for themselves—in this manner: our overseer had, about two miles off, a field of near twenty acres, planted in cotton, on his own account. He was the owner of this land; but as he had no slaves, he was obliged to hire people to work it for him, or let it lie waste. He had procured this field to be cleared, as I was told, partly by letting white men make tar and turpentine from the pine wood grew on it; and partly by hiring slaves to work upon it on Sunday. About twenty of our people went to work for him to-day, for which he gave them fifty cents each. Several of the others, perhaps forty in all, went out through the neighbourhood, to work for other planters.

On every plantation, with which I ever had any acquaintance, the people are allowed to make patches, as they are called—that is, gardens, in some remote and unprofitable part of the estate, generally in the woods, in which they plant corn, potatoes, pumpkins, melons, &c. for themselves.

These patches they must cultivate on Sunday, or let them go uncultivated. I think, that on this estate, there were about thirty of these patches, cleared in the woods, and fenced—some with rails, and others with brush—the property of the various families.

The vegetables that grow in these patches, were always consumed in the families of the owners; and the money that was earned by hiring out, was spent in various ways; sometimes for clothes, sometimes for better food than was allowed by the overseer, and sometimes for rum; but those who drank rum, had to do it by stealth.

By the time the sun was up an hour, this morning, our quarter was nearly as quiet and clear of inhabitants, as it had been at the same period on the previous day.

As I had nothing to do for myself, I went with Lydia, whose husband was still sick, to help her to work in her patch, which was about a mile and a half from our dwelling. We took with us some bread, and a large bucket of water; and worked all day. She had onions, cabbages, cucumbers, melons, and many other things in her garden.

In the evening, as we returned home, we were joined by the man who prayed five times a day; and at the going down of the sun, he stopped and prayed aloud in our hearing, in a language I did not understand.

This man told me, he formerly lived on the confines of a country, which had no trees, nor grass upon it; and that in some places, no water was to be found for several days' journey. That this barren country was, nevertheless, inhabited by a race of men, who had many camels and goats, and some horses. They had no settled place of residence; but removed from one part of the country to another, in quest of places Where green herbage was to be found—their chief food being the milk of their camels, and goats; but that they also ate the flesh of these animals, sometimes. The hair of those people, was not short and woolly, like that of the negroes; nor were they of a shining black. They were continually at war with some of the neighbouring people, and very often with his own countrymen. He was himself once taken prisoner by them, when a lad, in a great battle fought between them and his own people, in which his party were defeated. The victors kept him in their possession, more than two years, compelling him to attend to their camels and goats.

Whilst he was with these people, they travelled a great way towards the rising sun; and came to a river, running through a country inhabited by yellow people, where the land was very rich, and produced great quantities of rice, such as grows here— and many other kinds of grain.

The people who had taken him prisoner, professed the same religion that he did; and it was forbidden by its precepts, for one an to sell another into slavery, who held the same faith with himself; otherwise he should have been sold to these yellow people. In the river of this country be saw alligators, in great abundance, like those that he had seen in Carolina; and the musquitos were, in some places, so numerous, that it was difficult to breathe without inhaling them.

"When we turned the camels out to graze, we used tie their fore-feet together, with a rope made of the hair of this animal, spun upon small sticks, and twisted into a rope. Sometimes they broke these ropes, and slipped their feet out of its coils; and it was then very difficult to retake them. They would sometimes strike off at a trot, across the open country, and we would be obliged to mount other camels, and follow them for a day or two, before we could retake them. I had been with these people so long, and being of the same religion with themselves, had become so familiar with their customs and manner of life, that they seemed almost to regard me as one of their own nation; and frequently sent me alone, in pursuit of the stray camels, giving me instructions how to direct my course, so as to rejoin them; for they never waited for me, to return to them, at the place where I left them, if the beasts had consumed the bushes, and green herbage, growing there, before I came back.

"When I had been a captive with them fully two years, we came one evening, and encamped at a little well, the mouth of which was about a yard over; and the water in which was very sweet and good.

"This well, seemed to have been scooped out of the hard and flinty sand, with men's hands, and was scarcely more than four feet deep; though it contained an abundant supply of water. We encamped by this fountain all night; and I remembered that we had been at the same place, soon after I was made a prisoner; and that when we had formerly come to it, we travelled with our backs to the mid-day sun. There was no herbage hereabout, except a few stunted and thorny bushes; and in wandering abroad in quest of something to eat, one of the best and fleetest camels, entangled the rope which bound his fore-feet, amongst these bushes, and broke it. I found part of the rope fast to a bush in the morning; but the camel was at a great distance from us, towards the setting sun.

"The chief of our party ordered me to mount another camel, and go with a long rope, in pursuit of the stray; and told me that they should travel towards the south, that day, and encamp at a place where there was much grass. I went in pursuit of the lost camel; but when I came near him, he took off at a great trot over the country, — and I pursued him until noon, without ever being able to overtake him, or even to change the line of his march. His course was towards the south-west; and when I found it impossible to overtake him, as his speed was superior to that of the beast I rode, I resolved to strive to accomplish that, by stratagem, which force could not effect. I knew the beasts were both hungry; and that having received as much water as they could drink, the night before, they would devour with the utmost avidity, the first green herbage that they might meet with.

"I slackened the speed of my camel, and followed at a leisure gait, after the one I pursued, suffering him to leave me behind him at a considerable distance. He still, however, kept on in the same direction, and with nearly the same speed, with which he had advanced all the morning; so that it became necessary for me to quicken my pace, to prevent him from passing out of my sight, and escaping from me altogether.

About five o'clock in the afternoon, I came in sight of trees, the tops of which were only visible across the open plain. The camel I rode was now as desirous to advance rapidly, as his leader had been throughout the day. I was carried forward as quickly as the swiftest horse could trot; and awhile before sundown, I approached a small grove of tall straight trees, which are greatly valued in Africa, and which bear large quantities of nuts, of a very good quality. Under and about these trees, was a small tract of ground, covered with long green grass; and here my stray camel stopped.

"I have no doubt that he had scented the odour of this grass, soon after I first gave chase to him in the morning; though the distance at which he was from it, was so great, that the best horse could not have travelled it in one day. When I came up to the trees, I dismounted from the camel I rode, and tying its feet together with a short rope, preserved my long one, for the purpose of taking the runaway. I gathered as many nuts as I could eat, and after satisfying my hunger, lay down to sleep.

"This was the first time that I had ever attempted to pass a night alone, in this open country; and after I had made my bed in the grass, I became fearful that some wild beast might fall in with me before morning, as I had often heard lions, and other creatures of prey, breaking the stillness of night, in those desolate regions, by their yells and roaring. I therefore ascended a tree, and placed myself amongst some spreading limbs, in such a position as to be in no danger of falling, even if I should be overtaken by sleep.

"The moon was now full; and in that country where there are no clouds, and where there is seldom any dew, objects can be distinguished at the distance of several miles over the plains, by moonlight. When I had been in the tree about an hour, I heard at a great distance, a loud sullen noise, between a growl and a roar, which I knew to proceed from a lion; for I was well acquainted with the habits and noise of this animal; having frequently assisted in hunting him, in my own country.

"I was greatly terrified by this circumstance; not for my own safety, for I knew that no beast of prey could reach me in the tree, but I feared that my camels might be devoured, and I be left to perish in the desert.

"My fears were in part, well founded; for keeping my eye steadily directed towards the point from which the sound had proceeded, it was not long before I saw some object, moving over the naked plain.

"The runaway camel now joined his tethered companion, and both quitting the herbage, came and stood at the root of the tree, upon the branches of which I was. I still kept my eye steadily fixed upon the moving body which was evidently advancing nearer to me over the plain. I had no longer any doubt that it was coming to the grove of trees, which were only twelve or fifteen in number; and so bare of branches that I could distinctly see in every direction around me.

"In a few minutes, the animal approached me. It was a monstrous lion, of the black maned species. It was now within one hundred paces of me, and the poor camels raised their heads, as high as they could, towards me, and crouched close to the trunk of the tree, apparently so stupified by fear, as to be incapable of attempting to fly. The lion approached with a kind of motion; and at length dropping on its belly, glided along the ground, until within about ten yards of the tree, when uttering a terrific roar, which shook the stillness of the night for many a league around, he sprang upon and seized the unbound camel by the neck.

"Finding that I afforded no protection, the animal, after striving in vain to shake off his assailant, rushed out upon the open plain, carrying on his back the lion, which I could perceive, had already fastened upon the throat of his victim, which did not go more than a stone's cast from the trees, before he fell, and after a short struggle, ceased to move his limbs. The lion held the poor beast by the throat for some time after he was dead, and until, I suppose, the blood had ceased to flow from his veins—then, quitting the neck, he turned to the side of the slain, and tearing a hole into the cavity of the body, extracted the intestines, and devoured the liver and heart, before he began to gorge himself with the flesh.

"The moon was now high in the heavens, and shone with such exceeding brilliancy, that I could see distinctly for many miles round me. In that country, the smooth and glittering surface of the hard and baked sandy plains, reflects the light of the moon, as strongly as a sheet of snow in winter does in this; and the atmosphere being, free from all humidity, is so clear and transparent, that I could perceive the quivering motion of the camel's lips, in his last agony, as well as the tongue of the lion, when he licked the blood from his paws.

"As soon my fright had a little subsided, I looked for my surviving camel, which, to my terror, I could not see, either at the foot of the tree on which I was, and where I had last seen it, or any where in the grove.

"I now concluded, that in the alarm caused by the lion, and the destruction of his companion, my surviving beast had broken the cord which bound its feet, and had taken to flight, leaving me alone, and without any means of escaping from the desert; for I had no hope of being able to reach, on foot, either the people with whom I had so long lived, or the inhabitants of the woody countries, lying far to the south of me. No condition can be more miserable than that to which I was now reduced.

"My late masters were distant from me, at least one day's journey, on a swift camel; and were removing farther from me every day, as fast as their beasts could carry them; and I had no knowledge of the various watering places, and spots of herbage, which lie scattered over the wide expanse of those unfrequented regions, in the midst of which I then was. I had not seen any water at this place, since I came to it; and had not the poor consolation of knowing, that I could remain here, and live on the fruit of the trees, until some chance should bring hither some of the wandering tribes, that roam over those solitudes.

"After a lapse of two or three hours, not being able to discover my living camel anywhere, although the moon had now passed her meridian, and shone with a splendour which enabled me to distinguish small pebbles at some distance, I gave him up for lost, and again turned my attention to the lion, which still continued at intervals, to utter deep and sullen growls over his prey. I expected, that at the approach of day, the lion would leave the dead carcass, and retire to his lair in some distant place; and I determined to await the period of his departure, to descend the tree, and search for water amongst the grass, which rose in some places to the height of my shoulders.

"I slept none this night,—but from my couch in the boughs, watched the motions of the lion, which, after swallowing at least one third of the camel, stretched himself at full length on his belly, about twenty paces from it, and laying his head between his fore-feet, prepared to guard his spoil against all the intruders of the night. In this position he remained, until the sun was up in the morning, and began to dart his rays across the naked and parched plain, upon which he lay— when rising and stretching himself, he walked slowly towards the grove— passed under me—went to the other side of the trees and entered some very tall herbage, where I heard him lap water. I now knew that I was in no danger of dying from thirst, provided I could escape wild beasts, on my way to and from the fountain.

"The trees afforded me both food and shelter; but I quickly found myself deprived of lasting water, at the present—for the lion, after slaking his thirst, returned by the same way that he had gone to the water, and coming to the tree in the boughs of which I lay, rubbed himself against its trunk, raising his tail, and exposing his sides alternately to the friction of the rough bark. After continuing this exercise for some time, he rested his weight on his hind-feet, licked his breast, fore-legs and paws, and then lying down on his side in the shade, appeared to fall into a deep sleep. Great as my anxiety was to leave my present lodgings, I dared not attempt to pass the sentinel that kept guard at the root of the tree, even though he slept on his post: for whenever I made the least rustling it, the branches, I perceived that he moved his ears, and opened his eyes, but closed the latter again, when the, noise ceased.

"The lion lay all day under the tree, only removing so as to place himself in the shade in the afternoon; but soon after the sun descended below the horizon, in the evening, he aroused himself, and resting upon his hind-feet, as he had done in the morning, uttered a roar that shook all the leaves about my head, and caused a tremulous motion in the branches upon which I rested. This horrid noise, together with the sight of the great beast that uttered it, so agitated my whole frame, that I was near leaping from my seat, and falling to the ground. I was so overcome with fear, that all prudence and self-possession forsook me; and I uttered a loud shout, as if in defiance of the monster below me.

"The moment the lion heard my voice, he raised his head, looked directly at me, with his fiery eyes; and crouched down in the attitude of springing; but perceiving me to be quite out of the reach of his longest leap, he walked slowly off, and lay down about half way between me and the dead camel, with his head towards my tree. I had no doubt that his object was to watch me, until my descent from the tree, that he might make his supper of me this night, as he had of my camel, the night before.

"I had now been without water two days—my thirst was tormenting, and I had no prospect before me but of remaining in this tree, until driven to delirium for water, I should voluntarily descend, and deliver myself into the jaws of my enemy.

"The moon did not rise this night until long after the disappearance of daylight; but in the country where I then was, the stars shed such abundant light, that objects of magnitude can be seen at a great distance by their rays, without the aid of the moon. The lion moved frequently from place to place, but I could perceive that his attention was still fixed upon me: at last, however, be started away across the plain, and went farther and farther from me, until at length I lost sight of him in the distance; and all remained as quiet and noiseless, in the immense expanse around me, as the land of the dead.

"I now thought of descending, to go in quest of water; but whilst I deliberated upon this subject the moon rose, and cast her broad and glorious light upon these wide fields of desolation. As I could now see every thing, I resolved to descend; but before doing this, thought it prudent to cast a look about me, to see if there might not be some other beast of prey near. This thought saved my life; for on turning my eyes in a direction quite different from that in which the lion had departed, I saw him returning, within two or three stone's cast, creeping along the ground. I watched him, and he came and placed himself between me and the water.

"All was again silent; and I remained in the tree, burning with thirst, until the moon was elevated high in the heavens, when the silence was interrupted by the roaring of a lion, at a great distance, which was again repeated after a short interval. At the end of half an hour I again heard the same lion, apparently not far off. Casting my eye in the direction of the sound, I saw the beast advancing rapidly, as I thought towards me, and began to apprehend that a whole den of lions were lying in wait for me.

"The stranger soon undeceived me, for he was coming to partake of the dead camel, whose flesh or blood he had doubtlessly smelled, though it was not putrid, for, in this dry atmosphere, flesh is preserved a long time free from taint, and is sometimes dried in the sun, in a state of perfect soundness. I knew the nature of the lion too well, to suppose that the stranger was going to get his supper free of cost; and before he had reached the carcass, my jailer quitted his post, and set off to defend his acquisition of the last night.

"The new comer arrived first, and fell upon the dead camel, with the fury of a hungry lion—as he was; but he had scarcely swallowed a second morsel when the rightful owner, uttering a roar yet more dreadful than any that had preceded it, leaped upon the intruder, and brought him to the ground. For a moment I heard nothing but the gnashing of teeth, the clashing of talons, and the sounds caused by the laceration of the flesh and hides of the combatants; but anon, they rolled along the ground, and filled the whole canopy of heaven with their yells of rage—then the roaring would cease, and only the rending of the flesh of these lords of the waste could be heard—then the roaring would again burst forth, with renewed energy.

"This battle lasted more than an hour; but at length both appearing to be exhausted, they lay for some minutes on their sides, each with the other wrapped in his fierce embrace. In the end, I perceived that one of them rose and walked away, leaving the other upon the ground. The victor, which I could perceive was the stranger, for his mane was not black, returned to the remnant of the camel, and lay down panting beside it. After he had taken time to breathe, he recommenced his attack, and consumed far the larger part of the carcass. Having eaten to fulness, he took up the bones and remaining flesh of the camel, and set out across the desert,—I followed him with my eye for more than an hour.

"Parched as my throat was, but still afraid to descend from my place of safety, I remained on the tree until the light of the next morning, when I examined carefully around, to see that there was no beast of prey lurking about the place, where I knew the water to be. Perceiving no danger, I descended before the sun was up, and going to the water, knelt down, and drank as long and as much as I thought I could with safety.

"I then proceeded to make a more minute examination of this place, and saw numerous tracks of wild goats, and of other animals, that had come here, as well to drink as to eat the grass. I also saw the tracks of lions, and other beasts of prey, which satisfied me that these had come to lie in wait for other animals coming to drink: it also convinced me that it was not safe for me to remain in this grove alone; but I knew of no means by which I could escape from it.

"It now occurred to my mind that if my living camel had not escaped from me, I might have made my way to my own country, for on my camel I had two leather bottles, which I had neglected to fill with water, the morning I left the company of my former masters. By replenishing these from the fountain, giving my camel as much as he could drink, and filling two small sacks attached to my saddle with the nuts from these trees, I should have been equipped for a journey of ten days, within which period, I had no doubt, I should have been able to reach my own people; but my camel was gone and reflections served only to aggravate the bitterness of my anguish.

"I walked out upon the desert, and prayed to be delivered from the perils that environed me. At the distance of two or three miles from me, I now observed small sand hill, rising to the height of eight or ten feet; easily perceived when looking along the level surface of the ground, but which had escaped my observation from my elevated post in the tree. Such sand hills are often found in those deserts, and sometimes contain the bones of men and animals that have been buried in them.

"In my situation, I could not remain idle; and urged forward by restlessness, bordering on despair, resolved to go to the little hill before me, without having any definite object in view. I soon approached the hill, and having reached its foot, walked along its base for some distance. I then turned to go back to the trees; but after advancing a few steps, was seized with a sudden impulse, which urged me to go to the top of the sand hill. I again turned and walked slowly to the summit, beyond which I saw only the same dreary expanse that I was so well used to look upon. Advancing along the top of this sand hill, which had been blown up by the wind in a long narrow ridge, I saw a recess or hollow place, on the side opposite to that by which I had ascended it; and on coming to this spot, beheld my camel crouched down close to the ground, with his neck extended at full length. My joy was unbounded—I leaped with delight, and was wild for some minutes, with a delirium of gladness.

"My camel had fled from the grove, at the time his companion was killed by the lion, and reaching this place, had here taken refuge, and had not moved since. I hastened to loose his feet from the cords with which I had bound them, mounted upon his back, and was quickly at the watering place. I filled my two water skins with water, and gathering any nuts as my sacks would contain, caused my camel to take a full draught, and fill his stomach with grass, and then directed my course to the south, with a quick pace.

"It was now noon when I left this watering place; and I travelled hard all that day and the succeeding night, until the moon rose. I then alighted, and causing my camel to lie down, crept close to his side, and betook myself to sleep. I rested well this night, and recommencing my journey at the dawn of day, I pursued my route, without any thing worthy of relating happening to me until the eighth day, when I discovered trees, and all the appearance of a woody country, before me.

"Soon after entering the forest, I came to a small stream of water. Descending this stream a few miles, I found some people, who were cutting grass for the purpose of making mats to sleep on. These people spoke my own language, and told me that one of them had been in my native village lately. They took me and my camel to their village, and treated me very kindly; promising me that after I had recovered from my fatigue, they would go with me to my friends.

"My protectors were at war with a nation whose religion was different from ours and about a month after I came to the village we were alarmed one morning, just at break of day, by the horrible uproar caused by mingled shouts of men, and blows given with heavy sticks upon large wooden drums. The village was surrounded by enemies, who attacked us with clubs, long wooden spears, and bows and arrows. After fighting for more than an hour, those who were not fortunate enough to run away, were made prisoners. It was not the object of our enemies to kill; they wished to take us alive, and sell us as slaves. I was knocked down by a heavy blow of a club, and when I recovered from the stupor that followed, I found myself tied fast with the long rope that I had brought from the desert, and in which I had formerly led the camels of my masters.

"We were immediately led away from this village, through the forest, and were compelled to travel all day, as fast as we could walk. We had nothing to eat on this journey, but a small quantity of grain, taken with ourselves. This grain we were compelled to carry on our backs, and roast by the fires which we kindled at nights, to frighten away the wild beasts. We travelled three weeks in the woods,— sometimes without any path at all; and arrived one day at a large river, with a rapid current. Here we were forced to help our conquerors, to roll a great number of dead trees into the water, from a vast pile that had been thrown together by high floods.

These trees being dry and light, floated high out of the water; and when several of the were fastened together, with the tough branches of young trees, formed a raft, upon which we all placed ourselves, and descended the river for three days, when we came in sight of what appeared to me the most wonderful object in the world; this was a large ship, at anchor, in the river. When our raft came near the ship, the white people—for such they were on board—assisted to take us on deck, and the logs were suffered to float down the river.

"I had never seen white people before; and they appeared to me the ugliest creatures in the world. The persons who brought us down the river received payment for us of the people in the ship, in various articles, of which I remember that a keg of liquor, and some yards of blue and red cotton cloth, were the principal. At the time we came into this ship, she was full of black people, who were all confined in a dark and low place, in irons. The women were in irons as well as the men.

"About twenty persons were seized in our village, at the time I was; and amongst these were three children, so young that they were not able to walk, or to eat any hard substance. The mothers of these children had brought them all the way with them; and had them in their arms when we were taken on board this ship.

"When they put us in irons, to be sent to our place of confinement in the ship, the men who the irons on these others, took the children out of their hands, and threw the over the side of the ship, into the water. When this was done, two of the women leaped overboard after the children— the third was already confined by a chain to another woman, and could not get into the water, but in struggling to disengage herself she broke her arm, and died a few days after, of a fever. One of the two women who were in the river, was carried down by the weight of her irons, before she could be rescued; but the other was taken up by some men in a boat, and brought on board. This woman threw herself overboard one night, when we were at sea.

"The weather was very hot, whilst we lay in the river, and many of us died every day; but the number brought on board greatly exceeded those who died, and at the end of two weeks the place in which we were confined was so full that no one could lie down; and we were obliged to sit all the time, for the room was not high enough for us to stand. When our prison would hold no more, the ship sailed down the river, and on the night of the second day after she sailed, I heard the roaring of the ocean, as it dashed against her sides.

"After we had been at sea some days, the irons were removed from the women, and they were permitted to go upon deck; but whenever the wind blew high, they were driven down amongst us.

"We had nothing to eat but yams, which were thrown amongst us at random—and of these we had scarcely enough to support life. More than one-third of us died on the passage; and when we arrived at Charleston, I was not able to stand. It was more than a week after I left the ship, before I could straighten my limbs. I was bought by a trader, with several others; brought up the country, and sold to our present master. I have been here five years."

CHAPTER XI.

It was dusky twilight when this narrative was ended, and we hastened home to the quarter. When we arrived, the overseer had not yet come. He had been at his cotton field, with the people he had hired in the morning to work for him; but he soon made his appearance, and going into his house, came out with a small bag of money, and paid each one the price he had a right to receive. In this transaction the overseer acted with entire fairness to the people who worked for him; and with the exception of the moral turpitude of violating the Sabbath, in this shameful manner, the business was conducted with propriety.

I must here observe, that when the slaves go out to work for wages on Sunday, their employers never flog them; and so far as I know never give them abusive language. I have often hired myself to work on Sunday, and have been employed in this way by more than twenty different persons, not one of whom ever insulted or maltreated me in any way. They seldom took the trouble of coming to look at me until towards evening, and sometimes not them. I worked faithfully, because I knew that if I did not, I could not expect payment; and those who hired me, knew that if I did not work well, they need not employ me.

The practice of working on Sunday, is so universal amongst the slaves on the cotton plantations, that the immorality of the matter is never spoken of.

We retired to test this evening at the usual hour; and no one could have known, by either our appearance or our manners, that this was Sunday evening. There were no clean clothes amongst us; for few of our people were acquainted with the luxury of a suit of clean vestments, and those who could afford a clean garment, reserved it for Monday morning. Sunday is the customary wash-day on cotton plantations.

It is here proper to observe, that it is usual, on the cotton estates, to deal out the weekly allowance of corn to the slaves, on Sunday evening; but our overseer, at this period, had changed this business from Sunday to Monday morning, for the reason, I believe, that he wished to keep the hired people at work, in his own cotton field, until night. He, however, soon afterwards resumed the practice of distributing the allowance on Sunday evening, and continued it as long as I remained on the estate. The business was conducted in the same manner, when performed on Sunday, as when attended to on Monday, only the time was changed.

On Monday morning I heard the sound of the horn, at the usual hour, and repairing to the front of the overseer's house, found that he had already gone to the corn crib, for the purpose of distributing corn amongst the people, for the bread of the week; or rather, for the week's subsistence; for this corn was all the provision that our master, or his overseer, usually made for us;—I say usually, for whatever was given to us beyond the corn, which we received on Sunday evening, was considered in the light of a bounty bestowed upon us, over and beyond what we were entitled to, or had a right to expect to receive.

When I arrived at the crib, the door was unlocked and open, and the distribution had already commenced. Each person was entitled to half a bushel of ears of corn, which was measured out by several of the men who were in the crib. Every child above six months old drew this weekly allowance of corn; and in this way, women who had several small children, had more corn than they could consume, and sometimes bartered small quantities with the other people, for such things as they needed, and were not able to procure.

The people received their corn in baskets, old bags, or any thing with which they could most conveniently provide themselves. I had not been able since I came here, to procure a basket, or any thing else to put my corn in, and desired the man with whom I lived to take my portion in his basket, with that of his family. This he readily agreed to do, and as soon as we had received our share we left the crib.

The overseer attended in person to the measuring of this corn; and it is only justice to him to say that he was careful to see that justice was done us. The men who measured the corn always heaped the measure as long as an ear would lie on; and he never restrained their generosity to their fellow- slaves.

In addition to this allowance of corn, we received a weekly allowance of salt, amounting, in general, to about half a gill to each person; but this article was not furnished regularly, and sometimes we received none for two or three weeks.

The reader must not suppose, that, on this plantation we had nothing to eat beyond the corn and salt. This was far from the case. I have already described the gardens, or patches, cultivated by the people, and the practice which they universally followed of working on Sunday, for wages. In addition to all these, an industrious, managing slave would contrive to gather up a great deal to eat.

I have before observed, that the planters are careful of the health of their slaves, and in pursuance of this rule, they seldom expose them to rainy weather, especially in the sickly seasons of the year, if it can be avoided.

In the spring and early parts of the summer, the rains are frequently so violent, and the ground becomes so wet, that it is injurious to the cotton to work it, at least whilst it rains. In the course of the year there are many of these rainy days, in which the people cannot go to work with safety; and it often happens that there is nothing for them to do in the house. At such time they make baskets, brooms, horse collars, and other things, which they are able to sell amongst the planters.

The baskets are made of wooden splits, and the brooms of young white oak or hickory trees. The mats are sometimes made of splits, but more frequently of flags as they are called—a kind of tall rush, which grows in swampy ground. The horse or mule collars are made of husks of corn, though sometimes of rushes, but the latter are not very durable.

The money procured by these, and various other means, which I shall explain hereafter, is laid out by the slaves in purchasing such little articles of necessity or luxury, as it enables the to procure. A part is disbursed in payment for sugar, molasses, and sometimes a few pounds of coffee, for the use of the family; another part is laid out for clothes for winter; and no inconsiderable portion of his pittance is squandered away by the misguided slave for tobacco, and an occasional bottle of rum. Tobacco is deemed so indispensable to comfort, nay to existence that hunger and nakedness are patiently endured to enable the slave to indulge in this highest of enjoyments.

There being few towns in the cotton country, the shops, or stores, are frequently kept at some cross road, or other public place, in or adjacent to a rich district of plantations. To these shops the slaves resort, sometimes with, and at other times without, the consent of the overseer, for the purpose of laying out the little money they get. Notwithstanding all the vigilance that is exercised by the planters, the slaves, who are no less vigilant than their masters, often leave the plantation after the overseer has retired to his bed, and go to the store.

The store-keepers are always ready to accommodate the slaves, who are frequently better customers than any white people; because the former always pay cash, whilst the latter almost always require credit. In dealing with the slave, the shop-keeper knows he can demand whatever price he pleases for his goods, without danger of being charged with extortion; and he is ready to rise at any time of the night to oblige friends who are of so much value to him.

It is held highly disgraceful, on the part of store-keepers, to deal with the slaves for any thing but money, or the coarse fabrics that it is known are the usual products of the ingenuity and industry of the negroes; but, notwithstanding this, a considerable traffic is carried on between the shop-keepers and slaves, in which the latter make their payments by barter. The utmost caution and severity of masters and overseers, are sometimes insufficient to repress the cunning contrivances of the slaves.

After we had received our corn, we deposited it in our several houses, and immediately followed the overseer to the same cotton field, in which we had been at work on Saturday. Our breakfast this morning, was bread, to which was added a large basket of apples, from the orchard of our master. These apples served us for a relish with our bread, both for breakfast and dinner, and when I returned to the quarter in the evening, Dinah (the name of the woman who was at the head of our family) produced at supper, a black jug, containing molasses, and gave me some of the molasses for my supper.

I felt grateful to Dinah for this act of kindness, as I well knew that her children regarded molasses as the greatest of human luxuries, and that she was depriving them of their highest enjoyment to afford me the means of making a gourd full of molasses and water, I therefore proposed to her and her husband, whose name was Nero, that whilst I should remain a member of the family, I would contribute as much towards its support as Nero himself; or, at least, that I would bring all my earnings into the family stock, provided I might be treated as one of its members, and be allowed a portion of the proceeds of their patch or garden. This offer was very readily accepted, and from this time we constituted one community, as long as I remained among the field hands on this plantation. After supper was over, we had to grind our corn; but as we had to wait for our turn at the mill, we did not get through this indispensable operation before one o'clock in the morning. We did not sit up all night to wait, for our turn at the mill, but as our several turns were assigned us by lot, the person who had the first turn, when done with the with the mill, gave notice to the one entitled to the second, and so on. By this means nobody lost more than half an hour's sleep, and in the morning every one's grinding was done.

We worked very hard this week. We were now laying by the cotton, as it is termed; that is we were giving the last weeding and hilling to the crop, of which there was, on this plantation, about five hundred acres, which looked well, and promised to yield a fine picking.

In addition to the cotton, there was on this plantation, one hundred acres of corn, about ten acres of indigo, ten or twelve acres in sweet potatoes, and a rice swamp of about fifty acres. The potatoes and indigo had been laid by, at (that is, the season of working in them was past,) before I came upon the estate; and we were driven hard by the overseer to get done with the cotton, to be ready to give the corn another harrowing, and hoeing, before the season should be too far advanced. Most of the corn in this part of the country, was already laid by, but the crop here had been planted late, and yet required to be worked.

We were supplied with an abundance of bread, for a peck of corn is as much as a man call consume in a week, if he has other vegetables with it; but we were obliged to provide ourselves with the other articles, necessary for our subsistence. Nero had corn in his patch, which was now hard enough to be fit for boiling, and my friend Lydia had beans in her garden. We exchanged corn for beans, and had a good supply of both; but these delicacies we were obliged to reserve for supper. We took our breakfast in the field, from the cart, which seldom afforded us any thing better than bread, and some raw vegetables from the garden. Nothing of moment occurred amongst us, in this first week of my residence here. On Wednesday evening, called settlement-night, two men and a woman were whipped; but circumstances of this kind were so common, that I shall, in future, not mention them, unless something extraordinary attended them.

I could make wooden bowls and ladles, and went to work with a man who was clearing some new land about two miles off—on the second Sunday of my sojourn here, and applied the money I earned in purchasing the tools necessary to enable me to carry on my trade. I occupied all my leisure hours, for several months after this, in making wooden trays, and such other wooden vessels as were most in demand. These I traded off, in part, to a storekeeper, who lived about five miles from the plantation; and for some of my work I obtained money before Christmas, I had sold more than thirty dollars worth of my manufactures; but the merchant with whom I traded, charged such high prices for his goods, that I was poorly compensated for my Sunday toils, and nightly labours; nevertheless, by these means, I was able to keep our family supplied with molasses, and some other luxuries, and at the approach of winter, I purchased three coarse blankets to which Nero added as many, and we had all these made up into blanket-coats for Dinah, ourselves, and the children.

About ten days after my arrival, we had a great feast at the quarter. One night, after we had returned from the field, the overseer sent for me by his little son, and when I came, to his house, he asked me if I understood the trade of a butcher— told him I was not a butcher by trade, but that I had often assisted my master and others, to kill hogs and cattle, and that I could dress a hog, or a bullock, as well as most people. He then told me he was going to have a beef killed in the morning at the great house, and I must do it—that he would not spare any of the hands to go with me, but he would get one of the house-boys to help me.

When the morning came, I went, according to orders, to butcher the beef, which I expected to find in some enclosure on the plantation; but the overseer told me I must take a boy named Toney, from the house, whose business it was to take care of the cattle, and go to the woods and look for the beef. Toney and I set out sometime before sunrise, and went to a cow-pen, about a mile from the house, where he said he had seen the young cattle only a day or two before. At this cow-pen, we saw several cows waiting to be milked, I suppose, for their calves were in an adjoining field, and separated from them only by a fence. Toney then said, we should have to go to the long savanna, where the dry cattle generally ranged, and thither we set off. This long savanna lay at the distance of three miles from the cow-pen, and when we reached it, I found it to be literally what it was called, a long savanna. It was a piece of low, swampy ground, several miles in extent, with an open space in the interior part of it, about a mile long, and perhaps a quarter of a mile in width. It was manifest that this open space was covered with water through the greater part of the year, which prevented the growth of timber in this place; though at the time it was dry, except a pond near one end, which covered, perhaps, an acre of ground. In this natural meadow, every kind of wild grass, common to such places in the southern country, abounded.

Here I first saw the scrub and saw grasses—the first of which is so hard and rough, that it is gathered to scrub coarse wooden furniture, or even pewter and the last is provided with edges, somewhat like saw teeth, so hard and sharp that, it would soon tear the skin off the legs of any one who should venture to walk through it with bare limbs.

As we entered this savanna, we were enveloped in clouds of musquitos, and swarm of galinippers, that threatened to devour us. As we advanced through the grass, they rose up until the air was thick, and actually darkened with them. They rushed upon us with the fury of yellow-jackets, whose hive has been broken in upon, and covered every part of our persons. The clothes I had on, which were nothing but a shirt and trousers of tow linen, afforded no protection, even against the musquitos, which were much larger than those found along the Chesapeake Bay; and nothing short of a covering of leather could have defended me against the galinippers.

I was pierced by a thousand stings at a time, and verily believe I could not have lived beyond a few hours in this place. Toney ran into the pond, and rolled himself in the water to get rid of his persecutors; but he had not been long there before he came running out, as fast as he had gone in, hallooing and clamouring in a manner wholly unintelligible to me. He was terribly frightened; but I could not imagine what could be the cause of his alarm, until he reached the shore, when he turned round with his face to the water, and called out— "the biggest alligator in the whole world—did not you see him?" I told him I had not seen any thing but himself in the water; but he insisted that he had been chased in the pond by an alligator, which had followed him until he was close to the shore. We waited a few minutes for the alligator to rise to the surface, but were soon compelled by the musquitos, to quit this place.

Toney said, we need not look for the cattle here; no cattle could live amongst these musquitos, and I thought he was right in his judgment. We then proceeded into the woods and thickets, and after wandering about for an hour or more, we found the cattle, and after much difficulty, succeeded in driving a part of the back to the cow-pen, and enclosing them in it. I here selected the one that appeared to me to be the fattest, and securing it with ropes, we drove the animal to the place of slaughter.

This beef was intended as a feast for the slaves, at the laying by of the corn and cotton; and when I had it hung up, and had taken the hide off, my young master, who I had seen on the day of my arrival, came out to me, and ordered me to cut off the head, neck, legs, and tail, and lay them, together with the empty stomach and the harslet, in a basket. This basket was sent home, to the kitchen of the great house, by a woman and a boy, who attended for that purpose. I think there was at least one hundred and twenty or thirty pounds of this offal. The residue of the carcass I cut into four quarters, and we carried it to the cellar of the great house. Here one of the hind quarters was salted in a tub, for the use of the family, and the other was sent, as a present, to a planter, who lived about four miles distant. The two fore-quarters were cut into very small pieces, and salted by themselves. These, I was told, would be cooked for our dinner on the next day, (Sunday,) when there was to be a general rejoicing amongst all the slaves of the plantation.

After the beef was salted down, I received some bread and milk for my breakfast, and went to join the hands in the corn field, where they were now harrowing and hoeing the crop for the last time. The overseer had promised us that we should have holiday, after the completion of this work, and by great exertion, we finished it about five o'clock in the afternoon.

On our return to the quarter, the overseer, at roll-call— which he performed this day before night told us that every family must send a bowl to the great house, to get our dinners of meat. This intelligence diffused as much joy amongst us, as if each one had drawn a prize in a lottery. At the assurance of a meat dinner, the old people smiled and showed their teeth, and returned thanks to master overseer; but many of the younger ones shouted, clapped their hands, leaped, and ran about with delight.

Each family, or mess, now sent its deputy, with a large wooden bowl in his hand, to receive the dinner at the great kitchen. I went on the part of our family, and found that the meat dinner of this day, was made up of the basket of tripe, and other offal, that I had prepared in the morning. The whole had been boiled in four great iron kettles, until the flesh had disappeared from the bones, which were broken in small pieces—a flitch of bacon, some green corn, squashes, tomatos, and onions, had been added, together with other condiments, and the whole converted into about a hundred gallons of soup, of which I received in my bowl, for the use of our family more than two gallons. We had plenty of bread, and a supply of black-eyed peas, gathered from our garden, some of which Dinah had boiled in our kettle, whilst I was gone for the soup; of which there was as much as we could consume, and I believe that every one in the quarter had enough.

I doubt if there was in the world a happier assemblage than ours, on this Saturday evening. We had finished one of the grand divisions of the labours of a cotton plantation, and were supplied with a dinner, which to the most of my fellow-slaves, appeared to be a great luxury, and most liberal donation on the part of our master, who they regarded with sentiments of gratitude, for this manifestation of his bounty.

In addition to present gratification, they looked forward to the enjoyments of the next day, when they were to spend a whole Sunday in rest and banqueting; for it was known that the two fore-quarters of the bullock, were to be dressed for Sunday's dinner; and I had told them that each of these quarters weighed at least one hundred pounds.

Our quarter knew but little quiet this night; singing— playing on the banjoe, and dancing, occupied nearly the whole community, until the break of day. Those who were too old to take any part in our active pleasures, beat time with their hands, or recited stories of former times. Most of these stories referred to affairs that had been transacted in Africa, and were sufficiently fraught with demons, miracles, and murders, to fix the attention of many hearers.

To add to our happiness, the early peaches were now ripe, and the overseer permitted us to send, on Sunday morning, to the orchard, and gather at least ten bushels of very fine fruit.

In South Carolina they have very good summer apples, but they fall from the trees, and rot immediately after they are ripe; indeed, very often they speck-rot on the trees, before they become ripe. This "speck-rot," as it is termed, appears to be a kind of epidemic disease amongst apples; for in some seasons whole orchards are subject to it, and the fruit is totally worthless, whilst in other years, the fruit in the same orchard continues sound and good, until it is ripe. The climate of Carolina is, however, not favourable to the apple, and this fruit of so much value in the north, is in the cotton region, only of a few weeks continuance—winter apples being unknown. Every climate is congenial to the growth of some kind of fruit tree; and in Carolina and Georgia, the peach arrives at its utmost perfection; the fig also ripens well, and is a delicious fruit.

None of our people went out to work for wages, to-day. Some few, devoted a part of the morning to such work as they deemed necessary, in or about their patches, and some went to the woods, or the swamps, to collect sticks for brooms, and splits, or to gather flags for mats; but far the greater number remained at the quarter, occupied in some small work, or quietly awaiting the hour of dinner, which we had been informed, by one of the house-servants, would be at one o'clock. Every family made ready some preparation of vegetables, from their own garden, to enlarge the quantity, if not to heighten the flavour of the dinner of this day.

One o'clock at length arrived, but not before it had been long desired; and we proceeded with our bowls a second time, to the great kitchen. I acted, as I had done yesterday, the part of commissary for our family; but when we were already at the place, where we were to receive our soup and meat, into our bowls, (for it was understood that we were, with the soup, to have an allowance of both beef and bacon, to-day,) we were told that puddings had been boiled for us, and that we must bring dishes to receive them in. This occasioned some delay, until we obtained vessels from the quarter. In addition to at least two gallons of soup, about a pound of beef, and a small piece of bacon, I obtained nearly two pounds of pudding, made of corn meal, mixed with lard, and boiled in large bags. This pudding, with the molasses that we had at home, formed a very palatable second course, to our bread, soup, and vegetables.

On Sunday afternoon, we had a meeting, at which many of our party attended. A man named Jacob, who had come from Virginia, sang and prayed; but a great many of the people went out about the plantation, in search of fruits; for there were many peach and some fig trees, standing along the fences, on various parts of the estate. With us, this was a day of uninterrupted happiness.

A man cannot well be miserable, when he sees every one about him immersed in pleasure; and though our fare of to-day, was not of a quality to yield me much gratification, yet such was the impulse given to my feelings, by the universal hilarity and contentment, which prevailed amongst my fellows that I forgot for the time, all the subjects of grief that were stored in my memory, all the acts of wrong that had been perpetrated against me, and entered with the most sincere and earnest sentiments, in the participation of the felicity of our community.

CHAPTER XII.

At the time of which I now speak, the rice was ripe, and ready to be gathered. On Monday morning, after our feast, the overseer took the whole of us to the rice field, to enter upon the harvest of this crop. The field lay in a piece of low ground, near the river, and in such a position that it could be flooded by the water of the stream, in wet seasons. The rice is planted in drills, or rows, and grows more like oats than any of the other grain, known in the north.

The water is sometimes let in to the rice fields, and drawn off again, several times, according to the state of the weather. Watering and weeding the rice is considered one of the most unhealthy occupations on a southern plantation, as the people are obliged to live for several weeks in the mud and water, subject to all the unwholesome vapours that arise from stagnant pools, under the rays of a summer sun, as well as the chilly autumnal dews of night. At the time we came to cut this rice, the field was quite dry; and after we had reaped and bound it, we hauled it upon wagons, to a piece of hard ground where we made a threshing floor, and threshed it. In some places, they tread out the rice, with mules or horses, as they tread wheat in Maryland; but this renders the grain dusty, and is injurious to its sale.

After getting in the rice, we were occupied for some time in clearing and ditching swampy land, preparatory to a more extended culture of rice, the next year; and about the first of August, twenty or thirty of the people, principally women and children, were employed for two weeks in making cider, of apples which grew in an orchard of nearly two hundred trees, that stood on a part of the estate. After the cider was made, a barrel of it was one day brought to the field, and distributed amongst us; but this gratuity was not repeated. The cider that was made by the people, was converted into brandy, at a still in the corner of the orchard.

I often obtained cider to drink, at the still, which was sheltered from the weather by a shed, of boards and slabs. We were not permitted to go into the orchard at pleasure; but as long as the apples continued, we were allowed the privilege of sending five or six persons every evening, for the purpose of bringing apples to the quarter, for our common use; and by taking large baskets, and filling them well, we generally contrived to get as many as we could consume.

When the peaches ripened, they were guarded with more rigour—peach brandy being an article which is nowhere more highly prized than in South Carolina. There were on the plantation, more than a thousand peach trees, growing on poor sandy fields which were no longer worth the expense of cultivation. The best peaches grow upon the poorest sandhills.

We were allowed to take three bushels of peaches every day, for the use of the quarter; but we could, and did eat, at least three times that quantity, for we stole at night that which was not given us by day. I confess, that I took part in these thefts, and I do not feel that I committed any wrong, against either God or man, by my participation in the common danger that we ran, for we well knew the consequences that would have followed detection.

After the feast at laying by the corn and cotton, we had no meat for several weeks; and it is my opinion that our master lost money, by the economy he practised at this season of the year.

In the month of August, we had to save the fodder. This fodder-saving is the most toilsome, and next to working in the rice swaps, the most unhealthy job, that has to be performed on a cotton plantation, in the whole year. The manner of doing it is to cut the tops from the corn, as is done in Pennsylvania; but in addition to this, the blades below the ear, are always pulled off by the hand. Great pains is taken with these corn-blades. They constitute the chosen food of race, and all other horses, that are intended to be kept with extraordinary care, and in superior condition. For the purpose of procuring the best blades, they are frequently stripped from the stock, sometimes before the corn is ripe enough in the ear, to permit the top of the stalk to be cut off, without prejudice to the grain. After the blades are stripped from the stem, they are stuck between the hills of corn until they are cured, ready for the stack. They are then cut, and bound in sheaves, with small bands of the blades themselves. This binding, and the subsequent hauling from the field, must be done either early in the morning, before the dew is dried up, or in the night, whilst the dew is falling.

This work exposes the people who do it, to the fogs and damps of the climate, at the most unhealthy season of the year. Agues, fevers, and all the diseases which follow in their train, have their dates at the time of fodder-saving. It is the only work, appertaining to a cotton estate, which must of necessity be done in the night, or in the fogs of the morning; and the people at this season of the year, and whilst engaged in this very fatiguing work, would certainly be better able to go through with it, if they were regularly supplied, with proper portions of sound and wholesome salted provisions.

If every master would, through the months of August and September, supply his people with only a quarter of a pound of good bacon flitch to each person, daily, I have no doubt but that he would save money by it; to say nothing of the great comfort it would yield to the slaves, at this period, when the human frame is so subject to debility and feebleness.

Early in August, disease made its appearance amongst us. Several were attacked by the ague, with its accompanying fever; but in South Carolina the "ague," as it is called, is scarcely regarded as a disease, and if a slave, has no ailment that is deemed more dangerous, he is never withdrawn from the roll of the field hands. I have seen many of our poor people compelled to pick cotton, when their frames were shaken so violently, by the ague, that they were unable to get hold of the cotton in the burs, without difficulty. In this, masters commit a great error. Many fine slaves are lost, by this disease, which superinduces the dropsy, and sometimes the, consumption, which could have been prevented by arresting the ague at its onset. When any of our people were taken so ill that they were not able to go to the field, they were removed to the great house, and placed in the "sick room," as it was termed. This sick room was a large, airy apartment, in the second story of a building, which stood in the garden.

The lower part of this building was divided into two apartments, in one of which was kept the milk, butter, and other things connected with the dairy. In the other, the salt provisions of the family, including fish, bacon, and other articles, were secured. This apartment also constituted the smoke house; but as the ceiling was lathed, and plastered with a thick coat of lime and sand, no smoke could penetrate the "sick room," which was at all seasons of the year, a very comfortable place to sleep in. Though I was never sick myself, whilst on this plantation, I was several times in this "sick room," and always observed, when there, that the sick slaves were well attended to. There a hanging partition, which could be let down at pleasure, and which was let down when it was necessary, to divide the rooms into two apartments, which always happened when there were several slaves of different sexes, sick at the same time. The beds, upon which the sick lay, were of straw, but clean and wholesome, and the patients when once in this room, were provided with every thing necessary for persons in their situation. A physician attended them daily, and proper food, and even wines, were not wanting.

The contrast between the cotton and rice fields, and this little hospital, was very great; and it appeared to me at the time, that if a part of the tenderness and benevolence, displayed here, had been bestowed upon the people whilst in good health, very many of the inmates of this infirmary, would never have been here.

I have often seen the same misapplication of the principles of philanthropy in Pennsylvania,—the subjects only being varied, from slaves to horses. The finest, and most valuable horses, are often overworked, or driven beyond their capacity of endurance, (it cannot be said that horses are not generally well fed in Pennsylvania,) without mercy or consideration, on the part of their owners; or more frequently of unfeeling hirelings, who have no interest in the life of the poor animal; and when his constitution is broken, and his health gone, great care and even expense, are bestowed upon him, for the purpose of restoring him to his former strength; the one half of which care or expense, would have preserved him in beauty and vigour, had they been bestowed upon him before he had suffered the irreparable injuries, attendant upon his cruel treatment. In Pennsylvania, the horse is regarded, and justly regarded, only on account of the labour he is able to perform. Being the subject of property, his owner considers, not how he shall add most to the comforts and enjoyments of his horse, but by what means he shall be able to procure the greatest amount of labour from him, with the least expense to himself. In devising the means of saving expense, the life of the horse, and the surest and cheapest method of its preservation, are taken into consideration. Precisely in this way, do the cotton planters reason and act, in relation to their slaves. Regarding the negroes merely as objects of property, like prudent calculators, they study how to render this property of the greatest value, and to obtain the greatest yearly income, from the capital invested in the slaves, and the lands they cultivate.

Experience has proved to me, that a man who eats no animal food, may yet be healthy, and able to perform the work usually done on a cotton plantation. Corn bread, sweet potatoes, some garden vegetables, with a little molasses and salt, assisted by the other accidental supplies that a thrifty slave is able to procure, on a plantation, are capable of sustaining life and health; and a slave who lives on such food and never tastes flesh, stands at least an equal chance, for long life, with his master or mistress, "who are clad in purple and fine linen, and fare sumptuously every day." More people are killed by eating and drinking too much, than die of the effects of starvation, in the south; but the diseases of the white man, do not diminish the sufferings of the black one. A man who lives upon vegetable diet, may be healthy, and active; but I know he is not so strong and vigorous, as if he enjoyed a portion of animal food.

The labour usually performed by slaves, on a cotton plantation, does not require great bodily strength, but rather superior agility, and wakefulness. The hoes in use, are not heavy, and the art of picking cotton depends not upon superior strength, but upon the power of giving quick and accelerated motion to the fingers, arms, and legs. The fences have to be made, and repaired, and ditches dug—wood must also be cut, for many purposes, and all these operations call for strength; but they consume only a very small portion of the whole year,—more than three fourths of which is spent in the, cotton, corn, rice, and indigo fields, where the strength of a boy, or a woman is sufficient to perform any kind of labour, necessary in the culture of the plants; but men are able to do more, even of this work, than either boys or women.

We scarcely had time to complete the securing of the fodder, and working up the apples, and peaches, when the cotton was ready for picking. This business of picking cotton, constitutes about half the labour of the year, on a large plantation. In Carolina, it is generally commenced about the first of September; though in some years, much cotton is picked in August. The manner of doing the work is this. The cotton being planted in hills, in straight rows, from four to five feet apart, each hand or picker, provided with a bag, made of cotton bagging, holding a bushel or more, hung round the neck, with cords, proceeds from one side of the field to the other between two of these rows, picking all the cotton from the open burs, on the right and left, as he goes. It is the business of the picker to take all the cotton from each of the rows, as far as the lines of the rows or hills. In this way he picks half the cotton from each of the rows, and the pickers who come on his right and left, take the remainder from the opposite sides of the rows.

The cotton is gathered into the bag, and when it becomes burdensome by its weight, it is deposited in some convenient place, until night, when it is taken home, either in a large bag or basket, and weighed under the inspection of the overseer. A day's work is not estimated by the number of hills, or rows, that are picked in the day, but by the number of pounds of cotton in the seed, that the picker brings into the cotton house, at night.

In a good field of cotton, fully ripe, a day's work is sixty pounds; but where the cotton is of inferior quality, or the burs are not in full blow, fifty pounds is the day's work; and where the cotton is poor, or in bad order, forty, or even thirty pounds, is as much as one hand can get in a day.

The picking of cotton, continues from August until December, or January; and in some fields, they pick from the old plants, until they are ploughed up in February or March, to make room for the planting of the seeds of another crop.

On all estates, the standard of a day's work is fixed by the overseer, according to the quality of the cotton; and if a hand gathers more than this standard, he is paid for it; but if, on the other hand, when his or her cotton is weighed at the cotton-house, in the evening, it is found that the standard quantity has not been picked, the delinquent picker is sure to receive a whipping.

On some estates, settlements are made every evening, and the whipping follows immediately; on others, the whipping does not occur until the next morning, whilst on a few plantations, the accounts are closed twice, or three times a week.

I have stated heretofore, that our overseer whipped twice a week, for the purpose of saving time; but if this method saved time to the overseer and the hands, it also saved the latter of a great many hard stripes; for very often, when one of us had displeased the overseer, he would tell us that on Wednesday or Saturday night, as the case might be, we should be remembered; yet the matter was either forgotten, or the passion of the overseer subdued, before the time of retribution arrived, and the delinquent escaped altogether from the punishment, which would certainly have fallen upon him, if it had been the custom of the overseer to chastise for every offence, at the moment, or even on the day, of its perpetration. A short day's work was always punished.

The cotton does not all ripen at the same time, on the same plant, which is picked and repicked, from six to ten times. The burs ripen, and burst open on the lower branches of the plant, whilst those at the top are yet in flower; or perhaps only in leaf or bud. The plant grows on, taller and larger, until it is arrested by the frost, or cool weather in autumn, continually throwing out new branches, new stems, new blossoms, and new burs, ceasing only with the first frost, at which time there are always some green burs, at the top of the plant, that never arrive at maturity. This state of things is, however, often prevented by topping the plant, in August or September, which prevents it from throwing out new branches, and blossoms, and forwards the growth and ripening of those already formed.

The first picking, takes the cotton from the burs of the lowest branches; the second from those a little higher, and so on, until those of the latest growth, at the top of the plant, are reached.

When the season has been bad, or from any other cause, the crop is light, the picking is sometimes complete, and the field clear of the cotton, before the first of January; but when the crop is heavy, or the people have been sickly in the fall, the picking is frequently protracted until February, or even the first of March. The winter does not injure the cotton, standing in the field, though the wind blows some of it out of the expanded burs, which is thus scattered over the field and lost.

An acre of prime land, will yield two thousand pounds of cotton in the seed. I have heard of three thousand pounds having been picked from an acre, but have not seen it. Four pounds of cotton in the seed, yields one pound when cleaned, and prepared for market.

It is estimated by the planters, or rather by the overseers, that a good hand can cultivate and pick five acres of cotton, and raise as much corn as will make his bread, and feed a mule or a horse. I know this to be a very hard task for a single hand, if the land is good, and the crops at all luxuriant. One man may, with great diligence, and continued good health, be able to get through with the cotton, and two or three, or even five acres of corn, up to the time when the cotton is ready to be picked; but from this period, he will find the labour more than he can perform, if the cotton is to be picked clean from the plants. Five acres of good cotton will yield ten thousand pounds of rough, or seed cotton. If he can pick sixty pounds a day, and works twenty-five days in a month, the picking of ten thousand pounds will occupy him more than six months.

From my own observations, on the plantations of South Carolina and Georgia, I am of opinion, that the planters in those states, do not get more than six or seven thousand pounds of cotton in the seed, for each hand employed; and I presume, that fifteen hundred pounds of clean cotton, is a full average of the product of the labour of each hand.

I now entered upon a new scene of life. My true value had not yet been ascertained by my present owner; and whether I was to hold the rank of a first, or second rate hand, could only be determined by an experience of my ability to pick cotton; nor was this important trait in my character, to be fully understood by a trial of one, or only a few days. It requires some time to enable a stranger, or new hand, to acquire the sleight of picking cotton.

I had ascertained, that at the hoe, the spade, the axe, the sickle, or the flan, I was a full match for the best hands on the plantation; but soon discovered, when we came to the picking of cotton, that I was not equal to a boy of twelve or fifteen years of age. I worked hard the first day, and made every effort to sustain the character that I had acquired, amongst my companions, but when evening came, and our cotton was weighed, I had only thirty-eight pounds, and was vexed to see that two younger men, about my own age, had, one fifty-eight, and the other fifty-nine pounds. This was our first day's work; and the overseer had not yet settled the amount of a day's picking. It was necessary for him to ascertain, by the experience of a few days, how much the best hands could pick in a day, before he established the standard of the season. I hung down my head, and felt very much ashamed of myself, when I found that my cotton was so far behind that of many, even of the women, who had heretofore regarded me as the strongest and most powerful man of the whole gang.

I had exerted myself to-day, to the utmost of my power; and as the picking of cotton seemed to be so very simple a business, I felt apprehensive that I should never be able to improve myself, so far as to become even a second rate hand. In this posture of affairs, I looked forward to something still more painful than loss of character which I must sustain, both with my fellows and my master; for I knew that the lash of the overseer would soon become familiar with my back, if I did not perform as much work as any of the other young men.

I expected, indeed, that it would go hard with me even now, and stood by with feelings of despondence and terror, whilst the other people were getting their cotton weighed. When it was all weighed, the overseer came to me where I stood, and told me to show him my hands. When I had done this, and he had looked at them, he observed—"You have a pair of good hands—you will make a good picker." This faint praise of the overseer revived my spirits greatly, and I went home with a lighter heart than I had expected to possess, before the termination of cotton-picking.

When I came to get my cotton weighed, on the evening of the second day, I was rejoiced to find that I had forty-six pounds, although I had not worked harder than I did the first day. On the third evening I had fifty-two pounds; and before the end of the week, there were only three hands in the field—two men and a young woman—who could pick more cotton in a day, than I could.

On the Monday morning of the second week when we went to the field, the overseer told us, that he fixed the days work at fifty pounds; and that all those who picked more than that, would be paid a cent a pound, for the overplus. Twenty-five pounds was assigned as the daily task of the old people, as well as a number of boys and girls, whilst some of the women, who had children, were required to pick forty pounds, and several children had ten pounds each as their task.

Picking of cotton may almost be reckoned among the arts. A man who has arrived at the age of twenty-five, before he sees a cotton field, will never, in the language of the overseer, become *a crack picker*.

By great industry and vigilance, I was able, at the end of a month, to return every evening a few pounds over the daily rate, for which I received my pay; but the business of picking cotton was an irksome, and fatiguing labour to me, and one to which I could never become thoroughly reconciled; for the reason, I believe, that in every other kind of work in which I was engaged in the south, I was able to acquire the character of a first rate hand; whilst in picking cotton, I was hardly regarded as a *prime hand*.

CHAPTER XIII.

In a community of near three hundred persons, governed by laws as severe and unbending as which regulated our actions, it is not to be expected that universal content can prevail, or that crimes will not be imagined, and even sometimes perpetrated. Ignorant men estimate those things which fortune has placed beyond their reach, not by their real value, but by the strength of their own desires and passions. Objects in themselves indifferent, which they are forbidden to touch, or even approach, excite in the minds of the unreflecting, ungovernable impulses. The slave, who is taught from infancy, to regard his condition as unchangeable, and his fate as fixed, by the laws of nature, fancies that he sees his master in possession of that happiness which he knows has been denied to himself. The lower men are sunk in the scale of civilization, the more violent become their animal passions. The native Africans are revengeful, and unforgiving in their tempers, easily provoked, and cruel in their designs. They generally place little, or even no value, upon fine houses, and superb furniture of their masters; and discover no beauty in the fair complexions, and delicate forms of their mistresses. They feel indignant at the servitude that is imposed upon them, and only want power to inflict the most cruel retribution upon their oppressors; but they desire only the means of subsistence, and temporary gratification in this country, during their abode here.

They are universally of opinion, and this opinion is founded in their religion, that after death they shall return to their own country, and rejoin their former companions and friends, in some happy region, in which they will be provided with plenty of food, and beautiful women, from the lovely daughters of their own native land.

The case is different with the American negro, who knows nothing of Africa, her religion, or customs, and who has borrowed all his ideas of present and future happiness, from the opinions and intercourse of white people, and of Christians. He is, perhaps, not so impatient of slavery, and excessive labour, as the native of Congo; but his mind is bent upon other pursuits, and his discontent works out for itself other schemes, than those which agitate the brain of the imported negro. His heart pants for no heaven beyond the waves of the ocean; and he dreams of no delights in the arms of sable beauties, in groves of immortality, on the banks of the Niger, or the Gambia; nor does he often solace himself with the reflection, that the clay wilt arrive when all men will receive the awards of immutable justice, and live together in eternal bliss, without any other distinctions than those of superior virtue, and exalted mercy. Circumstances oppose great obstacles in the way of these opinions.

The slaves who are natives of the country, (I now speak of the mass of those on the cotton plantations, as I knew them,) like all other people, who suffer wrong in this world, are exceedingly prone to console themselves with the delights of a future state, when the evil that has been endured in this life, will not only be abolished, and all injuries be compensated by proper rewards, bestowed upon the sufferers, but, as they have learned that wickedness is to be punished, as well as goodness compensated, they do not stop at the point of their own enjoyments and pleasures, but believe that those who have tormented them here, will most surely be tormented in their turn hereafter. The gross and carnal minds of these slaves, are not capable of arriving at the sublime doctrines taught by the white preachers; in which they are encouraged to look forward to the day when all distinctions of colour, and of condition, will be abolished, and they shall sit down in the same paradise, with their masters, mistresses, and even with the overseer. They are ready enough to receive the faith, which conducts them to heaven, and eternal rest, on account of their present sufferings; but they by no means so willingly admit the master and mistress to an equal participation in their enjoyments— this would only be partial justice, and half way retribution. According to their notions, the master and mistress are to be, in future, the companions of wicked slaves, whilst an agreeable recreation of the celestial inhabitants of the negro's heaven, will be a return to the overseer of the countless lashes that he has lent out so liberally here.

It is impossible to reconcile the mind of the native slave to the idea of living in a state of perfect equality, and boundless affection, with the white people. Heaven will be no heaven to him, if he is not to be avenged of his enemies. I know, from experience, that these are the fundamental rules of his religious creed; because I learned them in the religious meetings of the slaves themselves. A favourite and kind master or mistress, may now and then be admitted into heaven, but this rather as a matter of favour, to the intercession of some slave, than as matter of strict justice to the whites, who will, by no means, be of an equal rank with those who shall be raised from the depths of misery, in this world.

The idea of a revolution in the conditions of the whites and the blacks, is the corner-stone of the religion of the latter; and indeed, it seems to me, at least, to be quite natural, if not in strict accordance with the precepts of the Bible; for in that book, I find it every where laid down, that those who have possessed an inordinate portion of the good things of this world, and have lived in ease and luxury, at the expense of their fellow men will surely have to render an account of their stewardship, and be punished, for having withheld from others the participation of those blessings, which they themselves enjoyed.

There is no subject which presents the mind of the male slave a greater contrast between his own condition and that of his master, than the relative station and appearance of his wife and his mistress. The one, poorly clad, poorly fed, and exposed to all the hardships of the cotton field; the other dressed in clothes of gay and various colours, ornamented with jewelry, and carefully protected from the rays of the sun, and the blasts of the wind.

As I have before observed, the Africans have feelings peculiar to themselves; but with an American slave, the possession of the spacious house, splendid furniture, and fine horses of his master, are but the secondary objects of his desires. To fill the measure of his happiness, and crown his highest ambition, his young and beautiful mistress must adorn his triumph, and enliven his hopes.

I have been drawn into the above reflections, by the recollection of an event of a most melancholy character, which took place when I had been on this plantation about three months. Amongst the house-servants of my master, was a young man, named Hardy, of a dark yellow complexion—a quadroon, or mulatto—one fourth of whose blood was transmitted from white parentage.

Hardy was employed in various kinds of work about the house, and was frequently sent of errands; sometimes on horseback. I had become acquainted with the boy, who had often come to see me at the quarter, and had sometimes staid all night with me, and often told me of the ladies and gentlemen, who visited at the great house.

Amongst others, he frequently spoke of a young lady, who resided six or seven miles from the plantation, and often came to visit the daughters of the family, in company with her brother, a lad about twelve or fourteen years of age. He described the great beauty of this girl, whose mother was a widow, living on a small estate of her own. This lady did not keep a carriage; but her son and daughter, when they went abroad, travelled on horseback.

One Sunday, these two young people came to visit at the house of my master, and remained until after tea in the evening. As I did not go out to work that day, I went over to the great house, and from the house to a place in the woods, about a mile distant, where I had set snares for rabbits. This place was near the road, and I saw the young lady and her brother, on their way home. It was after sundown, when they passed me; but, as the evening was clear and pleasant, I supposed they would get home soon after dark, and that no accident would befall them.

No more was thought of the matter this evening, and I heard nothing further of the young people, until the next day, about noon, when a black boy came into the field, where we were picking cotton, and went to the overseer with a piece of paper. In a short time the overseer called me to come with him; and, leaving the field with the hands under the orders of Simon, the first captain, we proceeded to the great house.

As soon as we arrived at the mansion, my master, who had not spoken to me since the day we came from Columbia, appeared at the front door, and ordered me to come in and follow him. He led me through a part of the house, and passed into the back yard, where I saw the young gentleman, his son, another gentleman, whom I did not know, the family doctor, and the overseer, all standing together, and in earnest conversation. At my appearance, the overseer opened a cellar door, and ordered me to go in. I had no suspicion of evil, and obeyed the order immediately: as, indeed, I must have obeyed it, whatever might have been my suspicions.

The overseer, and the gentlemen, all followed; and as soon as the cellar door was closed after us, by some one whom I could not see, I was ordered to pull off my clothes, and lie down on my back. I was then bound by the hands and feet, with strong cords, and extended at full length between two of the beams that supported the timbers of the building.

The stranger, who, I now observed, was much agitated, spoke to the doctor, who then opened a small case of surgeons' instruments, which he took from his pocket, and told me he was going to skin me, for what I had done last night; "But," said the doctor, "before you are skinned, you had better confess your crime." "What crime, master, shall I confess? I have committed no crime—what has been done, that you are going to murder me?" was my reply. My master then asked me, why I had followed the young lady and her brother, who went from the house the evening before, and murdered her? Astonished and terrified at the charge of being a murderer, I knew not what to say; and only continued the protestations of my innocence, and my entreaties not to be put to death. My young master was greatly enraged against me, and loaded me with maledictions, and imprecations; and his father appeared to be as well satisfied as he was, of my guilt, but was more calm, and less vociferous in his language.

The doctor, during this time, was assorting his instruments, and looking at me—then stooping down, and feeling my pulse, he said, it would not do to skin a man so full of blood as I was. I should bleed so much that he could not see to do his work; and he should probably cut some large vein, or artery, by which I should bleed to death in a few minutes; it was necessary to bleed me in the arms, for some time, so as to reduce the quantity of blood that was in me, before taking my skin off. He then bound a string round my right arm, and opened a vein near the middle of the arm, from which the blood ran in a large and smooth stream. I already began to feel faint, with the loss of blood, when the cellar door was thrown open, and several persons came down, with two lighted candles.

I looked at these people attentively, as they came near, and stood around me, and expressed their satisfaction at the just and dreadful punishment that I was about to undergo. Their faces were all new, and unknown to me, except that of a lad, whom I recognized as the same, who had ridden by me, the preceding evening, in company with his sister.

My old master spoke to this boy, by name, and told him to come and see the murderer of his sister receive his due. The boy was a pretty youth, and wore his hair long, on the top of his head, in the fashion of that day. As he came round near my head, the light of a candle, which the doctor held in his hand, shone full in my face, and seeing that the eyes of the boy met mine, I determined to make one more effort to save my life, and said to him, in as calm a tone as I could, "Young master, did I murder young mistress, your sister?" The youth immediately looked at my master, and said, "This is not the man,—this man has short wool, and he had long wool, like your Hardy."

My life was saved. I was snatched from the most horrible of tortures; and from a slow and painful death. I was unbound, the bleeding of my arm stopped, and I was suffered to put on my clothes, and go up into the back yard of the house, where I was required to tell what I knew of the young lady and her brother, on the previous day. I stated that I had seen them in the court yard of the house, at the time I was in the kitchen; that I had then gone to the woods, to set my snares, and had seen them pass along the road, near me, and that this was all the knowledge I had of them. The boy was then required to examine me particularly, and ascertain whether I was, or was not, the man who had murdered his sister. He said, he had not seen me at the place, where I stated I was, and that he was confident I was not the person who had attacked him and his sister. That my hair, or wool, as he called it, was short; but that of the man who committed the crime was long, like Hardy's, and that he was about the size of Hardy—not so large as I was, but black like me, and not yellow like Hardy. Some one now asked where Hardy was, and he was called for, but could not be found in the kitchen. Persons were sent to the quarter, and other places in quest of him, but returned without him. Hardy was nowhere to be found. Whilst this inquiry, or rather search, was going on, perceiving that my old master had ceased to look upon me as a murderer, I asked him to please to tell me what had happened, that had been so near proving fatal to me.

I was now informed, that the young lady, who had left the house on the previous evening, in company with her brother, had been assailed on the road, about four miles off, by a black man, who had sprung from a thicket, and snatched her horse, as she was riding at a short distance behind her brother. That the assassin, as soon as she was on the ground, struck her horse a blow with a long stick, which, together with the fright caused by the screams of its rider, when torn from it, had caused it to fly off at full speed; and the horse of the brother also taking flight, followed in pursuit, notwithstanding all the exertions of the lad to stop it. All the account the brother could give of the matter was, that as his horse ran with him, he saw the negro drag his sister into the woods, and heard her screams for a short time. He was not able to stop his horse, until he reached home, when he gave information to his mother, and her family. That people had been scouring the woods all night, and all the morning, without being able to find the young lady.

When intelligence of this horrid crime was brought to the house of my master, Hardy was the first to receive it; he having gone to take the horse of the person,—a young gentleman of the neighbourhood,— who bore it, and who immediately returned to join his friends, in their search for the dead body.

As soon as the messenger was gone, Hardy had come to my master, and told him, that if he would prevent me from murdering him, he would disclose the perpetrator of the crime. He was then ordered to communicate all he knew, on the subject; and declared, that, having gone into the woods the day before, to hunt squirrels, he staid until it was late, and on his return home, hearing the shrieks of a woman, he had proceeded cautiously to the place; but before he could arrive at the spot, the cries had ceased; nevertheless, he had found me, after some search, with the body of the young lady, whom I had just killed, and that I was about to kill him too, with a hickory club, but he had saved his life by promising that he would never betray me. He was glad to leave me; and what I had done with the body, he did not know.

Hardy was known in the neighbourhood, and his character had been good. I was a stranger, and on inquiry, the black people in the kitchen supported Hardy, by saying, that I had been seen going to the woods, before night, by the way of the road, which the deceased had travelled. These circumstances were deemed conclusive against me by my master; and as the offence, of which I was believed to be guilty, was the highest that can be committed by a slave, according to the opinion of owners, it was determined to punish me in a way unknown to the law, and to inflict tortures upon me which the law would not tolerate. I was now released, and though very weak from the effects of bleeding, I was yet able to return to my own lodgings.

I had no doubt, that Hardy was the perpetrator of the crime, for which I was so near losing my life; and now recollected, that when I was at the kitchen of the great house, on Sunday, he had disappeared, a short time before sundown, as I had looked for him, when I was going to set my snares, but could not find him. I went back to the house, and communicated this fact to my master.

By this time, nearly twenty white men had collected about the dwelling, with the intention of going to search for the body of the lost lady; but it was now resolved to make the look-out double, and to give it the twofold character of a pursuit of the living, as well as a seeking for the dead.

I now returned to my lodgings, in the quarter, and soon fell into a profound sleep, from which I did not awake until long after night, when all was quiet, and the stillness of undisturbed tranquillity prevailed over our little community. I felt restless, and sunk into a labyrinth of painful reflections, upon the horrid and perilous condition, from which I had this day escaped, as it seemed, merely by chance; and as I slept until all sensations of drowsiness had left me, I rose from my bed, and walked out by the light of the moon, which was now shining. After being in the open air some time, I thought of the snares that I had set on Sunday evening, and determined to go, and see if they had taken any game. I sometimes caught oppossums in my snares; and as these animals were very fat, at this season of the year, I felt a hope that I might be fortunate enough to get one tonight. I had been at my snares, and had returned, as far as the road, near where I had seen the young lady and her brother, on horseback, on Sunday evening, and had seated myself under the boughs of a holly bush, that grew there. It so happened, that the place where I sat, was in the shade of the bush, within a few feet of the road, but screened from it by some small boughs. In this position, which I had taken by accident, I could see a great distance along the road, towards the end of my master's lane. Though covered as I was, by the shade, and enveloped in boughs, it was difficult for a person in the road to see me.

The occurrence that had befallen me, in the course of the previous day, had rendered me nervous, and easily susceptible of all the emotions of fear. I had not been long in this place, when I thought I heard sounds, as of a person walking on the ground at a quick pace; and looking along the road, towards the lane, I saw the form of some one, passing through a space in the road, where the beams of the moon, piercing between two trees, reached the ground. When the moving body passed into the shade, I could not see it; but in a short time, it came so near, that I could distinctly see that it was a man, approaching me by the road. When he came opposite me, and the moon shone full in his face, I knew him to be a young mulatto, named David, the coachman of a widow lady, who resided somewhere near Charleston; but who had been at the house of my master, for two or three weeks, as a visiter, with her two daughters.

This man passed on at a quick step, without observing me; and the suspicion instantly riveted itself in my mind, that he was the murderer, for whose crime I had already suffered so much, and that he was now on his way to the place where he had left the body, for the purpose of removing, or burying it in the earth. I was confident, that no honest purpose could bring him to this place, at this time of night, alone. I was about two miles from home, and an equal distance from the spot, where the girl had been seized.

Of her subsequent murder, no one entertained a doubt; for it was not to be expected, that the fellow who had been guilty of one great crime, would flinch from the commission of another, of equal magnitude, and suffer his victim to exist, as a witness to identify his person.

I felt animated, by a spirit of revenge, against the wretch, whoever he might be, who had brought me so near to torture and death; and feeble and weak as I was, resolved to pursue the foot-steps of this coachman, at a wary and cautious distance, and ascertain, if possible, the object of his visit to these woods, at this time of night.

I waited until he had passed me, more than a hundred yards; and until I could barely discover his form, in the faint light of the deep shade of the trees, when stealing quietly into the road, I followed, with the caution of a spy, traversing the camp of an enemy. We were now in a dark pine forest, and on both sides of us, were tracts of low swampy ground, covered with thickets so dense, as to be difficult of penetration, even by a person on foot. The road led along a neck of elevated, and dry ground, that divided these swamps for more than a mile, when they terminated, and were succeeded by ground that produced scarcely any other timber, than a scrubby kind of oak, called black jack. It was amongst these black jacks, about half a mile beyond the swamps, that the lady had been carried off. I had often been here, for the purpose of snaring, and trapping, the small game of these woods, and was well acquainted with the topography of this forest, for some distance, on both sides of the road.

It was necessary for me to use the utmost caution, in the enterprise I was now engaged in. The road we were now travelling, was in no place very broad, and at some points, barely wide enough to permit a carriage to pass between the trees, that lined its sides. In some places, it was so dark that I could not see the man, whose steps I followed: but was obliged to depend on the sound, produced by the tread of his feet, upon the ground. I deemed it necessary to keep as close as possible, to the object of my pursuit, lest he should suddenly turn into the swamp, on one side or the other of the road, and elude my vigilance; for I had no doubt that he would quit the road, somewhere. As we approached the termination of the low grounds, my anxiety became intense, lest he should escape me; and at one time, I could not have been more than one hundred feet behind him; but he continued his course, until he reached the oak woods, and came to a place where an old cart-road led off to the left, along the side of the Dark Swamp, as it was termed in the neighbourhood.

This road, the mulatto took, without turning to look behind him. Here my difficulties, and perils increased, for I now felt myself in danger, as I had no longer any doubt, that I was on the trail of the murderer, and that, if discovered by him, my life would be the price of my curiosity. I was too weak to be able to struggle with him, for a minute; though if the blood which I had lost, through his wickedness, could have been restored to my veins, I could have seized him by the neck, and strangled him.

The road I now had to travel was so little frequented, that bushes of the ground oak, and bilberry, stood thick, in almost every part of it. Many of these bushes were full of dry leaves, which had been touched by the frost, but had not yet fallen. It was easy for me to follow him, for I pursued by the noise he made, amongst these bushes; but it was not so easy for me to avoid, on my part, the making of a rustling, and agitation of the bushes, which might expose me to detection. I was now obliged to depend wholly on my ears, to guide my pursuit, my eyes being occupied in watching my own way, to enable me to avoid every object, the touching of which was likely to produce sound.

I followed this road more than a mile, led by cracking of the sticks, or the shaking of the leaves. At length, I heard a loud, shrill whistle, and then a total silence succeeded. I now stood still, and in a few seconds, heard a noise in the swamp like the drumming of a pheasant. Soon afterwards, I heard the breaking of sticks, and the sounds caused by the bending of branches of trees. In a little time, I was satisfied, that something having life was moving in the swamp, and coming towards the place where the mulatto stood.

This was at the end of the cart-road, and opposite some large pine trees, which grew in the swamp, at the distance of two or three hundred yards from its margin. The noise in the swamp, still approached us; and at length a person came out of the thicket, and stood for a minute, or more, with the mulatto whom I had followed; and then they both entered the swamp, and took the course of the pine trees, as I could easily distinguish by my ears.

When they were gone, I advanced to the end of the road, and sat down upon a log, to listen to their progress, through the swamp. At length, it seemed that they had stopped, for I no longer heard any thing of them. Anxious, however, to ascertain more of this mysterious business, I remained in silence on the log, determined to stay there until day, if I could not sooner learn something to satisfy me, why these men had gone into the swamp. All uncertainty upon this subject was, however, quickly removed from my mind; for within less than ten minutes, after I had ceased to hear them, moving in the thicket, I was shocked by the faint, but shrill wailings of a female voice, accompanied with exclamations, and supplications, in a tone so feeble, that I could only distinguish a few solitary words.

My mind comprehended the whole ground of this matter, at a glance. The lady supposed to have been murdered, on Sunday evening, was still living; and concealed by the two fiends who had passed out of my sight, but a few minutes before. The one I knew, for I had examined his features, within a few feet of me, in the full light of the moon; and, that the other was Hardy, I was as perfectly convinced, as if I had seen him also.

I now rose to return home; the cries of the female in the swamp, still continuing; but growing weaker; and dying away, as I receded from the place where I had sat.

I was now in possession of the clearest evidence, of the guilt of the two murderers; but I was afraid to communicate my knowledge to my master, lest he should suspect me of being an accomplice in this crime; and, if the lady could not be recovered alive, I had no doubt, that Hardy and his companion, were sufficiently depraved, to charge me as a participator with themselves, to be avenged upon me. I was confident that the mulatto, David, would return to the house before day, and be found in his bed in the morning; which he could easily do, for he slept in a part of the stable loft; under pretence of being near the horses of his mistress.

I thought it possible, that Hardy might also return home, that night, and endeavour to account for his absence from home on Monday afternoon, by some ingenious lie; in the invention of which I knew him to be very expert. In this case, I saw that I should have to run the risk, of being overpowered by the number of my false accusers; and, as I stood alone, they might yet be able to sacrifice my life, and escape the punishment due to their crimes. After much consideration, I came to the resolution of returning, as quick as possible, to the quarter— calling up the overseer—and acquainting him with all that I had seen, heard, and done, in the course of this night.

As I did not know what time of night it was, when I left my bed, I was apprehensive that day might break before I could so far mature my plans, as to have persons to way-lay, and arrest the mulatto, on his return home; but when I roused the overseer, he told me it was only one o'clock, and seemed but little inclined to credit my story; but, after talking to me several minutes, he told me he now, more than ever, suspected me to be the murderer; but he would go with me, and see if I had told the truth. When we arrived at the great house, some members of the family had not yet gone to bed, having been kept up by the arrival of several gentlemen, who had been searching the woods all day for the lost lady, and who had come here to seek lodgings, when it was near midnight. My master was in bed, but was called up and listened attentively to my story—at the close of which, he shook his head, and said with an oath, "You—, I believe you to be the murderer; but we will go and see if all you say is a lie; if it is, the torments of—will be pleasure to what awaits you. You have escaped once, but you will not get off a second time." I now found that somebody must die; and if the guilty could not be found, the innocent would have to atone for them. The manner in which my master had delivered his words, assured me, that the life of somebody must be taken.

This new danger aroused my energies,—and I told them I was ready to go, and take the consequences. Accordingly, the overseer, my young master, and three other gentlemen, immediately set out with me. It was agreed that we should all travel on foot; the overseer and I going a few paces in advance of the others. We proceeded silently, but rapidly, on our way; and as we passed it, I shewed them the place where I sat under the holly bush, the mulatto passed me. We neither saw nor heard any person on the road, and reached the log at the end of the cart-road, where I sat, when I heard the cries in the swamp. All was now quiet, and our party lay down in the bushes, on each side of a large gum tree; at the root of which the two murderers stood, when they talked together, before they entered the thicket. We had not been here more than an hour, when I heard, as I lay with my head near the ground, a noise in the swamp, which I believed could only be made by those whom we sought.

I, however, said nothing, and the gentlemen did not hear it. It was caused, as I afterwards ascertained, by dragging the fallen branch of a tree, along the ground, for the purpose of lighting the fire.

The night was very clear and serene—its silence only being broken at intervals, by the loud hooting of the great long-eared owls, which are numerous in these swamps. I felt oppressed by the cold, and was glad to hear the crowing of a cock, at a great distance, announcing the approach of day. This was followed, after a short interval, by the cracking of sticks, and by other tokens, which I knew could proceed only from the motions of living bodies. I now whispered to the overseer, who lay near me, that it would soon appear whether I had spoken the truth or not.

All were now satisfied that people were coming out of the swamp, for we heard them speak to each other. I desired the overseer to advise the other gentlemen to let the culprits come out of the swamp, and gain the high ground, before we attempted to seize them; but this counsel was, unfortunately, not taken; and when they came near to the gum-tree, and it could be clearly seen that there were two men, and no more, one of the gentlemen called out to them to stop, or they were dead. Instead, however, of stopping, they both sprang forward, and took to flight. They did not turn into the swamp, for the gentleman who ordered them to stop, was in their rear—they having already passed him. At the moment they had started to run, each of the gentlemen fired two pistols at them. The pistols made the forest ring, on all sides; and I supposed it was impossible for either of the fugitives to escape from so many balls. This was, however, not the case; for only one of them was injured. The mulatto, David, had one arm and one leg broken, and fell about ten yards from us; but Hardy escaped, and when the smoke cleared away, he was nowhere to be seen. On being interrogated, David acknowledged that the lady was in the swamp, on a small island, and was yet alive—that he and Hardy had gone from the house on Sunday, for the purpose of waylaying and carrying her off; and intended to kill her little brother—this part of the duty being assigned to him, whilst Hardy was to drag the sister from her horse. As they were both mulattos, they blacked their faces with charcoal, taken from a pine stump, partially burned. The boy was riding before his sister, and when Hardy seized her and dragged her from her horse, she screamed and frightened both the horses, which took off at full speed, by which means the boy escaped. Finding that the boy was out of his reach, David remained in the bushes, until Hardy brought the sister to him. They immediately tied a handkerchief round her face, so as to cover her mouth and stifle her shrieks; and taking her in their arms, carried her back toward my master's house, for some distance, through the woods, until they came to the cart-road leading along the swamp. They then followed this road as far as it led, and, turning into the swamp, took their victim to a place they had prepared for her the Sunday before, on a small knoll in the swamp, where the ground was dry.

Her hands were closely confined, and she was tied by the feet to a tree. He said he had stolen some bread, and taken it to her this night; but when they unbound her mouth to permit her to eat, she only wept and made a noise, begging them to release her, until they were obliged again to bandage her mouth.

It was now determined by the gentlemen, that as the lady was still alive, we ought not to lose a moment in endeavouring to rescue her from her dreadful situation. I pointed out the large pine trees, in the direction of which I heard the cries of the young lady, and near which I believed she was—undertaking, at the same time, to act as pilot, in penetrating the thicket. Three of the gentlemen and myself, accordingly set out, leaving the other two with the wounded mulatto, with directions to inform us when we deviated from a right line to the pine trees. This they were able to do by attending to the noise we made, with nearly as much accuracy as if they had seen us.

The atmosphere had now become a little cloudy, and the morning was very dark, even in the oak woods; but when we had entered the thickets of the swamp, all objects became utterly invisible and the obscurity was as total as if our eyes had been closed. Our companions on the dry ground, lost sight of the pine trees, and could not give us any directions in our journey. We became entangled in briers, and vines, and mats of bushes, from which the greatest exertions were necessary to disengage ourselves.

It was so dark, that we could not see the fallen trees; and, missing these, fell into quagmires, and sloughes of mud and water, into which we sunk up to the arm-pits, and from which we were able to extricate ourselves, only be seizing upon the hanging branches of the surrounding trees. After struggling in this half-drowned condition, for at least a quarter of an hour, we reached a small dry spot, where the gentlemen again held a council, as to ulterior measures. They called to those left on the shore, to know if we were proceeding toward the pine trees; but received for answer that the pines were invisible, and they knew not whether we were right or wrong. In this state of uncertainty, it was thought most prudent to wait the coming of day, in our present resting place.

The air was frosty, and in our wet clothes, loaded as we were with mud, it may be imagined that our feelings were not pleasant; and when the day broke, it brought us but little relief, for we found, as as it was light enough to enable us to see around, that we were on one of those insulated dry spots, called "*tussocks,*" by the people of the south. These *tussocks* are formed by clusters of small trees, which, taking root in the mud, are, in process of time, surrounded by long grass, which, entwining its roots with those of the trees, overspread and cover the surface of the muddy foundation, by which the superstructure is supported. These tussocks are often several yards in diameter. That upon which we now were, stood in the midst of a great miry pool, into which we were again obliged to launch ourselves, and struggle onward for a distance of ten yards, before we reached the line of some fallen and decaying trees.

It was now broad daylight, and we saw the pine trees, at the distance of about a hundred yards from us; but even with the assistance of the light, we had great difficulty in reaching them,—to do which, we were compelled to travel at least a quarter of a mile by the angles and curves of the fallen timber, upon which alone we could walk; this part of the swamp being a vast half-fluid bog.

It was sunrise when we reached the pines, which we found standing upon a small islet of firm ground, containing, as well as I could judge, about half an acre, covered with a heavy growth of white maples, swamp oaks, a few large pines, and a vast mat of swamp laurel, called in the south *ivy*. I had no doubt, that the object of our search was somewhere on this little island; but small as it was, it was no trifling affair to give every part of it a minute examination, for the stems and branches of the ivy were so minutely interwoven with each other, and spread along the ground in so many curves and crossings, that it was impossible to proceed a single rod, without lying down and creeping along the earth.

The gentlemen agreed, that if any one discovered the young lady, he should immediately call to the others; and we all entered the thicket. I, however, turned along the edge of the island, with the intention of making its circuit, for the purpose of tracing, if possible, the footsteps of those who had passed between it and the main shore. I made my way more than half round the island, without much difficulty, and without discovering any signs of persons having been here before me; but in crossing the trunk of a large tree which had fallen, and the top of which extended far into the ivy, I perceived some stains of mud, on the bark of the log. Looking into the swamp, I saw that the root of this tree was connected with other fallen timber, extending beyond the reach of my vision which was obstructed by the bramble of the swamp, and the numerous ever-greens, growing here. I now advanced along the trunk of the tree, until I reached its topmost branches, and here discovered evident signs of a small trail, leading into the thicket of ivy. Creeping along, and following this trail, by the small bearberry bushes that had been trampled down, and had not again risen to an erect position, I was led almost across the island, and found that the small bushes were discomposed, quite up to the edge of a vast heap of the branches of ever-green trees, produced by the falling of several large juniper cypress trees, which grew in the swamp in a cluster, and, having been blown down, had fallen with their tops athwart each other, and upon the almost impervious mat of ivies, with which the surface of the island was coated over.

I stood and looked at this mass of entangled green brush, but could not perceive the slightest marks of any entrance into its labyrinths: nor did it seem possible for any creature, larger than a squirrel, to penetrate it. It now for the first time struck me as a great oversight in the gentlemen, that they had not compelled the mulatto, David, to describe the place where they had concealed the lady; and, as the forest was so dense, that no communication could be had with the shore, either by words or signs, we could not now procure any information on this subject. I therefore called to the gentlemen, who were on the island with me, and desired them to come to me without delay.

Small as this island was, it was after the lapse of many minutes, that the overseer, and the other gentlemen, arrived where I stood; and when they came, they would have been the subjects of mirthful emotions, had not the tragic circumstances, in which I was placed, banished from my heart, every feeling but that of the most profound melancholy.

When the gentlemen had assembled, I informed them of signs of footsteps, that I had traced from the other side of the island; and told them, that I believed the young lady lay somewhere under the heap of brushwood, before us. This opinion obtained but little credit, because there was no opening in the brush, by which any one could enter it; but on going a few paces round the heap, I perceived a small, shaggy pole, resting on the brush, and nearly concealed by it, with the lower end stuck in the ground. The branches had been cut from this pole, at the distance of three or four inches from the main stem, which made it a tolerable substitute for a ladder. I immediately ascended the pole, which led me to the top of the pile; and here I discovered an opening in the brush, between the forked top of one of the cypress trees, through which a man might easily pass. Applying my head to this aperture, I distinctly heard a quick, and laborious breathing, like that of a person in extreme illness; and again called the gentlemen to follow me.

When they came up the ladder, the breathing was audible to all; and one of the gentlemen, whom I now perceived to be the stranger, who was with us in my master's cellar, when I was bled, slid down into the dark and narrow passage, without uttering a word. I confess, that some feelings of trepidation passed through my nerves, when I stood alone; but now that a leader had preceded me, I followed, and glided through the smooth and elastic cypress tops to the bottom of this vast labyrinth of green boughs.

When I reached the ground, I found myself in contact with the gentleman, who was in advance of me, and near one end of a large concave, oblong, open space, formed by the branches of the trees, having been supported and kept above the ground, partly by a cluster of very large and strong ivies, that grew here, and partly by a young gum tree, which had been bent into the form of in arch, by the falling timber.

Though we could not see into this leafy cavern from above, yet when we had been in it, a few moments, we had light enough to see the objects around us, with tolerable clearness; but that which surprised us both greatly, was, that the place was totally silent, and we could not perceive the appearance of any living thing, except ourselves.

After we had been here some minutes, our vision became still more distinct; and I saw, at the other end of the open space, ashes of wood, and some extinguished brands. but there was no smoke. Going to these ashes, and stirring them with a stick, I found coals of fire carefully covered over, in a hole six or eight inches deep.

When he saw the fire, the gentleman spoke to me, and expressed his astonishment, that we heard the breathing no longer; but he had scarcely uttered these words, when a faint groan, as of a woman in great pain, was heard to issue, apparently from the ground, but a motion of branches on our right, assured me that the sufferer was concealed there. The gentleman sprung to the spot, pushed aside the pendant boughs, stooped low beneath the bent ivies, and came out, bearing in his hands, a delicate female figure. As he turned round, and exposed her half-closed eye and white forehead, to the light, he exclaimed, "Eternal God, Maria, is it you?" He then pressed her to his bosom, and sunk upon the ground, still holding her closely in his embrace.

The lady lay motionless in his arms, and I thought she was dead. Her hair hung matted and dishevelled from her head; a handkerchief, once white, but now soiled with dust, and stained with blood, was bound firmly round her head, covering her mouth and chin, and was fastened at the back of the neck, by a double knot, and secured by a ligature of cypress bark.

I knew not whom most to pity,—the lady, who now lay insensible, in the arms that still clasped her tenderly; or the unhappy gentleman, who having cut the cords from her limbs, and the handkerchief from her face, now sat, and silently gazed upon her death-like countenance. He uttered not a sigh, and moved not a joint; but his breast heaved with agony; the sinews, and muscles of his neck rose and fell, like those of a man in convulsions; all the lineaments of his face were, alternately, contracted and expanded, as if his last moments were at hand; whilst great drops of sweat rolled down his forehead, as though he struggled against an enemy, whose strength was more than human.

Oppressed by the sight of so much wretchedness, I turned from its contemplation; and called aloud to the gentlemen without, (who had all this time been waiting to hear from us,) to come up the ladder, to the top of the pile of boughs. The overseer was quickly at the top of the opening, by which I had descended; and I now informed him that we had found the lady. He ordered me to hand her up—and I desired the gentleman, who was with me, to permit me to do so; but this he refused—and mounting the boughs of the fallen trees, and support himself by the strong branches of the ivies, he quickly reached the place, where the overseer stood.

He even here refused to part from his charge, but bore her down the ladder alone. He was, however, obliged to accept aid, in conveying her through the swamp, to the place where we had left the two gentlemen, with the wounded mulatto, whose sufferings, demon as he was, were sufficient to move the hardest heart. His right arm, and left leg were broken; and he had lost much blood, before we returned from the island; and as he could not walk, it was necessary to carry him home. We had not brought any horses; and until the lady was recovered, no one seemed to think any more about the mulatto, after he was shot down.

It was proposed to send for a horse, to take David home; but it was finally agreed, that we should leave him in the woods where he was, until a man could be sent for him, with a cart. At the time we left him, his groans and lamentations seemed to excite no sympathy, in the breast of any. More cruel sufferings yet awaited him.

The lady was carried home, in the arms of the gentlemen; and she did not speak, until after she was bathed, and put to bed in my master's house, as I afterwards heard. I know she did not speak on the way. She died on the fourth day after her rescue, and before her death, related the circumstances of her misfortune, as I was told by a coloured woman, who attended her in her illness, in the following manner:

As she was riding in the dusk of the evening, at a rapid trot, a few yards behind her brother, a black man sprang from behind a tree standing close by the side of the road; seized her by her riding dress, and dragged her to the ground, but failed to catch the bridle of the horse, which sprang off at full speed. Another negro immediately came to the aid of the first, and said, "I could not catch him—we must make haste." They carried her as fast as they could go, to the place where we found her; when they bound her hands, feet, and mouth, and left her until the next night; and had left her the second morning, only a few minutes, when she heard the report of guns. Soon after this, by great efforts, she extricated one of her feet from the bark, with which she was bound; but finding herself too weak to stand, she crawled, as far as she could, under the boughs of the trees, hoping that when her assassins returned again, they would not be able to find her, and that she might there die alone.

Exhausted by the efforts she had made, to remove herself, she fell into the stupor of sleep, from which she was aroused by the noise we made, when we descended into the cavern. She then, supposing us to be her destroyers returned again, lay still, and breathed as softly as possible, to prevent us from hearing her; but when she heard the voice of the gentleman who was with me, the tones of which were familiar to her, she groaned, and moved her feet, to let us know where she was. This exertion, and the idea of her horrid condition, overcame the strength of her nerves; and when her deliverer raised her from the ground, she had swooned, and was unconscious of all things.

We had no sooner arrived at the house, than inquiry was made for Hardy; but it was ascertained in the kitchen, that he had not been seen, since the previous evening, at night fall, when he had left the kitchen for the purpose of going to sleep at the stable, with David, as he had told one of the black women; and preparation was immediately made, to go in pursuit of him.

For this purpose all the gentlemen present equipped themselves with pistols, fowling pieces, and horns—such as are used by fox hunters. Messengers were despatched round the country, to give notice to all the planters, within the distance of many miles, of the crime that had been committed, and of the escape of one of its perpetrators, with a request to them to come without delay, and join in the pursuit, intended to be given. Those who had dogs, trained to chase thieves, were desired to bring them; and a gentleman who lived twelve miles off, and who owned a blood hound, was sent for, and requested to come with his dog, in all haste.

In consequence, I suppose, of the information I had given, I was permitted to be present at these deliberations; and though my advice was not asked, I was often interrogated, concerning my knowledge of the affair. Some proposed to go at once, with dogs and horses, into the woods, and traverse the swamp and thickets, for the purpose of rousing Hardy from the place of concealment, he might have chosen; but the opinion of the overseer prevailed, who thought, that from the intimate knowledge possessed by him, of all the swamps and coverts in the neighbourhood, there would be little hope of discovering him in this manner. The overseer advised them, to wait the coming of the gentleman with his blood hound, before they entered the woods; for the reason, that if the blood hound could be made to take the trail, he would certainly find his game, before he quit it, if not thrown off the scent by the men, horses, and dogs crossing his course; but if the blood hound, could not take the scent, they might then adopt the proposed plan of pursuit, with as much success as at present. This counsel being adopted, the horses were ordered into the stable; and the gentlemen entered the house to take their breakfast, and wait the arrival of the blood hound.

Nothing was said of the mulatto, David, who seemed to be forgotten—not a word being spoken by any one of bringing him from the woods. I knew that he was suffering the most agonizing pains, and great as were his crimes, his groans and cries of anguish still seemed to echo in my ears; but I was afraid to make any application in his behalf, lest, even yet, I might be suspected of some participation in his offences; for I knew that the most horrid punishments were often inflicted upon slaves, merely on suspicion.

As the morning advanced, the number of men and horses in front of my master's mansion increased; and before ten o'clock, I think there were, at least, fifty of each—the horses standing hitched and the men conversing in groups without, or as-together within the house.

At length the owner of the blood hound came, bringing with him his dog, in a chaise, drawn by one horse, The harness was removed from the horse, its place supplied by a saddle and bridle, and the whole party set off for the woods. As they rode away, my master, who was one of the company, told me to follow them; but we had proceeded only a little distance, when the gentlemen stopped, and my master, after speaking with the owner of the dog told the overseer to go back to the house, and get some piece of the clothes of Hardy, that had been worn by him lately. The overseer returned, and we all proceeded forward to the place where David lay.

We found him where we had left him, greatly weakened by the loss of blood, and complaining that the cold air caused his wounds to smart intolerably. When I came near him, he looked at me and told me I had betrayed him. None of the gentlemen seemed at all moved by his sufferings, and when any of them spoke to him, it was with derision; and every epithet of scorn and contumely. As it was apparent that he could not escape, no one proposed to remove him to a place of greater safety; but several of the horsemen, as they passed, lashed him with the thongs of their whips; but I do not believe he felt these blows—the pain he endured from his wounds being so great, as to drown the sensation of such minor afflictions.

The day had already become warm, although the night had been cold; the sun shone with great clearness and many carrion crows, attracted by the scent of blood, were perched upon the trees near where we now were.

When the overseer came up with us, he brought an old blanket, in which Hardy had slept for some time, and handed it to the owner of the dog; who having first caused the hound to smell of the blanket, untied the cord in which he had been led, and turned him into the woods. The dog went from us fifty or sixty yards, in a right line, then made a circle around us; again commenced his circular movement, and pursued it nearly half round. Then he dropped his nose to the ground, snuffed the tainted surface, and moved off through the woods, slowly, almost touching the earth with his nose. The owner of the dog, and twelve or fifteen others followed him, whilst the residue of the party dispersed themselves along the edge of the swamp; and the overseer ordered me to stay, and watch the horses of those who dismounted, going himself on foot in the pursuit.

When the gentlemen were all gone out of sight, I went to David, who lay all this time within my view, for the purpose of asking him if I could render him any assistance. He begged me to bring him some water, as he was dying of thirst, no less than with the pain of his wounds. One of the horsemen had left a large tin horn, hanging on his saddle; this I took, and stopping the small end closely with leaves, filled it with water from the swamp, and gave it to the wounded man, who drank it, and then turning his head towards me, said—"Hardy and I had laid plan to have this thing brought upon you, and to have you hung for it—but you have escaped." He then asked me if they intended to leave him to die in the woods, or to take him home and hang him. I told him I had heard them talk of taking him home in a cart, but what was to be done with him I did not know. I felt a horror of the crimes committed by this man; was pained by the sight of his sufferings, and being unable to relieve the one, or to forgive the other, went to a place where I could neither see nor hear him, and sat down to await the return of those who had gone in pursuit of Hardy.

In the circumstances which surrounded me, it cannot be supposed that my feelings were pleasant, or that time moved very fleetly; but painful as my situation was, I was obliged to bear it for many hours. From the time the gentlemen left me, I neither saw nor heard them, until late in the afternoon, when five or six of them returned, having lost their companions in the woods.

Toward sundown, I heard a great noise of horns blown, and of men shouting at a distance in the forest; and soon after, my master, the owner of the blood hound, and many others returned, bringing with them, Hardy, whom the hound had followed ten or twelve miles, through the swamps and thickets; had at last caught him, and would soon have killed him, had he not been compelled to relinquish his prey. When the party had all returned, a kind of court was held in the woods, where we then were, for the purpose of determining what punishment should be inflicted upon Hardy and David. All agreed at once, that an example of the most terrific character ought to be made of such atrocious villains, and that it would defeat the ends of Justice to deliver these fellows up to the civil authority, to be hanged like common murderers. The next measure was, to settle upon the kind of punishment to be inflicted upon them, and the manner of executing the sentence.

Hardy was, all this time, sitting on the ground, covered with blood, and yet bleeding profusely, in hearing of his inexorable judges. The dog had mangled both his arms, and hands, in a shocking manner; torn a large piece of flesh entirely away from one side of his breast, and sunk his fangs deep in the side of his neck. No other human creature that I have ever seen, presented a more deplorable spectacle of mingled crime and cruelty.

It was now growing late, and the fate of these miserable men was to be decided before the company separated to go to their several homes. One proposed to burn them, another to flay them alive, and a third to starve them to death, and many other modes of slowly and tormentingly extinguishing life, were named; but that which was finally adopted was, of all others, the most horrible. The wretches were unanimously sentenced to be stripped naked, and bound down securely upon their backs, on the naked earth, in sight of each other; to have their mouths closely covered with bandages, to prevent them from making a noise to frighten away the birds, and in this manner to be left, to be devoured alive by the carrion crows and buzzards, which swarm in every part of South Carolina.

The sentence was instantly carried into effect, so far as its execution depended on us. Hardy, and his companion, were divested of their clothes, stretched upon their backs on the ground; their mouths bandaged with handkerchiefs—their limbs extended— and these, together with their necks, being crossed by numerous poles, were kept close to the earth by forked sticks driven into the ground, so as to prevent the possibility of moving any part of their persons; and in this manner these wicked men were left to be torn in pieces, by birds of prey. The buzzards, and carrion crows, always attack dead bodies by pulling out and consuming the eyes first. They then tear open the bowels, and feed upon the intestines.

We returned to my master's plantation, and I did not see this place again until the next Sunday, when several of my fellow-slaves went with me to see the remains of the dead, but we found only their bones. Great flocks of buzzards, and carrion crows, were assembled in the trees, giving a dismal aspect to the woods; and I hastened to abandon a place, fraught with so many afflicting recollections.

The lady, who had been the innocent sacrifice of the brutality of the men, whose bones I had seen bleaching in the sun, had died on Saturday evening, and her corpse was buried on Monday, in a graveyard on my master's plantation. I have never seen a large cotton plantation, in Carolina, without its burying ground. This burying ground is not only the place of sepulture of the family, who are the proprietors of the estate, but also of many other persons, who have lived in the neighbourhood. Half an acre, or an acre of ground, is appropriated as a grave-yard, on one side of which the proprietors of the estate, from age to age, are buried; whilst the other parts of the ground are open to strangers, poor people of their vicinity, and, in general, to all who choose to inter their dead within its boundaries. This custom prevails as far north as Maryland; and it seems to me to be much more consonant to the feelings of solitude and tender recollections, which we always associate with the memory of departed friends, than the practice of promiscuous interment in a church-yard, where all idea of seclusion is banished, by the last home of the dead being thrown open to the rude intrusions of strangers; where the sanctity of the sepulchre is treated as a common, and where the grave itself is, in a few years, torn up, or covered over, to form a temporary resting place for some new tenant.

The family of the deceased lady, though not very wealthy, was amongst the most ancient and respectable in this part of the country; and, on Sunday, whilst the body lay in my master's house, there was a continual influx and efflux of visiters, in carriages, on horse-back, and on foot. The house was open to all who chose to come; and the best wines, cakes, sweet-meats and fruits, were handed about to the company, by the servants; though I observed that none remained for dinner, except the relations of the deceased, those of my master's family, and the young gentleman who was with me on the island. The visiters remained but a short time when they came, and were nearly all in mourning. This was the first time that I had seen a large number of the fashionable people of Carolina assembled together, and their appearance impressed me with an opinion favourable to their character. I had never seen an equal number of people anywhere, whose deportment was more orderly and decorous, nor whose feelings seemed to be more in accordance with the solemnity of the event, which had brought them together.

I had been ordered by the overseer, to remain at the great house until the afternoon, for the purpose, as I afterwards learned, of being seen by those who came to see the corpse; and many of the ladies and gentlemen inquired for me, and when I was pointed out to them, commended my conduct and fidelity, in discovering the authors of the murder—condoled with me for having suffered innocently, and several gave me money. One old lady, who came in a pretty carriage, drawn by two black horses, gave me a dollar.

On Monday, the funeral took place, and several hundred persons followed the corpse to the grave, over which a minister delivered a short sermon. The young gentleman who was with me when we found the deceased on the island, walked with her Mother to the grave-yard, and the little brother followed, with a younger sister.

After the interment, wines and refreshments were handed round to the whole assembly, and, at least a hundred persons remained for dinner, with my master's family. At four o'clock in the afternoon, the carriages and horses were ordered to the door of the court-yard of the house, and the company retired. At sundown, the plantation was as quiet as if its peace had never been disturbed.

CHAPTER XIV.

I have before observed, that the negroes of the cotton plantations are exceedingly superstitious; and they are indeed, prone, beyond all other people that I have ever known, to believe in ghosts, and the existence of an infinite number of supernatural agents. No story of a miraculous character, can be too absurd to obtain credit with them; and a narrative is not the less eagerly listened to, nor the more cautiously received, because it is impossible in its circumstances. Within a few weeks after the deaths of the two malefactors, to whose horrible crimes were awarded equally horrible punishments, the forest that had been the scene of these bloody deeds, was reported, and believed to be visited at night by beings of unearthly make, whose groans, and death-struggles, were heard in the darkest recesses of the woods, amidst the flapping of the wings of vultures, the fluttering of carrion crows, and the dismal croaking of ravens. In the midst of this nocturnal din, the noise caused by the tearing of the flesh from the bones was heard, and the panting breath of the agonized sufferer, quivering under the beaks of his tormentors, as they consumed his vitals, floated audibly upon the evening breeze.

The murdered lady was also seen walking by moonlight, near the spot where she had been dragged from her horse, wrapped in a blood-stained mantle; overhung with gory and dishevelled locks.

The little island in the swamp, was said to present spactacles too horrible for human eyes to look upon, and sounds were heard to issue from it, which no human ear could bear. Terrific and ghastly fires were seen to burst up, at midnight, amongst the ever-greens that clad this lonely spot, emitting scents too suffocating and sickly to be endured; whilst demoniac yells, shouts of despair and groans of agony mingled their echos in the solitude of the woods.

Whilst I remained in this neighbourhood, no coloured person ever travelled this road, alone, after night-fall; and many white men would have ridden ten miles round the country, to avoid the passage of the ridge road, after dark. Generations must pass away, before the tradition of this place will be forgotten and many a year will open and close, before the last face will be pale, or the last heart beat, as the twilight traveller, skirts the borders of the Murderers' Swamp.

We had allowances of meat distributed to all the people twice this fall—once when we had finished the saving of the fodder, and again soon after the murder of the young lady. The first time we had beef, such as I had driven from the woods went to the alligator pond; but now we had two hogs given to us, which weighed, one a hundred and thirty, and the other a hundred and fifty-six pounds. This was very good pork, and I received a pound and a quarter as my share of it. This was the first pork that I had tasted in Carolina, and it afforded a real feast. We had, in our family, full seven pounds of good fat meat; and as we now had plenty of sweet potatoes, both in our gardens and in our weekly allowance, we had on the Sunday following the funeral, as good a dinner of stewed pork and potatoes, as could have been found in all Carolina. We did not eat all our meat on Sunday, but kept part of it until Tuesday, when we warmed it in a pot, with an addition of parsley and other herbs, and had another very comfortable meal.

I had, by this time, become in some measure, acquainted with the country, and began to lay and execute plans to procure supplies of such things as were not allowed me by my master. I understood various methods of entrapping rackoons, and other wild animals that abounded in the large swamps of this country; and besides the skins, which were worth something for their furs, I generally procured as many rackoons, opossums; and rabbits, as afforded us two or three meals in a week. The woman with whom I lived, understood the way of dressing an opossum, and I was careful to provide one for our Sunday dinner every week, so long as these animals continued fat and in good condition.

All the people on the plantation did not live as well as our family did, for many of the men did not understand trapping game, and others were too indolent to go far enough from home to find good places for setting their traps. My principal trapping ground was three miles from home, and I went three times a week, always after night, to bring home my game, and keep my traps in good order. Many of the families in the quarter caught no game, and had no meat, except that which we received from the overseer, which averaged about six or seven meals in the year.

Lydia, the woman whom I have mentioned heretofore was one of the women whose husbands procured little or nothing for the sustenance of their families, and I often gave her a quarter of a rackoon or a small opossum, for which she appeared very thankful.

Her health was not good—she had a bad cough, and often told me, she was feverish and restless at night. It appeared clear to me that this woman's constitution was broken by hardships, and sufferings, and that she could not live long in her present mode of existence. Her husband, a native of a country far in the interior of Africa, said he had been a priest in his own nation, and had never been taught to do any kind of labour, being supported by the contributions of the public; and he now maintained, as far as he could, the same kind of lazy dignity, that he had enjoyed at home. He was compelled by the overseer to work, with the other hands, in the field, but as soon as he had come into his cabin, he took his seat, and refused to give his wife the least assistance in doing any thing. She was consequently obliged to do the little work that it was necessary to perform in the cabin, and also to bear all the labour of weeding and cultivating the family patch or garden. The husband was a morose, sullen man, and said, he formerly had ten wives in his own country, who all had to work for, and wait upon him; and he thought himself badly off here, in having but one woman to do any thing for him. This man was very irritable, and often beat and otherwise maltreated his wife, on the slightest provocation, and the overseer refused to protect her, on the ground, that he never interfered in the family quarrels of the black people. I pitied this woman greatly, but as it was not in my power to remove her from the presence and authority of her husband, I thought it prudent not to say nor do any thing to provoke him further against her. As the winter approached, and the autumnal rains set in, she was frequently exposed in the field, and was wet for several hours together: this, joined to the want of warm and comfortable woollen clothes, caused her to contract colds, and hoarseness, which increased the severity of her cough. A few days before Christmas, her child died, after an illness of only three days. I assisted her and her husband to inter the infant—which was a little boy —and its father buried with it, a small bow, and several arrows; a little bag of parched meal; a miniature canoe, about a foot long, and a little paddle, (with which he said it would cross the ocean to his own country) a small stick, with an iron nail, sharpened, and fastened into one end of it; and a piece of white muslin, with several curious and strange figures painted on it in blue and red, by which, he said, his relations and countrymen would know the infant to be his son, and would receive it accordingly, on its arrival amongst them.

Cruel as this man was to his wife, I could not but respect the sentiments which inspired his affection for his child; though it was the affection of a barbarian. He cut a lock of hair from his head, threw it upon the dead infant, and closed the grave with his own hands. He then told us the God of his country was looking at him, and was pleased with what he had done. Thus ended the funeral service.

As we returned home, Lydia told me she was rejoiced that her child was dead, and out of a world in which slavery and wretchedness must have been its only portion. I am now, said she, ready to follow my child, and the sooner I go, the better for me. She went with us to the field until the month of January, when, as we were returning from our work, one stormy and wet evening, she told me she should never pick any more cotton—that her strength was gone, and she could work no more. When we assembled, at the blowing of the horn, on the following morning, Lydia did not appear. The overseer, who had always appeared to dislike this woman, when he missed her, swore very angrily, and said he supposed she was pretending to be sick, but if she was, he would soon cure her. He then stepped into his house and took some copperas front a little bag, and mixed it with water. I followed him to Lydia's cabin, where he compelled her to drink this solution of copperas. It caused her to vomit violently, and made her exceedingly sick. I think to this day, that this act of the overseer, was the most inhuman of all those that I have seen perpetrated upon defenceless slaves.

Lydia was removed that same day to the sick room, in a state of extreme debility and exhaustion. When she left this room again she was a corpse. Her disease was a consumption of the lungs, which terminated her life early in March. I assisted in carrying her to the grave, which I closed upon her, and covered with green turf. She sleeps by the side of her infant, in a corner of the negro grave-yard, of this plantation. Death was to her a welcome messenger who came to remove her from toil that she could not support, and from misery that she could not sustain.

Her life had been a morning of pleasure, but a day of bitterness, upon which no sunlight had fallen. Had she known no other mode of existence than that which she saw on this plantation, her lot would have been happiness itself, in comparison with her actual destiny. Trained up as she had been in Maryland, no greater cruelty could have been devised by the malice of her most cunning enemy, than to transfer her from the service, and almost companionship of

155

an indulgent and affectionate mistress, to the condition in which I saw her, and knew her, in the cotton fields of South Carolina.

In Maryland, it is a custom as widely extended as the state itself, I believe, to give the slaves a week of holidays; at Christmas; and the master, who should attempt to violate this usage, would become an object of derision amongst his neighbours. But I learned, long before Christmas, that the force of custom was not so binding here, as it is farther north. In Maryland, Christmas comes at a season of leisure, when the work of the farm, or the tobacco plantation, is generally closed for the year; and, if a good supply of firewood has been provided, there seems to be but little for the people to do, and a week lost to the master, is a matter of little moment, at a period when the days are short and cold; but in the cotton country, the case is very different.

Christmas comes in the very midst of cotton picking. The richest and best part of the crop has been secured before this period, it is true; but large quantities of cotton still remain in the field, and every pound that can be saved from the winds, or the plough of the next spring, is a gain of its value, to the owner of the estate.

For these reasons, which are very powerful on the side of the master, there is but little Christmas on a large cotton plantation. In lieu of the week of holiday, which formerly prevailed even in Carolina, before cotton was cultivated as a crop, the master now gives the people a dinner of meat, on Christmas-day, and distributes amongst them their annual allowance of winter clothes, on estates where such an allowance is made; and where it is not, some small gratuity supplies its place.

There are cotton planters who give no clothes to their slaves, but expect them to supply themselves with apparel, out of the proceeds of their Sunday labour and nightly earnings. Clothes of a certain quality were given to the people of the estate on which I lived, at the time of which I now speak; but they were not at all sufficient to keep us warm and comfortable in the winter; and the residue, we had to procure for ourselves. In Georgia, I lived three years with one master, and the best master, too, that I ever had in the south, who never gave me any clothes during that period, except an old great coat, and a pair of boots.—I shall have occasion to speak of him hereafter.

As Christmas of the year 1805, approached, we were all big with hope of obtaining three or four days, at least, if not a week of holiday; but when the day at length arrived, we were sorely disappointed, for on Christmas eve, when we had come from the field, with our cotton, the overseer fell into a furious passion, and swore at us all for our laziness, and many other bad qualities. He then told us that he had intended to give us three days, if we had worked well, but that we had been so idle, and had left so much cotton yet to be picked in the field, that he found it impossible to give us more than one day; but that he would go to the house, and endeavour to procure a meat dinner for us, and a dram in the morning. Accordingly, on the next morning, we received a dram of peach brandy, for each person; and two hogs, weighing together more than three hundred, were slaughtered and divided amongst us.

I went to the field and picked cotton all day, for which I was paid by the overseer, and at night I had a good dinner of stewed pork and sweet potatoes.—Such were the beginning and end of my first Christmas on a cotton plantation. We went to work as usual the next morning, and continued our labour through the week, as if Christmas had been stricken from the calender. I had already saved and laid by a little more than ten dollars in money, but part of it had been given to me at the funeral. I was now much in want of clothes, none having been given me since I came here. I had, at the commencement of the cold weather, cut up my old blanket, and, with the aid of Lydia, who was a very good seamstress, converted it into a pair of trousers, and a long roundabout jacket; but this deprived me of my bed, which was imperfectly supplied by mats, which I made of rushes. The mats were very comfortable things to lie upon, but they were by no means equal to blankets for covering.

A report had been current amongst us, for some time, that there would be a distribution of clothes, to the people, at new-year's-day; but how much, or what kind of clothes we were to get, no one pretended to know, except that we were to get shoes, in conformity to a long-established rule of this plantation. From Christmas to new-year, appeared a long to week to me, and I have no doubt that it longer to some of my fellow-slaves, most of whom were entirely barefoot. I had made mockasins for myself, of the skins of squirrels, that I had caught in my traps, and by this means protected my feet from the frost, which was sometimes very heavy and sharp, in the morning.

On the first day of January, when we met at the blowing of the morning horn, the overseer told us, we must all proceed to the great house, where we were to receive our winter clothes; and surely, no order was ever more willingly obeyed. When we arrived at the house, our master was up, and we were all called into the great court yard in front of the dwelling. The overseer now told us, that shoes would be given to all those who were able to go to the field, to pick cotton. This deprived of shoes, the children, and several old persons, whose eye-sight was not sufficiently clear, to enable them to pick cotton. A new blanket was then given to every one above seven years of age—children under seven, received no blanket, being left, to be provided for by their parents. Children of this age, and under, go entirely naked, in the day-time, and sleep with their mothers at night, or are wrapped up together, such bedding as the mother may possess. Children under seven years of age are of little use in picking cotton, and it is not supposed that their labour can repay the expense of clothing them in a manner to fit them to go to the field—they are, therefore, suffered to remain in the house or quarter, without clothes, from October to April. In summer they do not require clothes, and can perform such work as they are able to do, as well without garments as with them.

At the time we received our shoes, and blankets, there was not a good shirt in our quarter—but all the men, and women, had provided themselves with some sort of woollen clothes, out of their own savings. Woollen stuff, for a petticoat and shortgown had also been given, before Christmas, to each of the women who were mothers of small children or in such a condition as to render it certain, that they must, in a short time, become so. Many of the women could pick as much cotton as a man; and any good hand could earn sixty cents, by picking cotton on Sunday—the overseer paying us punctually for all the cotton we brought in, on Sunday evening. Besides this, a good hand could always, in a fine day, pick more cotton than was required to be brought home, as a day's work. I could not pick as much in a day, as some of the others, by four or five pounds; but I could generally carry home as much beyond the day's work, or task, as it is called, as, entitled me to receive from five to ten cents every evening, from the overseer. This money was punctually paid to me every Saturday night; and in some weeks I cleared, in this way, as high as fifty cents, over and above what I earned on Sunday. One of the men cleared to himself, including his Sunday work, two dollars a week, for several weeks; and his savings, on this entire crop of cotton, were thirty-one dollars—but he was a first-rate cotton picker, and worked late and early. One of the women cleared twenty-six dollars to herself in the same way. We were expected to clothe ourselves with these, and our other extra earnings; but some of the people performed no more work, through the week, than their regular task, and would not work constantly on Sunday. Such were not able to provide themselves with good clothes; and many of them suffered greatly from the cold, in the course of the winter. When the weather was mild and pleasant, some of the children, who were not required to go to the field, to do a day's work, would go out, in the warmest part of the day, and pick a few pounds of cotton, for which their parents received pay, and were obliged, in return, to find the children in bedding for the winter.

A man can plant and cultivate more cotton plants, than he is afterwards able to pick the wool from, if the season is good, and no disaster befalls the crop. Here every effort is made, from the commencement of the picking season until its close, to procure as much work as possible from the hands; and, spite of all that can be done, much cotton is lost—the people not being able to pick it all from the stalks, before the field is ploughed up to prepare the ground for the reception of the seeds of a new crop. In such cases, every pound that the hands can be induced to pick, beyond their daily task, is a clear gain to the master; and slaves often leave the fields of their masters, where the cotton is nearly all gathered, and the picking is poor, to go to the field of some neighbouring planter, where the cotton is more abundant, to work on Sunday. It is a matter of indifference to the slave, whether his master gets his cotton all picked or not; his object is to get employment in a field where he can make the best wages. In such cases, the masters often direct the overseers to offer their own slaves one half as much as the cotton is worth, for each pound they will pick on Sunday—and this, for the purpose of preventing them from going to some other field, to work on that day.

The usual price only, is paid for extra cotton, picked on working days; for after a hand has picked his task, he would not have time to go anywhere else to work; nor indeed, would he be permitted to leave his plantation. The slave is a kind of freeman on Sunday all over the southern country; and it is in truth, by the exercise of his liberty on this day, that he is enabled to provide himself and his family, with many of the necessaries of life that his master refuses to supply him with.

It is altogether impossible, to make a person residing in any of the middle or northern states of the Union, and who has never been in the south, throughly acquainted with all the minute particulars of the life of a slave on a cotton plantation; or to give him an idea of the system of parsimonious economy, that the slave is obliged to exercise and maintain in his little household. Poor as the slave is, and dependant at all times upon the arbitrary will of his master, or yet more fickle caprice of the overseer, his children look up to him in his little cabin, as their protector and supporter. There is always in every cabin, except in times of scarcity, after there has been a failure of the corn crop, a sufficient supply of either corn bread or sweet potatoes; and either of these, is sufficient to give health and vigour to children, who are not required to do any work; but a person who is grown up, and is obliged to labour hard, finds either bread or potatoes, or even both together, quite inadequate to sustain the body in the full and powerful tone of muscular action, that more generous food would bestow. A mother will imagine the painful feelings experienced by a parent, in the cabin of a slave, when a small portion of animal food is procured, dressed and made ready for the table. The father and mother know, that it is not only food, but medicine to them, and their appetites keenly court the precious morsel; whilst the children, whose senses are all acute, seem to be indued with taste and smell in a tenfold degree, and manifest a ravenous craving for fresh meat, which it is painful to witness, without being able to gratify it.

During the whole of this fall and winter, we usually had something to roast, at least twice a week, in our cabin. These roasts were rackoons, opossums, and other game—the proceeds of my trapping. All the time the meat was hanging at the fire, as well as while it was on the table, our house was surrounded by the children of our fellow-slaves; some begging for a piece, and all expressing, by their eager countenances the keen desire they felt to partake with us of our dainties. It was idle to think of sharing with them, the contents of our board; for they were often thirty or forty in number; and the largest rackoon would scarcely have made a mouthful for each of them. There was one little boy, four years old, a very fine little fellow, to whom I had become warmly attached; and who used to share with me in all the good things I possessed. He was of the same age with my own little son, whom I had left in Maryland; and there was nothing that I possessed in the world, that I would not have divided with him, even to my last crust.

It may well be supposed, that in our society, although we were all slaves, and all nominally in a condition of the most perfect equality, yet there was in fact a very great difference in the manner of living, in the several families. Indeed, I doubt, if there is as great a diversity in the modes of life, in the several families of any white village in New-York, or Pennsylvania, containing a population of three hundred persons, as there was in the several households of our quarter. This may be illustrated by the following circumstance: Before I came to reside in the family with whom I lived at this time, they seldom tasted animal food, or even fish, except on meat-days, as they were called; that is, when meat was given to the people by the overseer, under the orders of our master. The head of the family was a very quiet, worthy man; but slothful and inactive in his habits. When he had come from the field at night, he seldom thought of leaving the cabin again before morning. He would, and did, make baskets and mats, and earned some money by these means, he also did his regular day's work on Sunday; but all his acquirements were not sufficient to enable him to provide any kind of meat for his family. All that his wife and children could do, was to provide him with work at his baskets and mats; and they lived even then better than some of their neighbours. After I came among them and had acquired some knowledge of the surrounding country, I made as many baskets and mats as he did; and took time to go twice a week to look at all my traps.

As the winter passed away and spring approached, the proceeds of my hunting began to diminish. The game became scarce, and both rackoons and opossums grew poor and worthless. It was necessary for me to discover some new mode of improving allowance allotted to me by the overseer. I had all my life been accustomed to fishing, in Maryland, and I now resolved to resort to the water for a living; the land having failed to furnish me a comfortable subsistence. With these views, I set out one Sunday morning, early in February, and went to the river at a distance of three miles from home. From the appearance of the stream, I felt confident that it must contain many fish; and I went immediately to work to make a weir. With the help of an axe that I had with me, I had finished, before night, the frame work of a weir of pine sticks, lashed together with white oak splits. I had no canoe, but made a raft of dry logs, upon which I went to a suitable place in the river, and set my weir. I afterwards made a small net of twine, that I bought at the store; and on next Thursday night I took as many fish from my weir as filled a half bushel measure. This was a real treasure—it was the most fortunate circumstance that had happened with me since I came to the country.

I was enabled to show my generosity; but, like all mankind, even in my liberality, I kept myself in mind. I gave a large fish to the overseer, and took three more to the great house. These were the first fresh fish that had been in the family this season; and I was much praised by my master and young mistresses, for my skill and success in fishing but this was all the advantage I received from this effort to court the favour of the great:—I did not even get a dram. The part I had performed in the detection of the murderers of the young lady was forgotten; or, at least, not mentioned now. I went away from the house, not only disappointed, but chagrined, and thought with myself, that if my master and young mistresses had nothing but words to give me for my fish, we should not carry on a very large traffic.

On next Sunday morning, a black boy came from the house, and told me that our master wished to see me. This summons was not to be disobeyed. When I returned to the mansion, I went round to the kitchen, and sent word by one of the house-slaves, that I had come. The servant returned and told me, that I was to stay in the kitchen and get my breakfast; and after that, to come into the house. A very good breakfast was sent to me from my master's table, after the family had finished their morning meal; and when I had done with my repast, I went into the parlour. I was received with great affability by my master, who told me he had sent for me to know if I had been accustomed to fish in the place I had come from. I informed him, that I had been employed at a fishery on the Patuxent, every spring, for several years; and that I thought I understood fishing with a seine, as well as most people. He then asked me, if I could knit a seine; to which I replied in the affirmative. After some other questions, he told me, that as the picking of cotton was nearly over for this season, and the fields must soon be ploughed up for a new crop, he had a thought of having a seine made; and of placing me at the head of a fishing party, for the purpose of trying to take a supply of fish for his hands. No communication could have been more unexpected than this was, and it was almost as pleasing to me as it was unexpected by me. I now began to hope that there would be some respite from the labours of the cotton field, and that I should not be doomed to drag out a dull and monotonous existence within the confines of the enclosures of the plantation.

In Maryland, the fishing season was always one of hard labour, it is true; but also a time of joy and hilarity. We then had, throughout the time of fishing plenty of bread, and, at least, bacon enough to fry our fish with. We had also a daily allowance of whiskey, or brandy, and we always considered ourselves fortunate when we left the farm to go to the fishery.

A few days after this, I was again sent for by my master, who told me, that he had bought twine and ropes for a seine; and that I must set to work and knit it as quickly as possible; that as he did not wish the twine to be taken to the quarter, I must remain with the servants in the kitchen, and live with them whilst employed in constructing the seine. I was assisted in making the seine by a black boy, whom I had taught to work with me; and by the end of two weeks we had finished our job.

While at work on this seine, I lived rather better than I had formerly done, when residing at the quarter. We received amongst us—twelve in number, including the people who worked in the garden— the refuse of our master's table. In this way we procured a little cold meat every day; and when there were many strangers visiting the family, we sometimes procured considerable quantities of cold and broken meats.

My new employment afforded me a better opportunity, than I had hitherto possessed, of making correct observations upon the domestic economy of my master's household, and of learning the habits and modes of life of the persons who composed it. On a great cotton plantation, such as this of my master's the field hands, who live in the quarter, are removed so far from the domestic circle of their master's family, by their servile condition and the nature of their employment, that they know but little more of the transactions within the walls of the great house, than if they lived ten miles off. Many a slave has been born, lived to old age, and died on a plantation, without ever having been within the walls of his master's domicil.

My master was a widower and his house was in charge of his sister, a maiden lady, apparently of fifty- five or sixty. He had six children, three sons and three daughters, and all unmarried; but only one of the sons was at home, at the time I came upon the estate; the other two were in some of the northern cities: the one studying medicine, and the other at college. At the time of knitting the twine, these

young gentlemen had returned, on a visit, to their relations, and all
the brothers and sisters were now on the place. The young ladies
were all grown up, and marriageable; their father was known to be a
man of great wealth; and the girls were reputed very pretty in
Carolina; one of them, the second of the three, was esteemed a great
beauty.

The reader might deem my young mistress' pretty face and graceful
person, altogether impertinent to the narrative of my own life; but
they had a most material influence upon my fortunes, and changed
the whole tenor of my existence. Had she been less beautiful, or of a
temper less romantic and adventurous I should still have been a
slave in South Carolina if yet alive, and the world would have been
saved the labour of perusing these pages.

Any one at all acquainted with southern manners will at once see
that my master's house possessed attractions which would not fail to
draw within it numerous visiters; and that the head of such a family
as dwelt under its roof was not likely to be without friends.

I had not been at work upon the seine a week before I discovered, by
listening to the conversation of my master, and the other members of
the family, that they prided themselves not a little, upon the
antiquity of their house, and the long practice of a generous
hospitality to strangers, and to all respectable people, who chose to
visit their homestead. All circumstances seemed to conspire to
render this house one of the chief seats of the fashion, the beauty, the
wit, and the gallantry of South Carolina. Scarcely an evening came
but it brought a carriage, and ladies and gentlemen, and their
servants; and every day brought dashing young planters, mounted
on horseback, to dine with the family; but Sunday was the day of the
week on which the house received the greatest accession of
company. My master and family were members of the Episcopal
Church, and attended service every Sunday, when the weather was
fine, at a church eight miles distant. Each of my young masters and
mistresses had a saddlehorse, and in pleasant weather, they
frequently all went to church on horseback, leaving my old master
and mistress to occupy the family carriage alone. I have seen fifteen
or twenty young people come to my master's for dinner, on Sunday
from church; and very often the parson, a young man of handsome
appearance, was amongst them. I had observed these things long
before, but now I had come to live at the house, and became more
familiar with them. Three Sundays intervened while I was at work

upon the seine, and on each of these Sundays more than twenty persons, besides the family, dined at my master's. During these three weeks, my young masters were absent far the greater part of the time; but I observed that they generally came home on Sunday for dinner. My young mistresses were not from home much, and I believe they never left the plantation unless either their father or some one of their brothers was with them. Dinner parties were frequent in my master's house; and on these occasions of festivity, a black man, who belonged to a neighbouring estate, and who played the violin, was sent for. I observed that whenever this man was sent for, he came, and sometimes even came before night, which appeared a little singular to me, as I knew the difficulty that coloured people had to encounter in leaving the estate to which they were attached. I felt curious to ascertain how it happened that Peter (that was the name of the fiddler,) enjoyed such privileges and contrived to become acquainted with him, when he came to get his supper in the kitchen. He informed me that his master was always ready to let him go to a ball; and would permit him to leave the cotton field at any time for that purpose, and even lend him a horse to ride. I afterwards learned from this man, that his master compelled him to give him half the money that he received as gratuities from the gentlemen for whom he played at the dinner parties; but as his master had enjoined him, under pain of being whipped, not to divulge this circumstance, I never betrayed the poor fellow's confidence. Peter's master was a planter, who owned thirty slaves, and his children (several of whom were young ladies and gentlemen) moved in highly respectable circles of society; but I believe my master's family did not treat them as quite their equals; not so much on account of their inferiority in point of wealth, as because they were new in the country, having only been settled here but a few years, and the master of Peter having, when a young man, acted as overseer on a rice plantation near Charleston.

CHAPTER XV.

I have, though always in a very humble station in life, travelled more, and seen more of the people in the United States, than some who occupy elevated ranks, and claim for themselves a knowledge of the world far greater than I pretend to possess; but a man's knowledge is to be valued, not by that which he has imagined, but by that which experience has taught him; and in estimating his ability to give information to others, we are to judge him, not by what he says he would wish men and the world to be, but by what he has seen, and by the just inferences he draws from those actions, that he has witnessed in the various conditions of human society, that have passed in review before him. In this book I do not pretend to discuss systems, or advance theories. I am content to give facts as I saw them.

In the northern and middle states, so far as I have known them, very little respect is paid to family pretensions; and this disregard of ancestry seems to me to be the necessary offspring of the condition of things. In the states of New-York and Pennsylvania, there are so many ways by which men may and do arrive at distinction, and so many, and such various means of acquiring wealth, that all claim of superiority on account of the possession of any particular kind of property, is prohibited by public opinion. A great landholder is counterbalanced by a great manufacturer, and perhaps surpassed by a great merchant, whilst a successful and skilful mechanic is the rival of all these. Family distinction can obtain no place amongst these men. In the plantation states, the case is widely different. There, lands and slaves constitute the only property of the country that is worthy of being taken into an estimate of public wealth. Cattle and horses, hogs, sheep and mules exist, but in numbers so few, and of qualities so inferior, that the portion of them, possessed by any individual planter, would compose an aggregate value of sufficient magnitude only to raise him barely beyond the lines that divide poverty from mediocrity of condition.

The mechanic is a sort of journeyman to the planters, and works about the country as he may chance to find a job, in building a house, erecting a cotton-gin, or constructing a horse-mill, if he is a carpenter or mill-wright; if he is a tailor, he seeks employment from house to house, never remaining longer in one place than to allow himself time to do the work of the family. The mechanic holds a kind of half-way rank between the gentleman and the slave. He is not, and never can be, a gentleman, for the reason that he does, and must do his own work. Hence mechanics and artizans of every description avoid the southern country; or, if found there, they are only sojourners. The country they are in is not their home: they are there from necessity or with a hope of acquiring money to establish themselves in business, in places where their occupations are held more in honour. Manufacturers are not in existence in the cotton country, therefore no comparison can be instituted between them and the planters.

I believe, from what I saw, that all the commerce of the cotton country is in the hands of strangers, and that a large portion of these strangers are foreigners. The planters deal with them from necessity, as they must have such things as they need, and must obtain them somewhere, and from somebody. The store-keeper lives as well, dresses as well, and often lives in as good a house as the planter — perhaps in one that is better than that of the planter; but his wealth is not so material, his means of subsistence do not strike the eye so powerfully as a hundred field hands, and three hundred acres of cotton. The country has no hold on him, and he has no hold on the country. His habits of life are not similar to those of his neighbours — he is not "one of us."

All the families who visited at my master's were those of planters; and the families of the cotton planters have nothing to do but visit, or read, hunt, or fish, or run into some vicious amusements, or sit down and do nothing. Every kind of labour is as strictly prohibited to the sons and daughters of the planters, by universal custom, as if a law of the land made it punishable by fine and imprisonment, and gave one-half of the fine to a common informer. The only line that divides the gentleman from the simple man, is that the latter works for his living, whilst the former has slaves to work for him. No man who works with his hands, can or will be received into the highest orders of society, on a footing of equality, nor can he hope to see his family treated better than himself. This unhappy fiat of public opinion has done infinite mischief in the south.

Men of fortune will not work, nor permit their sons to work in the field, because this exemption from labour is their badge of gentility, and the circumstance that distinguishes them from the less favoured members of the community. As the wealthy, the great, and the fashionable, are never seen at labour and as it is known that they hold it to be beneath the rank of a gentleman to work in the field, those who are more sparingly endowed with the advantages of fortune, imbibe an opinion that it is disgraceful to plough, or to dig, and that it is necessary to lead a life of idleness, to maintain their caste in society.

No man works in South Carolina, except under the impulse of necessity. In this state of things, many men of limited fortunes rear up families of children without education, and without the means of supporting an expensive style of living. The sons, when grown up, of necessity, commingle with the other young people of the country, and bring with them into the affairs of the world, nothing upon which they can pride themselves, except that they are white men, and are not obliged to work for a living.

This false pride has infected the whole mass of the white population; and the young man, whose father has half a dozen children, and an equal number of slaves looks with affected disdain upon the son of his father's neighbour, who owns no slaves, because the son of the non-slaveholder must work for his bread, whilst the son of the master of half a dozen negroes, contrives to support himself in a sort of lazy poverty, only one remove from actual penury.

Every man who is able to procure a subsistence, without labour, regards himself a gentleman, from this circumstance alone, if he has nothing else to sustain his pretensions. These poor gentlemen, are the worst members of society, and the least productive of benefit, either to themselves or their country. They are prone to horse-racing, cock-fighting, gambling, and all sorts of vices common to the country. Having no livelihood, and being engaged in no pursuit, they hope to distinguish themselves by running to excess in what they call fashionable amusements, or sporting exercises. These people are universally detested by the slaves, and are indeed far more tyrannical than the great slave-holders themselves, or any other portion of the white population, the overseers excepted.

A man who is master of only four or five slaves, is generally the most ready of all to apprehend a black man, whom he may happen to catch straying from his plantation; and generally whips him the most unmercifully for this offence. The law gives him the same authority to arrest the person of a slave, seen travelling without his pass, that it vests in the owner of five hundred negroes; and the experience of all ages, that petty tyrants are the most oppressive, seems fully verified in the cotton country.

A person who has not been in the slave-holding states, can never fully understand the bonds that hold society together there, or appreciate the rules which prescribe the boundaries of the pretensions of the several orders of men who compose the body politic of those communities; and after all that I have written, and all that I shall write, in this book, the reader who has never resided south of the Potomac, will never be able to perceive things precisely as they present themselves to my vision, or to comprehend the spirit that prevails in a country, where the population is divided into three separate classes. Those will fall into great error, who shall imagine that in Carolina and Georgia there are but two orders of men; and that the artificial distinctions of society have only classified the people into white and black, freemen and slaves. It is true, that the distinctions of colour are the most obvious, and present themselves more readily than any others to the inspection of a stranger; but he who will take time to examine into the fundamental organization of society, in the cotton planting region, will easily discover that there is a third order of men located there, little known to the world, but who, nevertheless, hold a separate station, occupying a place of their own, and who do not come into direct contrast with either the master or the slave.

The white man, who has no property, no possession, and no education, is, in Carolina, in a condition no better than that to which the slave has been reduced; except only that he is master of his own person, and of his own time, and may, if he chooses, emigrate and transfer himself to a country where he can better his circumstances, whilst the slave is bound, by invisible chains, to the plantation on which his master may think proper to place him.

In my opinion, there is no order of men in any part of the United States, with which I have any acquaintance, who are in a more debased and humiliated state of moral servitude, than are those white people who inhabit that part of the southern country, where the landed property is all, or nearly all, held by the great planters. Many of these white people live in wretched cabins, not half so good as the houses which judicious planters provide for their slaves. Some of these cabins of the white men are made of mere sticks, or small poles notched, or rather thatched together, and filled in with mud, mixed with the leaves, or *shats*, as they are termed, of the pine tree.

Some fix their residence far in the pine forest, and gain a scanty subsistence by notching the trees and gathering the turpentine; others are seated upon some poor, and worthless point of land, near the margin of a river, or creek, and draw a precarious livelihood from the water, and the badly cultivated garden that surrounds, or adjoins the dwelling.

These people do not occupy the place held in the north by the respectable and useful class of day labourers, who constitute so considerable a portion of the numerical population of the country.

In the south, these white cottagers are never employed to work on the plantations for wages. Two things forbid this. The white man, however poor and necessitous he may be, is too proud to go to work in the same field with the negro slaves by his side; and the owner of the slaves is not willing to permit white men, of the lowest order, to come amongst them, lest the morals of the negroes should be corrupted, and illicit traffic should be carried on, to the detriment of the master.

The slaves generally believe, that however miserable they may be, in their servile station, it is nevertheless preferable to the degraded existence of these poor white people. This sentiment is cherished by the slaves, and encouraged by their masters, who fancy that they subserve their own interests in promoting an opinion amongst the negroes, that they are better off in the world than are many white persons, who are free, and have to submit to the burthen of taking care of, and providing for themselves.

I never could learn nor understand how, or by what means, these poor cottagers came to be settled in Carolina. They are a separate and distinct race of men from the planters, and appear to have nothing in common with them. If it were possible for any people to occupy a grade in human society below that of the slaves, on the cotton plantations, certainly the station would be filled by these white families, who cannot be said to possess any thing in the shape of property. The contempt in which they are held, and the contumely with which they are treated, by the great planters, to be comprehended, must be seen.

These observations are applicable in their fullest extent, only to the lower parts of Georgia and Carolina, and to country places. In the upper country, where slaves are not so numerous, and where less of cotton and more of grain is cultivated, there is not so great a difference between the white man, who holds slaves and a plantation, and another white man who has neither slaves nor plantation. In the towns, also, more especially in Charleston and Savannah, where the number of white men who have no slaves is very great, they are able, from their very numbers, to constitute a moral force sufficiently powerful to give them some degree of weight in the community.

I shall now return to my narrative. Early in March, or perhaps on one of the last days of February, my seine being now completed, my master told me I must take with me three other black men, and go to the river to clear out a fishery. This task of clearing out a fishery, was a very disagreeable job; for it was nothing less than dragging out of the river, all the old trees and brush that had sunk to the bottom, within the limits of our intended fishing ground. My master's eldest son had been down the river, and had purchased two boats, to be used at the fishery; but when I saw them I declared them to be totally unfit for the purpose. They were old batteaux, and so leaky, that they would not have supported the weight of a wet seine, and the men necessary to lay it out. I advised the building of two good canoes, from some of the large yellow pines, in the woods. My advice was accepted, and together with five other hands, I went to work at the canoes, which we completed in less than a week.

So far things went pretty well, and I flattered myself that I should become the head man at this new fishery, and have the command of the other hands. I also expected that I should be able to gain some advantage to myself, by disposing of a part of the small fish that might be taken at the fishery. I reckoned without my host.

My master had only purchased this place a short time before he bought me. Before that time he did not own any place on the river, fit for the establishment of a fishery. His lands adjoined the river for more than a mile in extent, along its margin; but an impassable morass separated the channel of the river, from the firm ground, all along his lines. He had cleared the highest parts of this morass, or swamp, and had here made his rice fields; but he was as entirely cut off from the river, as if an ocean had separated it from him.

On the day that we launched the canoes into the river, and while we were engaged in removing some snags, and old trees that had stuck in the mud, near the shore, an ill-looking stranger came to us, and told us that our master had sent him to take charge of the fishery, and superintend all the work that was to be done at it. This man, by his contract with my master, was to receive a part of all the fish caught, in lieu of wages; and was invested with the same authority over us that was exercised by the overseer in the cotton field.

I soon found that I had cause to regret my removal from the plantation. It was found quite impossible to remove the old logs, and other rubbish from the bottom of the river, without going into the water and wrenching them from their places with long hand-spikes. In performing this work we were obliged to wade up to our shoulders, and often to dip our very heads under water, in raising the sunken timber. However, within less than a week, we had cleared the ground, and now began to haul our seine. At first, we caught nothing but common river fish; but after two or three days, we began to take shad. Of the common fish, such as pike, perch, suckers, and others, we had the liberty of keeping as many as we could eat; but the misfortune was, that we had no pork, or fat of any kind, to fry them with; and for several days we contented ourselves with broiling them on the coals, and eating them with our corn bread, and sweet potatoes. We could have lived well, if we had been permitted to broil the shad on the coals, and eat them; for a fat shad will dress itself in being broiled, and is very good, without any oily substance added to it.

All the shad that we caught, were carefully taken away by a black man, who came three times every day to the fishery, with a cart.

The master of the fishery had a family that lived several miles up the river. In the summer time; he fished with hooks, and small nets, when not engaged in running turpentine, in the pine woods. In the winter he went back into the pine forest, and made tar of the dead pine trees; but returned to the river at the opening of the spring, to take advantage of the shad fishery. He was supposed to be one of the most skilful fishermen on the Congaree river, and my master employed him to superintend his new fishery, under an expectation, I presume, that as he was to get a tenth part of all the fish that might be caught, he would make the most of his situation. My master had not calculated with accuracy the force of habit, nor the difficulty which men experience, in conducting very simple affairs, of which they have no practical knowledge.

The fish-master did very well for the interest of his employer, for a few days; compelling us to work, in hauling the seine, night and day, and scarcely permitting us to take rest enough to obtain necessary sleep. We were compelled to work full sixteen hours every day, including Sunday; for in the fishing season, no respect is paid to Sunday by fishermen, anywhere. We had our usual quantity of bread and potatoes, with plenty of common fish; but no shad came to our lot; nor had we any thing to fry our fish with. A broiled fresh-water fish is not very good, at best, without salt or oil; and after we had eaten them every day, for a week, we cared very little for them.

By this time, our fish-master began to relax in his discipline; not that he became more kind to us, or required us to do less work; but to compel us to work all night, it was necessary for him to sit up all night and watch us. This was a degree of toil and privation to which he could not long submit; and one evening soon after dark, he called me to him and told me, that he intended to make me overseer of the fishery that night; and he had no doubt, I would keep the hands at work, and attend to the business as well without him as with him. He then went into his cabin, and went to bed; whilst I went and laid out the seine, and made a very good haul. We took more than two hundred shad at this draught; and followed up our work with great industry all night, only taking time to eat our accustomed meal at midnight.

Every fisherman knows that the night is the best time for taking shad; and the little rest that had been allowed us, since we began to fish, had always been from eight o'clock in the morning, until four in the afternoon; unless within that period there was an appearance of a school of fish in the river; when we had to rise, and lay out the seine, no matter at what hour of the day. The fish-master had been very severe with the hands, since he came amongst us; and had made very free use of a long hickory gad that he sometimes carried about with him; though at times he would relax his austerity, and talk quite familiarly with us: especially with me, whom he perceived to have some knowledge of the business in which we were engaged. The truth was, that this man knew nothing of fishing with a seine, and I had been obliged from the beginning to direct the operations of laying out and drawing in the seine; though the master was always very loud and boisterous in giving his commands, and directing us in what part of the river we should let down the seine.

Having never been accustomed to regular work, or to the pursuit of any constant course of personal application, the master was incapable of long continued exertion; and I feel certain, that he could not have been prevailed upon to labour twelve hours each day, for a year, if in return he had been certain of receiving ten thousand dollars. Notwithstanding this, he was capable of rousing himself, and of undergoing any degree of fatigue or privation, for a short time; even for a few days. He had not been trained to habits of industry, and could not bear the restraints of uniform labour.

We worked hard all night, the first night of my superintendence, and when the sun rose the next morning, the master had not risen from his bed. As it was now the usual time of dividing the fish, I called to him to come and see this business fairly done; but as he did not come down immediately to the landing, I proceeded to make the division myself, in as equitable a manner as I could: giving, however, a full share of large fish to the master. When he came down to us, and overlooked both the piles of fish— his own and that of my master— he was so well satisfied with what I had done, that he said, if he had known that I would do so well for him, he would not have risen. I was glad to hear this, as it led me to hope, that I should be able to induce him to stay in his cabin during the greater part of the time; to do which, I was well assured, he felt disposed.

When the night came, the master again told me he should go to bed, not being well; and desired me to do as I had done the night before. This night we cooked as many shad as we could all eat; but were careful to carry, far out into the river, the scale, and entrails of the stolen fish. In the morning I made a division of the fish before I called the master, and then went and asked him to come and see what I had done. He was again well pleased, and now proposed to us all, that if we would not let the affair be known to our master, he would leave us to manage the fishery at night according to our discretion. To this proposal we all readily agreed, and I received authority to keep the other hands at work, until the master would go and get his breakfast. I had now accomplished the object that I had held very near my heart, ever since we began to fish at this place.

From this time, to the end of the fishing season, we all lived well, and did not perform more work than we were able to bear. I was in no fear of being punished by the fish-master; for he was now a least as much in my power, as I was in his; for if my master had known the agreement, that he had made with us, for the purpose of enabling himself to sleep all night in his cabin, he would have been deprived of his situation, and all the profits of his share of the fishery.

There never can be any affinity of feeling between master and slave, except in some few isolated cases, where the master has treated his slave in such a manner, as to have excited in him strong feelings of gratitude; or where the slave entertains apprehensions, that by the death of his master, or by being separated from him in any other way, he may fall under the power of a more tyrannical ruler, or may in some shape be worsted by the change. I was never acquainted with a slave who believed, that he violated any rule of morality by appropriating to himself any thing that belonged to his master, if it was necessary to his comfort. The master might call it theft, and brand it with the name of crime; but the slave reasoned differently, when he took a portion of his master's goods, to satisfy his hunger, keep himself warm, or to gratify his passion for luxurious enjoyment.

The slave sees his master residing in a spacious mansion, riding in a fine carriage, and dressed in costly clothes, and attributes the possession of all these enjoyments to his own labour; whilst he who is the cause of so much gratification and pleasure to another, is himself deprived of even the necessary accommodations of human life. Ignorant men do not and cannot reason logically; and in tracing things from cause to effect, the slave attributes all that he sees in possession of his master, to his own toil, without taking the trouble to examine, how far the skill, judgment, and economy of his master may have contributed to the accumulation of the wealth by which his residence is surrounded. There is, in fact, a mutual dependence between the master and his slave. The former could not acquire any thing without the labour of the latter, and the latter would always remain in poverty, without the former in directing labour to a definite and profitable result.

After I had obtained the virtual command of the fishery, I was careful to awaken the master every morning at sunrise, that he might be present when the division of the fish was made; and when the morning cart arrived, that the carter might not report to my master, that the fish-master was in bed. I had now become interested in preserving the good opinion of my master in favour of his agent.

Since my arrival in Carolina I had never enjoyed a full meal of bacon; and now determined, if possible, to procure such a supply of that luxury, as would enable me and all my fellow-slaves at the fishery to regale ourselves at pleasure. At this season of the year, boats frequently passed up the river, laden with merchandise and goods of various kinds, amongst which were generally large quantities of salt, intended for curing fish, and for other purposes on the plantations. These boats also carried bacon and salted pork up the river, for sale; but they never moved at night, confining their navigation to daylight, and as none of them had hitherto stopped near our landing, we had not met with an opportunity of entering into a traffic with any of the boat masters. We were not always to be so unfortunate. One evening, in the second week of the fishing season, a large keel-boat was seen working up the river about sundown; and shortly after, came to for the night, on the opposite side of the river, directly against our landing. We had at the fishery a small canoe called a punt, about twelve feet long; and when we went to lay out the seine, for the first haul after night, I attached the punt to the side of the canoe, and when we had finished letting down the seine, I left the other hands to work it toward the shore, and ran over in the punt to the keel-boat. Upon inquiring of the captain if he had any bacon that he would exchange for shad, he said, he had a little; but, as the risk he would run in dealing with a slave was great, I must expect to pay him more than the usual price. He at length proposed to give me a hundred pounds of bacon for three hundred shad. This was at least twice as much as the bacon was worth; but we did not bargain as men generally do, where half of the bargain is on each side; for here the captain of the keel-boat settled the terms for both parties. However, he ran the hazard of being prosecuted for dealing with slaves, which is a very high offence in Carolina; and I was selling that which, in point of law, did not belong to me; but to which, nevertheless, I felt in my conscience that I had a better right than any other person. In support of the right, which I felt to be on my side in this case, came a keen appetite for the bacon, which settled the controversy, upon the question of the morality of this traffic, in my favour. It so happened, that we made a good haul with our seine this evening, and at the time I returned to the landing, the men were all on shore, engaged in drawing in the seine. As soon as we had taken out the fish, we placed three hundred of them in one of our canoes, and pushed over to the keel-boat, where the fish were counted out and the bacon was received into our craft with all possible despatch. One part of this small trade exhibited a trait of human character which I think worthy of being noticed. The captain of the boat was a middle-aged, thin, sallow man, with long bushy hair; and he looked like one who valued the opinions of men but little. I expected that he would not be scrupulous in giving me my full hundred pound of bacon; but in this I was mistaken; for he weighed the flitches with great exactness, in a pair of large steelyards, and gave me good weight. When the business was ended, and the bacon in my canoe, he told me, he hoped I was satisfied with him; and assured me, that I should find the bacon excellent. When I was about pushing from the boat, he told me in a low voice, though there was no one who could hear us, except his own people—that he should be down the river again in about two weeks, when he should be very glad to buy any produce that I had for sale; adding, "I will give you half as much for cotton as it is worth in Charleston, and pay you either in money or groceries, as you may choose. Take care, and do not betray yourself, and I shall be honest with you."

I was so much rejoiced, at being in possession of a hundred pounds of good flitch bacon, that I had no room in either my head or my heart, for the consideration of this man's notions of honesty, at the present time; but paddled with all strength for our landing, where we took the bacon from the canoe, stowed it away in an old salt barrel, and safely deposited it in a hole, dug for the purpose in the floor of my cabin.

About this time, our allowance of sweet potatoes was withheld from us altogether, in consequence of the high price paid for this article by the captains of the keel-boats; for the purpose, as I heard, of sending, them to New-York and Philadelphia. Ever since Christmas, we had been permitted to draw, on each Sunday evening, either a peck of corn, as usual, or half a peck of corn, and half a bushel of sweet potatoes at our discretion. The half a peck of corn, and the half a bushel of potatoes was worth much more than a peck of corn; but potatoes were so abundant this year, that they were of little value, and the saving of corn was an object worth attending to by a large planter. The boatmen now offered half a dollar a bushel for potatoes, and we were again restricted to our corn ration.

Notwithstanding the privation of our potatoes, we at the fishery lived sumptuously; although our master certainly believed, that our fare consisted of corn bread and river fish, cooked without lard or butter. It was necessary to be exceedingly cautious in the use of our bacon; and to prevent the suspicions of the master and others, who frequented our landing, I enjoined our people never to fry any of the meat, but to boil it all. No one can smell boiled bacon far; but fried flitch can be smelled a mile by a good nose.

We had two meals every night, one of bacon and the other of fried shad; which nearly deprived us of all appetite for the breakfasts and dinners that we prepared in the daytime; consisting of cold corn bread without salt, and broiled fresh water fish, without any sort of seasoning. We spent more than two weeks in this happy mode of life, unmolested by our master, his son, or the master of the fishery; when the latter complained, rather than threatened us, because we sometimes suffered our seine to float too far down the river, and get entangled amongst some roots and brush that lay on the bottom, immediately below our fishing ground. We now expected, every evening, to see the return of the boatman who had sold us the bacon; and the man who was with me in the canoe, at the time we received it, had not forgotten the invitation of the captain to trade with him in cotton on his return. My fellow-slave was a native of Virginia, as he told me and had been sold and brought to Carolina about ten years before this time. He was a good natured, kind hearted man, and did many acts of benevolence to me, such as one slave is able to perform for another, and I felt a real affection for him; but he had adopted the too common rule of moral action, that there is no harm in a slave robbing his master.

The reader may suppose, from my account of the bacon, that I, too, had adopted this rule as a part of my creed; but I solemnly declare, that this was not the case, and that I never deprived any one of all the masters that I have served, of any thing against his consent, unless it was some kind of food; and that of all I ever took, I am confident, I have given away more than the half to my fellow-slaves, whom I knew to be equally needy with myself.

The man who had been with me at the keelboat told me one day, that he had laid a plan by which we could get thirty or forty dollars, if I would join him in the execution of his project. Thirty or forty dollars was a large sum of money to me. I had never possessed so much money at one time in my life; and I told him that I was willing to do any thing by which we could obtain such a treasure. He then told me, that he knew where the mule and cart that were used by the man who carried away our fish, were kept at night; and that he intended to set out on the first dark night, and go to the plantation—harness the mule to the cart—go to the cotton-gin house—put two bags of cotton into the cart—bring them to a thicket of small pines that grew on the river bank, a short distance below the fishery, and leave them there until the keel-boat should return. All that he desired of me was, to make some excuse for his absence, to the other hands; and assist him to get his cotton into the canoe, at the coming of the boat.

I disliked the whole scheme, both on account of its iniquity, and of the danger which attended it; but my companion was not to be discouraged by all the arguments which I could use against it, and said, if I would not participate in it, he was determined to undertake it alone: provided I would not inform against him. To this I said nothing; but he had so often heard me express my detestation of one slave betraying another, that I presume he felt easy on that score. The next night but one after this conversation, was very dark; and when we went to lay out the seine after night, Nero was missing. The other people inquired of me, if I knew where he was, and when I replied in the negative, little more was said on the subject; it being common for the slaves to absent themselves from habitations at night, and if the matter is not discovered by the overseer or master, nothing is ever said of it by the slaves. The other people supposed that, in this instance, Nero had gone to see a woman whom he lived with as his wife, on a plantation a few miles down the river; and were willing to work a little harder to permit him to enjoy the pleasure of seeing his family. He returned before day, and said he had been to see his wife, which satisfied the curiosity of our companions. The very next evening after Nero's absence, the keel-boat descended the river, came down on our side, hailed us at the fishery, and, drawing in to the shore below our landing, made her ropes fast among the young pines of which I have spoken above. After we made our first haul, I missed Nero; but he returned to us before we had laid out the seine, and told us that he had been in the woods to collect some *light-wood*— dry, resinous pine,—which he brought on his shoulder. When the morning came, the keel-boat was gone, and every thing wore the ordinary aspect about our fishery; but when the man came with the mule and the cart, to take away the fish, he told us that there was great trouble on the plantation. The overseer had discovered, that some one had stolen two bags of cotton the last night, and all the hands were undergoing an examination on the subject. The slaves on the plantation, one and all, denied having any knowledge of the matter, and, as there was no evidence against any one, the overseer threatened, at the time he left the quarter, to whip every hand on the estate, for the purpose of making them discover who the thief was.

The slaves on the plantation differed in opinion as to the perpetrator of this theft; but the greater number concurred in charging it upon a free negro man, named Ishmael, who lived in a place called the White Oak Woods, and followed making ploughs and harrow frames. He also made handles for hoes, and the frame work of cart bodies.

This man was generally reputed a thief for a great distance round the country, and the black people charged him with stealing the cotton on no other evidence than his general bad character. The overseer, on the other hand, expressed his opinion without hesitation; which was, that the cotton had been stolen by some of the people of the plantation, and sold to a poor white man, who resided at the distance of three miles back in the pine woods, and was believed to have dealt with slaves, as a receiver of their stolen goods, for many years.

This white man was one of the class of poor cottagers to whom I have heretofore referred, in this narrative. The house, or cabin, in which he resided, was built of small poles of the yellow pine, with the bark remaining on them; the roof was of clap-boards of pine, and the chimney was made of sticks and mud, raised to the height of eight or ten feet. The appearance of the man and his wife was such as one might expect to find in such a dwelling. The lowest poverty had, through life, been the companion of these poor people, of which their clayey complexions, haggard figures, and tattered garments, gave the strongest proof. It appeared to me, that the state of destitution in which these people lived, afforded very convincing evidence that they were not in possession of the proceeds of the stolen goods of any person. I had often been at the cabin of this man, in my trapping expeditions, the previous autumn and winter; and I believe the overseer regarded the circumstance, that black people often called at his house, as conclusive evidence that he held criminal intercourse with them. However this might be, the overseer determined to search the premises of this harmless forester, whom he resolved, beforehand, to treat as a guilty man.

It being known that I was well acquainted with the woods, in the neighbourhood of the cabin, I was sent for, to leave the fishery, and come to assist in making search for the lost bags of cotton—perhaps it was also believed, that I was in the secrets of the suspected house. It was not thought prudent to trust any of the hands on the plantation in making the intended search, as they were considered the principal thieves; whilst we, of the fishery, against whom no suspicion had arisen, were required to give our assistance, in ferreting out the perpetrators of an offence of the highest grade that can be committed by a slave, on a cotton estate.

Before leaving the fishery, I advised the master to be very careful not to let the overseer, or my master know, that he had left us to manage the fishery at night, by ourselves; since, as a theft had been committed, it might possibly be charged upon him, if it were known that he had allowed us so much liberty. I said this to put the master on his guard against surprise; and to prevent him from saying any thing that might turn the attention of the overseer to the hands at the fishery; for I knew that if punishment were to fall amongst us, it would be quite as likely to reach the innocent as the guilty—besides, though I was innocent of the bags of cotton, I was guilty of the bacon, and, however I might make distinctions between the moral turpitude of the two cases, I knew that if discovered, they would both be treated alike.

When I arrived at the quarter, whither I repaired, in obedience to the orders I received, I found the overseer with my master's eldest son, and a young white man who had been employed to repair the cotton-gin, waiting for me. I observed when I came near the overseer, that he looked at me very attentively and afterwards called my young master aside, and spoke to him in a tone of voice too low to be heard by me. The white gentlemen then mounted their horses, and set off by the road for the cabin of the white man. I had orders to take a short route, through the woods and across a swamp, by which I could reach the cabin as soon as the overseer.

The attentive examination that the overseer had given me, caused me to feel uneasy, although I could not divine the cause of his scrutiny, nor of the subject of the short conversation between him and my young master. By travelling at a rapid pace, I arrived at the cabin of the suspected man before the gentlemen, but thought it prudent not to approach it before they came up, lest it might be imagined that I had gone in to give information to the occupants of the danger that threatened them.

Here I had a hard struggle with my conscience, which seemed to say to me, that I ought at once to disclose all I knew concerning the lost bags of cotton for the purpose of saving these poor people from the terror that they must necessarily feel at the sight of those who were coming to accuse them of a great crime, perhaps from the afflictions and sufferings attendant upon a prosecution in a court of justice.

These reflections were cut short by the arrival of the party of gentlemen, who passed me where I sat, at the side of the path, with no other notice than a simple command of the overseer to come on. I followed them into the cabin, where we found the man and his wife, with two little children, eating roasted potatoes.

The overseer saluted this family by telling them that we had come to search the house for stolen cotton. That it was well known that he had long been dealing with negroes, and they were now determined to bring him to punishment. I was then ordered to tear up the floor of the cabin, whilst the overseer mounted into the loft. I found nothing under the floor, and the overseer had no better success above. The wife was then advised to confess where her husband had concealed the cotton, to save herself from being brought in as a party to the affair; but this poor woman protested with tears that they were totally ignorant of the whole matter. Whilst the wife was interrogated, the father stood without his own door, trembling with fear, but, as I could perceive, indignant with rage.

The overseer, who was fluent in the use of profane language, exerted the highest degree of his vulgar eloquence upon these harmless people, whose only crime was their poverty, and whose weakness alone had invited the ruthless aggression of their powerful and rich neighbours.

Finding nothing in the house, the gentlemen set out to scour the woods around the cabin, and commanded me to take the lead in tracing out tree tops and thickets, where it was most likely that the stolen cotton might be found. Our search was in vain, as I knew it would be beforehand; but when weary of ranging in the woods, the gentlemen again returned to the cabin, which we now found without inhabitants. The alarm caused by our visit, and the manner in which the gentlemen had treated this lonely family, had caused them to abandon their dwelling, and seek safety in flight. The door of the house was closed and fastened with a string to a nail in the post of the door. After calling several times for the fugitives, and receiving no answer, the door was kicked open by my young master; the few articles of miserable furniture that the cabin contained, including a bed, made of flags, were thrown into a heap in the corner, and fire was set to the dwelling by the overseer.

We remained until the flames had reached the roof of the cabin, when the gentlemen mounted their horses and set off for home, ordering me to return by the way that I had come. When we again reached the house of my master, several gentlemen of the neighbourhood had assembled, drawn together by common interest that is felt amongst the planters to punish theft, and particularly a theft of cotton in the bag. My young master related to his neighbours, with great apparent satisfaction, the exploits of the morning; said he had routed one receiver of stolen goods out of the country, and that all others of his character ought to be dealt with in the same manner. In this opinion all the gentlemen present concurred, and after much conversation on the subject, it was agreed to call a general meeting for the purpose of devising the best, surest, and most peaceful method of removing from the country the many white men who, residing in the district without property, or without interest in preserving the morals of the slaves, were believed to carry on an unlawful and criminal traffic with the negroes, to the great injury of the planters in general, and of the masters of the slaves who dealt with the offenders in particular.

I was present at this preliminary consultation, which took place at my master's cotton-gin, whither the gentlemen had repaired for the purpose of looking at the place where the cotton had been removed. So many cases of this forbidden traffic between the slaves and these "white negro dealers," as they were termed, were here related by the different gentlemen, and so many white men were referred to by name as being concerned in this criminal business, that I began to suppose the losses of the planters in this way must be immense. This conference continued until I had totally forgotten the scrutinizing look that I had received from our overseer at the time I came up from the fishery in the morning; but the period had now come when I again was to be reminded of this circumstance, for on a sudden the overseer called me to come forward and let the gentlemen see me. I again felt a sort of vague and undefinable apprehension that no good was to grow out of this examination of my person, but a command of our overseer was not to be disobeyed. After looking at my face, with a kind of leer or side glance, one of the gentlemen, who was an entire stranger to me, and whom I had never before seen, said, "boy you appear to live well; how much meat does your master allow you in a week?" I was almost totally confounded at the name of meat, and felt the blood rush to my heart, but nevertheless forced a sort of smile upon my face, and replied, "My master has been very kind to all his people of late, but has not allowed us any meat for some weeks. We have plenty of good bread, and abundance of river fish, which, together with the heads and roes of the shad that we have salted at the landing, makes a very excellent living for us; though if master would please to give us a little meat now and then, we should be very thankful for it."

This speech, which contained all the eloquence I was master of at the time, seemed to produce some effect in my favour, for the gentleman said nothing in reply, until the overseer, rising from a board on which he had been sitting, came close up to me and said, "Charles, you need not tell lies about it; you have been eating meat, I know you have, no negro could look as fat, and sleek, and black, and greasy, as you, if he had nothing to eat but corn bread and river chubs. You do not look at all as you did before you went to the fishery; and all the hands on the plantation have had as many chubs and other river fish as they could eat, as well as you, and yet they are as poor as snakes in comparison with you. Come, tell us the truth, let us know where you get the meat that you have been eating, and you shall not be whipped." I begged the overseer and the other gentlemen not to ridicule or make sport of me, because I was a poor slave, and was obliged to live on bread and fresh water fish; and concluded this second harangue by expressing my thankfulness to God Almighty, for giving me such good health and strength as to enable me to do my work, and look so well as I did upon such poor fare; adding, that if I only had as much bacon as I could eat, they would soon see a man of a different appearance from that which I now exhibited. "None of your palaver," rejoined the overseer— "Why, I smell the meat in you this moment. Do I not see the grease as it runs out of your face?" I was by this time in a profuse sweat, caused by the anxiety of my feelings, and simply said, "Master sees me sweat, I suppose."

All the gentlemen present then declared, with one accord, that I must have been living on meat for a long time, as no negro, who had no meat to eat, could look as I did; and one of the company advised the overseer to whip me, and compel me to confess the truth. I have no doubt but this advice would have been practically followed, had it not been for a happy, though dangerous suggestion of my own mind, at this moment. It was no other than a proposal on my part, that I should be taken to the landing, and if all the people there did not look as well, and as much like meat-eaters as I did, then I would agree to be whipped in any way the gentlemen should deem expedient. This offer on my part was instantly accepted by the gentlemen, and it was agreed amongst them that they would all go to the landing with the overseer, partly for the purpose of seeing me condemned by the judgment to which I had voluntarily chosen to submit myself, and partly for the purpose of seeing my master's new fishery.

We were quickly at the landing, though four miles distant; and I now felt confident that I should escape the dangers that beset me, provided the master of the fishery did not betray his own negligence, and lead himself, as well as us, into new troubles.

Though on foot, I was at the landing as soon as the gentlemen, and was first to announce to the master the feats we had performed in the course of the day, adding, with great emphasis, and even confidence in my manner, "You know, master fish-master, whether we have had any meat to eat here or not. If we had meat here, would not you see it? You have been up with us every night, and know that we have not been allowed to take even shad, let alone having meat to eat." The fish-master supported me in all I said; declared we had been good boys—had worked night and day, of his certain knowledge, as he had been with us all night and every night since we began to fish. That he had not allowed us to eat any thing but fresh water fish, and the heads and roes of the shad that were salted at the landing. As to meat, he said he was willing to be qualified on a cart load of testaments that there had not been a pound at the landing since the commencement of the season, except that which he had in his own cabin. I had now acquired confidence, and desired the gentlemen to look at Nero and the other hands, all of whom had as much the appearance of bacon eaters as myself. This was the truth, especially with regard to one of the men, who was much fatter than I was.

The gentlemen now began to doubt the evidence of their own senses, which they had held infallible heretofore. I showed the fine fish that we had to eat; cat, perch, mullets, and especially two large pikes, that had been caught to-day, and assured them that upon such fare as this men must needs get fat. I now perceived that victory was with me for once. All the gentlemen faltered, hesitated, and began to talk of other affairs, except the overseer, who still ran about the landing, swearing and scratching his head, and saying it was strange that we were so fat, whilst the hands on the plantation were as lean as sand-hill cranes. He was obliged to give the affair over. He was no longer supported by my young master and his companions, all of whom congratulated themselves upon a discovery so useful and valuable to the planting interest; and all determined to provide, as soon as possible, a proper supply of fresh river fish for their hands.

The two bales of cotton were never once named, and, I suppose, were not thought of by the gentlemen when at the landing; and this was well for Nero; for such was the consternation and terror into which he was thrown, by the presence of the gentlemen and their inquiries concerning our eating of meat, that the sweat rolled off him like rain from the plant *never-wet*; his countenance was wild and haggard, and his knees shook like the wooden spring of a wheat-fan. I believe, that if they had charged him at once with stealing the cotton, he would have confessed the deed.

CHAPTER XVI.

After this, the fishing season passed off without any thing having happened, worthy of being noticed here. When we left the fishery, and returned to the plantation, which was after the middle of April, the corn and cotton had all been planted, and the latter had been replanted. I was set to plough, with two mules for my team; and having never been accustomed to ploughing with these animals, I had much trouble with them at first. My master owned more than forty mules, and at this season of the year, they were all at work in the cotton field, used instead of horses for drawing ploughs. Some of the largest were hitched single to a plough; but the smallest were coupled together.

On the whole, the fishery had been a losing affair with me; for although I had lived better at the landing, than I usually did at the plantation, yet I had been compelled to work all the time, by night and by day, including Sunday, for my master; by which I had lost all that I could have earned for my own benefit, had I been on the plantation. I had now become so well acquainted with the rules of the plantation, and the customs of the country where I lived, that I experienced less distress than I did at my first coming to the south.

We now received a shad every Sunday evening with our peck of corn. The fish were those that I had caught in the spring; and were tolerably preserved. In addition to all this, each one of the hands now received a pint of vinegar, every week. This vinegar was a great comfort to me. As the weather became hot, I gathered lettuce, and other salads, from my garden in the woods; which, with the vinegar and bread, furnished me many a cheerful meal. The vinegar had been furnished to us by our master, more out of regard to our health, than to our comfort; but it greatly promoted both.

The affairs of the plantation now went on quietly, until after the cotton had been ploughed, and hoed the first time, after replanting. The working of the cotton crop is not disagreeable labour—no more so than the culture of corn—but we were called upon to perform a kind of labour, than which none can be more toilsome to the body, or dangerous to the health.

I have elsewhere informed the reader, that my master was a cultivator of rice, as well as of cotton. Whilst I was at the fishery in the spring, thirty acres of swamp land had been cleared off, ploughed, and planted in rice. The water had now been turned off the plants, and the field was to be ploughed and hoed. When we were taken to the rice field, the weather was very hot, and the ground was yet muddy and wet. The ploughs were to be dragged through the wet soil, and the young rice had to be cleaned of weeds, by the hand, and hilled up with the hoe.

It is the common opinion, that no stranger can work a week in a rice swamp, at this season of the year, without becoming sick; and all the new hands, three in number, besides myself, were taken ill within the first five days, after we had entered this field. The other three were removed to the sick room; but I did not go there, choosing rather to remain at the quarter, where I was my own master, except that the doctor, who called to see me, took a large quantity of blood from my arm, and compelled pelted me to take a dose of some sort of medicine that made me very sick, and caused me to vomit violently. This happened on the second day of my illness, and from this time I recovered slowly, but was not able to go to the field again for more than a week. Here it is but justice to my master to say, that during all the time of my illness, some one came from the great house, every day, to inquire after me, and to offer me some kind of light and cool refreshment I might have gone to the sick room at any time, if I had chosen to do so.

An opinion generally prevails, amongst the people of both colours, that the drug *copperas* is very poisonous—and perhaps it may be so, if taken in large quantities—but the circumstance, that it is used in medicine, seems to forbid the notion of its poisonous qualities. I believe copperas was mingled with the potion the doctor gave to me. Some overseers keep copperas by them, as a medicine, to be administered to the hands whenever they become sick; but this I take to be a bad practice; for although, in some cases, this drug may be very efficacious, it certainly should be administered by a more skilful hand than that of an overseer. It, however, has the effect of deterring the people from complaining of illness, until they are no longer able to work; for it is the most nauseous and sickening medicine that was ever taken into the stomach. Ignorant, or malicious overseers may, and often do, misapply it; as was the case with our overseer, when he compelled poor Lydia to take a draught of its solution. After the restoration of my health, I resumed my accustomed labour in the field, and continued it without intermission, until I left this plantation.

We had, this year, as a part of our crop, ten acres of indigo. This plant is worked nearly after the manner of rice, except, that it is planted on high and dry ground, whilst the rice is always cultivated in low swamps, where the ground may be inundated with water; but notwithstanding its location on dry ground, the culture of indigo is not less unpleasant than that of rice. When the rice is ripe, and ready for the sickle, it is no longer disagreeable; but when the indigo is ripe and ready to cut, the troubles attendant upon it, have only commenced.

The indigo plant bears more resemblance to the weed called wild indigo, which is common in the woods of Pennsylvania, than to any other herb with which I am acquainted.

The root of the indigo plant is long and slender, and emits a scent somewhat like that of parsley. From the root issues a single stem, straight, hard, and slender, covered with a bark, a little cracked on its surface, of a gray colour towards the bottom, green in the middle, reddish at the extremity, and without the appearance of pith in the inside. The leaves ranged in pairs around the stalk, are of an oval form,—smooth, soft to the touch, furrowed above, and of a deep green on the under side. The upper parts of the plant are loaded with small flowers, destitute of smell. Each flower changes into a pod, enclosing seed.

This plant thrives best in a rich, moist soil. The seeds are black, very small, and sowed in straight drills. This crop requires very careful culture, and must be kept free from every kind of weeds and grass. It ripens within less than three months from the time it is sown. When it begins to flower, the top is cut off, and, as new flowers appear, the plant is again pruned, until the end of the season.

Indigo impoverishes land more rapidly than almost any other crop, and the plant must be gathered in with great caution, for fear of shaking off the valuable farina that lies in the leaves. When gathered, it is thrown into the steeping vat—a large tub filled with water—here it undergoes a fermentation which, in twenty-four hours, at farthest, is completed. A cock is then turned to let the water run into the second tub, called the mortar, or pounding tub: the steeping vat is then cleaned out, that fresh plants may be thrown in; and thus the work is continued, without interruption. The water in the pounding tub is stirred with wooden buckets, with holes in their bottoms, for several days; and, after the sediment contained in the water, has settled to the bottom of the tub, the water is let off, and the sediment, which is the indigo of commerce, is gathered into bags, and hung up to drain. It is afterwards pressed, and laid away to dry in cakes, and then packed in chests for market.

Washing at the tubs is exceedingly unpleasant, both on account of the filth and the stench, arising from the decomposition of the plants.

In the early part of June, our shad, that each one had been used to receive, was withheld from us, and we no longer received any thing but the peck of corn, and pint of vinegar. This circumstance, in a community less severely disciplined than ours, might have procured murmurs; but to us it was only announced by the fact of the fish not being distributed to us on Sunday evening.

This was considered a fortunate season by our people. There had been no exemplary punishment inflicted amongst us, for several months; we had escaped entirely upon the occasion of the stolen bags of cotton, though nothing less was to have been looked for, on that occurrence, than a general whipping of the whole gang.

There was more or less of whipping amongst us, every week; frequently, one was flogged every evening, over and above the punishments that followed on each settlement day; but these chastisements, which seldom exceeded ten or twenty lashes, were of little import. I was careful, for my own part, to conform to all the regulations of the plantation.

When I no longer received my fish from the overseer, I found it necessary again to resort to my own expedients, for the purpose of procuring something in the shape of animal food, to add to my bread and greens.

I had, by this time, become well acquainted with the woods and swamps, for several miles round our plantation; and this being the season when the turtles came upon the land, to deposite their eggs, I availed myself of it, and going out one Sunday morning, caught, in the course of the day, by travelling cautiously around the edges of the swamps, ten snapping turtles, four of which were very large. As I caught these creatures, I tied each one with hickory bark, and hung it up to the bough of a tree, so that I could come and carry it home at my leisure.

I afterwards carried my turtles home, and put them into a hole that I dug in the ground, four or five feet deep, and secured the sides by driving small pieces of split timber into the ground, quite round the circumference of the hole, the upper ends of the timber standing out above the ground. Into this hole I poured water at pleasure, and kept my turtles until I needed them.

On the next Sunday, I again went to the swamps to search for turtles; but as the period of laying their eggs had nearly passed, I had poor success to day, only taking two turtles of the species called skill-pots— a kind of large terrapin, with a speckled back and red belly.

This day, when I was three or four miles from home, in a very solitary part of the swamps, I heard the sound of bells, similar to those which wagoners place on the shoulders of their horses. At first, the noise of bells of this kind, in a place where they were so unexpected, alarmed me, as I could not imagine who or what it was that was causing these bells to ring. I was standing near a pond of water, and listening attentively; I thought the bells were moving in the woods, and coming toward me. I therefore crouched down upon the ground, under cover of a cluster of small bushes that were near me, and lay, not free from disquietude, to await the near approach of these mysterious bells.

Sometimes they were quite silent for a minute or more at a time, and then again would jingle quick, but not loud. They were evidently approaching me, and at length I heard footsteps distinctly in the leaves, which lay dry upon the ground. A feeling of horror seized me at this moment, for I now recollected that I was on the verge of the swamp, near which the vultures and carrion crows had mangled the living bodies of the two murderers; and my terror was not abated, when, a moment after, I saw come from behind a large tree, the form of a brawny, famished-looking black man, entirely naked, with his hair matted and shaggy, his eyes wild and rolling, and bearing over his head something in the form of an arch, elevated three feet above his hair, beneath the top of which were suspended the bells, three in number, whose sound had first attracted my attention. Upon a closer examination this frightful figure, I perceived that it wore a collar of iron about its neck, with a large padlock pendent from behind, and carried in its hand a long staff, with an iron spear in one end. The staff, like every thing else belonging to this strange spectre, was black. It slowly approached within ten paces of me, and stood still.

The sun was now down, and the early twilight produced by the gloom of the heavy forest, in the midst of which I was, added approaching darkness to heighten my dismay. My heart was in my mouth; all the hairs of my head started from their sockets; I seemed to be rising from my hiding place into the open air, in spite of myself, and I gasped for breath.

The black apparition moved past me, went to the water and kneeled down. The forest re-echoed with the sound of the bells, and their dreadful peals filled the deepest recesses of the swamps, as their bearer, drank the water of the pond, in which I thought I heard his irons hiss, when they came in contact with it. I felt confident that I was now in the immediate presence of an inhabitant of a nether fiery world, who had been permitted to escape, for a time, from the place of his torment, and come to revisit the scenes of his former crimes. I now gave myself up for lost, without other aid than my own, and began to pray aloud to heaven to protect me. At the sound of my voice, the supposed evil one appeared to be scarcely less alarmed than I was. He sprang to his feet, and, at a single bound, rushed into the water, then turning, he besought me in a suppliant and piteous tone of voice, to have mercy upon him, and not carry him back to his master.

The suddenness with which we pass from the extreme of one passion, to the utmost bounds of another, is inconceivable, and must be assigned to the catalogue of unknown causes and effects, unless we suppose the human frame to be an involuntary machine, operated upon by surrounding objects which give it different and contrary impulses, as a ball is driven to and fro by the batons of boys, when they play in troops upon a common. I had no sooner heard a human voice than all my fears fled, as a spark that ascends from a heap of burning charcoal, and vanishes to nothing.

I at once perceived, that the object that had well nigh deprived me of my reason, so far from having either the will or the power to injure me, was only a poor destitute African negro, still more wretched and helpless than, myself.

Rising from the bushes, I now advanced to the water side, and desired him to come out without fear, and to be assured that if I could render him any assistance I would do it most cheerfully. As to carrying him back to his master, I was more ready to ask help to deliver me from my own, than to give aid to any one in forcing him back to his.

We now went to a place in the forest, where the ground was, for some distance, clear of trees, and where the light of the sun was yet so strong that every object could be seen. My new friend now desired me to look at his back, which was seamed and ridged with scars of the whip, and the hickory, from the pole of his neck to the lower extremity of the spine. The natural colour of the skin had disappeared and was succeeded by a streaked and speckled appearance of dusky white and pale flesh colour, scarcely any of the original black remaining. The skin of this man's back had been again and again cut away by the thong, and renewed by the hand of nature, until it was grown fast to the flesh, and felt hard and turbid.

He told me his name was Paul; that he was a native of Congo, in Africa, and had been a slave five years; that he had left an aged mother, a widow, at home, as also a wife and four children; that it had been his misfortune to fall into the hands of a master, who was frequently drunk, and whose temper was so savage, that his chief delight appeared to consist in whipping and torturing his slaves, of whom he owned near twenty; but through some unaccountable caprice, he had contracted a particular dislike against Paul, whose life he now declared to me, was insupportable. He had then been wandering in the woods, more than three weeks, with no other subsistence than the land tortoises, frogs, and other reptiles that he had taken in the woods, and along the shores of the ponds, with the aid of his spear. He had not been able to take any of the turtles in the laying season, because the noise of his bells frightened them, and they always escaped to the water before he could catch them. He had found many eggs, which he had eaten raw, having no fire, nor any means of making fire, to cook his food. He had been afraid to travel much in the middle of the day, lest the sound of his bells should be heard by some one, who would make his master acquainted with the place of his concealment. The only periods when he ventured to go in search of food, were early in the morning, before people could have time to leave their homes and reach the swamp; or late in the evening, after those who were in pursuit of him had gone to their dwellings for the night.

This man spoke our language imperfectly, but possessed a sound and vigorous understanding; and reasoned with me upon the propriety of destroying a life which was doomed to continual distress. He informed me that he had first run away from his master more than two years ago, after being whipped, with long hickory switches, until he fainted. That he concealed himself in a swamp, at that time, ten or fifteen miles from this place, for more than six months, but was finally betrayed by a woman who he sometimes visited; that when taken, he was again whipped until he was not able to stand, an had a heavy block of wood chained to one foot, which he was obliged to drag after him at his daily labour, for more than three months, when he found an old file, with which he cut the irons from his ancle, and again escaped to the woods, but was retaken within little more than a week after his flight, by two men who were looking for their cattle, and came upon him in the woods where he was asleep.

On being returned to his master, he was again whipped; and then the iron collar that he now wore with the iron rod, extending from one shoulder over his head to the other, with the bells fastened at the top of the arch, were put upon him. Of these irons he could not divest himself, and wore them constantly from that time to the present.

I had no instruments with me, to enable we to release Paul from his manacles, and all I could do for him was to desire him to go with me to the place where I had left my terrapins, which I gave to him together with all the eggs that I had found to day. I also caused him to lie down, and having furnished myself with a flint-stone, (many of which lay in the sand near the edge of the pond) and a handful of dry moss, I succeeded in striking fire from the iron collar, and made a fire of sticks, upon which he could roast the terrapins and the eggs. It was now quite dark, and I was full two miles from my road, with no path to guide me towards home, but the small traces made in the woods by the cattle.

I advised Paul to bear his misfortunes as well as he could, until the next Sunday, when I would return and bring with me a file, and other things necessary to the removal of his fetters.

I now set out alone, to make my way home, not without some little feeling of trepidation, as I passed along in the dark shade of the pine trees, and thought of the terrific deeds that had been done in these woods.

This was the period of the full moon, which now rose, and cast her brilliant rays through the tops of the trees that overhung my way, and enveloped my path in a gloom more cheerless than the obscurity of total darkness. The path I travelled led by sinuosities around the margin of the swamp, and finally ended at the extremity of the cart-road terminating at the spot where David and Hardy had been given alive for food to vultures; and over this ground I was now obliged to pass, unless I chose to turn far to the left, through the pathless forest, and make my way to the high road near the spot where the lady had been torn from her horse. I hated the idea of acknowledging to my own heart, that I was a coward, and dared not look upon the bones of a murderer at midnight; and there was little less of awe attached to the notion of visiting the ground where the ghost of the murdered woman was reported to wander in the moonbeams, than in visiting the scene where diabolical crimes had been visited by fiend-like punishment.

My opinion is, that there is no one who is not at times subject to a sensation approaching fear, when placed in situations similar to that in which I found myself this night. I did not believe that those who had passed the dark line, which separates the living from the dead, could again return to the earth, either for good or for evil; but that solemn foreboding of the heart which directs the minds of all men to a contemplation of the just judgment, which a superior, and unknown power, holds in reservation for the deeds of this life, filled my soul with a dread conception of the unutterable woes which a righteous and unerring tribunal must award to the blood-stained spirits of the two men whose lives had been closed in such unspeakable torment by the side of the path I was now treading.

The moon had risen high above the trees, and shone with a clear and cloudless light; the whole firmament of heaven was radiant with the lustre of a mild and balmy summer evening. Save only the droppings of the early dew from the lofty branches of the trees into the water, which lay in shallow pools on my right, and the light trampling of my own footsteps; the stillness of night pervaded the lonely wastes around me. But there is a deep melancholy in the sound of the heavy drop as it meets the bosom of the wave in a dense forest at night, that revives in the memory the recollection of the days of other years, and fills the heart with sadness.

I was now approaching the unhallowed ground where lay the remains of the remorseless and guilty dead who had gone to their final account, reeking in their sins, unatoned, unblest, and unwept. Already I saw the bones, whitened by the rain, and bleached in the sun, lying scattered and dispersed, a leg here and an arm there, whilst a scull with the tinder jaw in its place, retaining all its teeth, grinned a ghastly laugh, with its front full in the beams of the moon, which, falling into the vacant sockets of the eye-balls, reflected a pale shadow from these deserted caverns, and played in twinkling lustre upon the bald, and skinless forehead.

In a moment, the night-breeze agitated the leaves of the wood and moaned in dreary sighs through the lofty pine tops; the gale shook the forest in the depth of its solitudes: a cloud swept across the moon, and her light disappeared; a flock of carrion crows disturbed in their roosts, flapped their wings and fluttered over my head; and a wolf, who had been gnawing the dry bones, greeted the darkness with a long and dismal howl.

I felt the blood chill in my veins, and all my joints shuddered, as if I had been smitten by electricity. At least a minute elapsed before I recovered the power of self-government. I hastened to fly from a place devoted to crime, where an evil genius presided in darkness over a fell assembly of howling wolves, and blood-snuffing vultures.

When I arrived at the quarter, all was quiet. The inhabitants of this mock-village were wrapped ill forgetfulness; and I stole silently into my little loft and joined my neighbours in their repose. Experience had made me so well acquainted with the dangers that beset the life of a slave, that I determined as a matter of prudence, to say nothing to any one, of the adventures of this Sunday; but went to work on Monday morning, at the summons of the overseer's horn, as if nothing unusual had occurred. In the course of the week, I often thought of the forlorn and desponding African; who had so terrified me in the woods, and, who seemed so grateful for the succour I gave him. I felt anxious to become better acquainted with this man, who possessed knowledge superior to the common race of slaves, and manifested a moral courage in the conversation that I had with him, worthy of a better fate than that to which fortune had consigned him. On the following Sunday, having provided myself with a large file, which I procured from the blacksmith shop, belonging to the plantation, I again repaired to the place, at the side of the swamp, where I had first seen the figure of this ill-fated man. I expected that he would be in waiting for me at the appointed place, as I had promised him that I would certainly come again, at this time; but on arriving at the spot where I had left him, I saw no sign of any person. The remains of the fire that I had kindled were here, and it seemed that the fire had been kept up for several days, by the quantity of ashes that lay in a heap, surrounded by numerous small brands. The impressions of human feet, were thickly disposed around this decayed fire: and the bones of the terrapins that I had given to Paul, as well as the skeletons of many frogs, were scattered upon the ground; but there was nothing that showed that any one had visited this spot, since the fall of the last rain, which I now recollected had taken place on the previous Thursday. From this circumstance I concluded that Paul had relieved himself of his irons, and gone to seek concealment in some other place; or that his master had discovered his retreat, and carried him back to the plantation.

Whilst standing at the ashes I heard the croaking of ravens at some distance in the woods, and immediately afterwards a turkey-buzzard passed over me pursued by an eagle, coming from the quarter in which I had just heard the ravens. I knew that the eagle never pursued the buzzard for the purpose of preying upon him, but only to compel him to disgorge himself of his own prey for the benefit of the king of birds. I therefore concluded that there was some dead animal in my neighbourhood that had called all these ravenous fowls together. It might be that Paul had killed a cow by knocking her down with a pine knot, and that he had removed his residence to this slaughtered animal. Curiosity was aroused in me, and I proceeded to examine the woods.

I had not advanced more than two hundred yards when I felt oppressed by a most sickening stench, and saw the trees swarming with birds of prey, buzzards perched upon their branches, ravens sailing their boughs, and clouds of carrion crows flitting about, and poising themselves in the air in a stationary position, after the manner of that most nauseous of all birds, when it perceives, or thinks it perceives, some object of prey. Proceeding onward, I came in view of a large sassafras tree, around the top of which was congregated a cloud of crows, some on the boughs and others on the wing, whilst numerous buzzards were sailing low and nearly skimming the ground. This sassafras tree had many low horizontal branches, attached to one of which I now saw the cause of so vast an assembly of the obscene fowls of the air. The lifeless and putrid body of the unhappy Paul hung suspended by a cord made of twisted hickory bark, passed in the form of a halter round the neck, and firmly bound to a limb of the tree.

It was manifest that he had climbed the tree, fastened the cord to the branch, and then sprung off. The smell that assailed my nostrils was too overwhelming to permit me to remain long in view of the dead body, which was much mangled and torn, though its identity was beyond question, for the iron collar, and the bells with the arch that bore them, were still in their place. The bells had preserved the corpse from being devoured; for whilst I looked at it I observed a crow descend upon it, and make a stroke at the face with its beak, but the motion that this gave to the bells caused them to rattle, and the bird took to flight.

Seeing that I could no longer render assistance to Paul, who was now beyond the reach of his master's tyranny, as well as of my pity, I returned without delay to my master's house, and going into the kitchen, related to the household servants that I had found a black man hung in the woods with bells upon him. This intelligence was soon communicated to my master, who sent for me to come into the house to relate the circumstance to him. I was careful not to tell that I had seen Paul before his death; and when I had finished my narrative, my master observed to a gentleman who was with him, that this was a heavy loss to the owner, and told me to go.

The body of Paul was never taken down, but remained hanging where I had seen it until the flesh fell from the bones, or was torn off by the birds. I saw the bones hanging in the sassafras tree more than two months afterwards, and the last time that I was ever in these swamps.

CHAPTER XVII.

An affair was now in progress, which, though the persons who were actors in it were far removed from me, had in its effects a great influence upon the fortunes of my life. I have informed the reader that my master had three daughters, and that the second of the sisters was deemed a great beauty. The eldest of the three was married about the time of which I now write to a planter of great wealth, who resided near Columbia; but the second had formed an attachment to a young gentleman whom she had frequently seen at the church attended by my master's family. As this young man, either from want of wealth, or proper persons to introduce him, had never been at my master's house, my young mistress had no opportunity of communicating to him the sentiments she entertained towards him, without violating the rules of modesty in which she had been educated. Before she would attempt any thing which might be deemed a violation of the decorum of her sex, she determined to take a new method of obtaining a husband. She communicated to her father, my master, a knowledge of the whole affair, with a desire that he would invite the gentleman of her choice to his house. This the father resolutely opposed, upon the ground that the young man upon whom his daughter had fixed her heart was without property, and consequently destitute of the means of supporting his daughter in a style suitable to the rank she occupied in society. A woman in love is not easily foiled in her purposes; my young mistress, by continual entreaties, so far prevailed over the affections, or more probably the fears of her father, that he introduced the young man to his family, and about two months afterwards my young mistress was a bride; but it had been agreed amongst all the parties, as I understood, before the marriage, that as the son-in-law had no land or slaves of his own, he should remove with his wife to a large tract of land that my master owned in the new purchase in the state of Georgia.

In the month of September, 1806, my master came to the quarter one evening, at the time of our return from the field, in company with his son-in-law, and informed me that he had given me, with a number of others of his slaves, to his daughter; and that I, with eight other men and two or three women, must set out on the next Sunday with my new master, for his estate in Georgia, whither we were to go, to clear land, build houses, and make other improvements necessary for the reception of the newly-married lady, in the following spring.

I was much pleased with the appearance and manners of my new master, who was a young man apparently about twenty-seven or eight years old, and of good figure. We were to take with us, in our expedition to Georgia, a wagon, to be drawn by six mules, and I was appointed to drive the team. Before we set off my young mistress came in person to the quarter, and told us that all those who were going to the new settlement must come to the house, where she furnished each of us with two full suits of clothes, one of coarse woollen, and the other of hempen cloth. She also gave a hat to each of us, and two pairs of shoes, with a trifle in money, and enjoined us to be good boys and girls, and get things ready for her, and that when she should come to live with us we should not be forgotten. The conduct of this young lady was so different from that which I had been accustomed to witness since I came to Carolina, that I considered myself highly fortunate in becoming her slave, and now congratulated myself with the idea that I should, in future, have a mistress who would treat me kindly, and if I behaved well, would not permit me to want.

At the time appointed we set out for Georgia, with all the tools and implements necessary to the prosecution of a new settlement. My young master accompanied us, and travelled slowly for several days to enable me to keep up with him. We continued our march in this order until we reached the Savannah river at the town of Augusta, where my master told me that he was so well satisfied with my conduct, that he intended to leave me with the team to bring on the goods and the women and children; but that he would take the men and push on, as fast as possible, to the new settlement, and go to work until the time of my arrival. He gave me directions to follow on and inquire for Morgan county Court House, and said that he would have a person ready there on my arrival to guide me to him and the people with him. He then gave me twenty dollars to buy food for the mules and provisions for myself and those with me, and left me on the high road master of myself and the team. I was resolved that this striking proof of confidence on the part of my master should not be a subject of regret to him, and pursued my route with the greatest diligence, taking care to lay out as little money as possible for such things as I had to buy. On the sixth day, in the morning, I arrived at our new settlement in the middle of a heavy forest of such timber as is common to that country, with three dollars and twenty-five cents in my pocket, part of the money given to me at Augusta. This I offered to return, but my master refused to take it, and told me to keep it for my good conduct. I now felt assured that all my troubles in this world were ended, and that, in future, I might look forward to a life of happiness and ease; for I did not consider labour any hardship, if I was well provided with good food and clothes, and my other wants properly regarded.

My master, and the people who were with him, had, before our arrival with the wagon, put up the logs of two cabins, and were engaged, when we came, in covering one of them with clapboards. In the course of the next day we completed both these cabins, with puncheon floors and small glass windows, the sash and glass for which I had brought in the wagon. We put up two other cabins, and a stable for the mules, and then began to clear land. After a few days, my master told me he meant to go down into the settlements to buy provisions for the winter, and that he should leave me to oversee the hands, and carry on the work in his absence. He accordingly left us, taking with him the wagon and two boys, one to drive the team, and another to drive cattle and hogs, which he intended to buy and drive to our settlement. I now felt myself almost proprietor of our new establishment, and believe the men left under my charge did not consider me a very lenient overseer. I in truth compelled them to work very hard, as I did myself. At the end of a week my master returned with a heavy load of meal and bacon, with salt and other things that we needed, and the day following a white man drove to our station several cows, and more than twenty hogs the greater part of which were breeders. At this season of the year neither the hogs nor the cattle required any feeding at our hands. The woods were full of nuts, and the grass was abundant; but we gave salt to our stock, and kept the hogs in a pen, two or three days, to accustom them to the place.

We now lived very differently from what we did on my old master's plantation. We had as much bacon every day as we could eat; which, together with bread and sweet potatoes, which we had at will, constituted our fare. My master remained with us more than two months; within which time we had cleared forty acres of ground, ready for the plough; but, a few days before Christmas, an event took place, which, in its consequences, destroyed all my prospects of happiness, and totally changed the future path of my life. A messenger one day came to our settlement, with a letter, which had been forwarded in this manner, by the postmaster at the Court House, where the post-office was kept. This letter contained intelligence of the sudden death of my old master; and that difficulties had arisen in the family which required the immediate attention of my young one. The letter was written by my mistress. My master, forthwith, took all account of the stock of provisions, and other things that he had on hand, and putting the whole under my charge, gave me directions to attend to the work, and set off on horseback that evening; promising to return within one month at furthest. We never saw him again, and heard nothing of him until late in the month of January, 1807, when the eldest son of my late master came to our settlement, in company with a strange gentleman. The son of my late master informed me, to my surprise and sorrow, that my young waster, who had brought us to Georgia, was dead; and that he, and the gentleman with him, were administrators of the deceased, and had come to Georgia for the purpose of letting out on lease, for the period of seven years, our place, with all the people on it, including me.

To me, the most distressing part of this news, was the death of my young master; and I was still more sorry when I learned, that he had been killed in a duel. My young mistress, whose beauty had drawn around her numerous suiters, many of whom were men of base minds and cowardly hearts, had chosen her husband, in the manner I have related; and his former rivals, after his return from Georgia, confederated together, for the dastardly purpose of revenging themselves, of both husband and wife, by the murder of the former.

In all parts of the cotton country, there are numerous taverns, which answer the double purpose of drinking and gambling houses. These places are kept by men who are willing to abandon all pretensions to the character and standing of gentlemen, for the hope of sordid gain; and are frequented by all classes of planters; though it is not to be understood, that all the planters resort to these houses. There are men of high and honourable virtue amongst the planters, who equally detest the mean cupidity of the men who keep these houses, and the silly wickedness of those who support them. Billiard is the game regarded as the most polite, amongst men of education and fashion; but cards, dice, and every kind of game, whether of skill or of hazard, are openly played in these sinks of iniquity. So far as my knowledge extends, there is not a single district of ten miles square, in all the cotton region, without at least one of these vile ordinaries, as they are frequently and justly termed. The keeping of these houses is a means of subsistence resorted to by men of desperate reputation, or reckless character; and they invite, as guests, all the profligate, the drunken, the idle, and the unwary of the surrounding country. In a community, where the white man never works, except at the expense of forfeiting all claim to the rank of a gentleman, and where it is beneath the dignity of a man, to oversee the labour of his own plantation, the number of those who frequent these gaming houses, may be imagined.

My young master, fortunately for his own honour, was of those who kept aloof from the precincts of the tavern, unless compelled by necessary business to go there; but the band of conspirators, who had resolved on his destruction, invited him through one of their number, who pretended to wish to treat with him concerning his property, to meet them at an ordinary, one evening. Here a quarrel was sought him, and he was challenged to fight with pistols over the table around which they sat.

My master, who, it appears, was unable to bear the reproach of cowardice, even amongst fools, agreed to fight; and as he had no pistols with him, was presented with a pair belonging to one of the gang; and accepted their owner, as his friend, or second in the business. The result was as might have been expected. My master was killed, at the first fire, by a ball which passed through his breast, whilst his antagonist escaped unharmed.

A servant was immediately despatched, with a letter to my mistress, informing her of the death of her husband. She was awakened in the night, to read the letter, the bearer having informed her maid that it was necessary for her to see it immediately. The shock drove her into a feverish delirium, from which she never recovered. At, periods, her reason resumed its dominion; but in the summer following, she became a mother, and died in child-bed, of puerperal fever. I obtained this account from the mouth of a black man, who was the travelling servant of the eldest son of my old master, and who was with his master at the time he came to visit the tenant, to whom he let his sister's estate in Georgia, in the year 1807.

The estate to which I was now attached, was advertised to be rented for the term of seven years, with all the stock of mules, cattle, and so forth, upon it—together with seventeen slaves, six of whom were too young to be able to work at present. The price asked, was one thousand dollars for the first year and two thousand dollars for each of the six succeeding years; the tenant to be bound to clear thirty acres of land annually.

Before the day on which the estate was to be let, by the terms of the advertisement, a man came from the neighbourhood of Savannah, and agreed to take the new plantation, on the terms asked. He was immediately put intop ossession of the premises, and from this moment, I became his slave for the term of seven years.

Fortune had now thrown me into the power of a new master, of whom, when I considered the part of the country from whence he came, which had always been represented to me, as distinguished for the cruelty with which slaves were treated in it, I had no reason to expect much that was good. I had indeed, from the moment I saw this new master, and had learned the place of his former residence, made up my mind to prepare myself for a harsh servitude; but as we are often disappointed for the worse, so it sometimes happens, that we are deceived for the better. This man was by no means so bad as I was prepared to find him; and yet, I experienced all the evils in his service, that I had ever apprehended: but I could never find in my heart, to entertain a revengeful feeling towards him, for he was as much a slave as I was; and I believe of the two, the greater sufferer. Perhaps the evils he endured himself, made him more compassionate of the sorrows of others; but notwithstanding the injustice that was done me while with him, I could never look upon him as a bad man.

At the time he took possession of the estate, he was alone, and did not let us know that he had a wife, until after he had been with us, at least two weeks. One day, however, he called us together, and told us that he was going down the country, to bring up his family—that he wished us to go on with the work on the place in the manner he pointed out; and telling the rest of the hands that they must obey my orders, he left us. He was gone full two weeks; and when he returned, I had all the cleared land planted in cotton, corn, and sweet potatoes, and had progressed with the business of the plantation so much to his satisfaction, that he gave me a dollar, with which I bought a pair of new trousers—my old ones having been worn out in clearing the new land, and burning logs.

My master's family, a wife and one child, came with him; and my new mistress soon caused me to regret the death of my former young master, for other reasons, than those of affection and esteem.

This woman (though she was my mistress, I cannot call her lady) was the daughter of a very wealthy planter, who resided near

Milledgeville, and had several children, besides my mistress. My master was a native of North Carolina—had removed to Georgia several years before this—had acquired some property and was married to my mistress more than two years, when I became his slave, for a term of years as I have stated. I saw many families, and was acquainted with the moral character of many ladies, while I lived in the south; but I must, in justice to the country, say, that my new mistress was the worst woman I ever saw amongst the southern people. Her temper was as bad as that of a speckled viper; and her language, when she was enraged, was a mere vocabulary of profanity and virulence.

My master and mistress brought with them when they came, twelve slaves, great and small, seven of whom were able to do field work. We now had on our new place, a very respectable force; and my master was a man, who understood the means of procuring a good day's work from his hands, as well as any of his neighbours. He was also a man who, when left to pursue his own inclinations, was kind and humane in his temper, and conduct towards his people; and if he had possessed courage enough, to whip his wife two or three times, as he sometimes whipped his slaves, and to compel her to observe a rule of conduct befitting her sex, I should have had a tolerable time of my servitude with him; and should, in all probability, have been a slave in Georgia until this day. Before my mistress came, we had meat in abundance; for my master had left his keys with me, and I dealt out the provisions to the people.

Lest my master should complain of me at his return, or suspect that I had not been faithful to my trust, I had only allowed ourselves (for I fared in common with the others) one meal of meat in each day. We had several cows, that supplied us with and a barrel of molasses was amongst the stores of provisions. We had mush, sweet potatoes, milk, molasses, and sometimes butter for breakfast and supper, and meat for dinner. Had we been permitted to enjoy this fine fare, after the arrival of our mistress, and had she been a woman of kindly disposition, and lady-like manners, I should have considered myself well off in the world; for I was now living in as good a country as I ever saw; and I much doubt if there is a better one anywhere.

Our mistress gave us a specimen of her character on the first morning after her arrival amongst us, by beating severely, with a raw cow-hide, the black girl who nursed the infant, because the child cried, and could not be kept silent. I perceived by this, that my mistress possessed no control over her passions; and that, when enraged, she would find some victim to pour her fury upon, without regard to justice or mercy.

When we were called to dinner to-day, we had no meat, and a very short supply of bread; our meal being composed of badly cooked sweet potatoes, some bread, and a very small quantity of sour milk. From this time our allowance of meat was withdrawn from us altogether, and we had to live upon our bread, potatoes, and the little milk that our mistress permitted us to have. The most vexatious part of the new discipline, was the distinction that was made between us, who were on the plantation before our mistress came to it, and the slaves that she brought with her. To these latter, she gave the best part of the sour milk, all the buttermilk, and I believe, frequently rations of meat.

We were not on our part (I mean us of the old stock) wholly without meat, for our master sometimes gave us a whole flitch of bacon at once; this he had stolen from his own smoke-house—I say stolen, because he took it without the knowledge of my mistress, and always charged us in the most solemn manner not to let her know that we had received it. She was as negligent of the duties of a good housewife, as she was arrogant in assuming the control of things not within the sphere of her domestic duties, and never missed the bacon that our master gave to us, because she had not taken the trouble of examining the state of the meat-house. Obtaining all the meat we ate by stealth, through our master, our supplies were not regular, coming once or twice a-week, according to circumstances. However, I was satisfied of the good intentions of my master towards me, I felt interested in his welfare, and in a short time became warmly attached to him. He fared but little better at the hands of my mistress than I did, except that as he ate at the same table with her, he always had enough of comfortable food; but in the matter of ill language, I believe my master and I might safely have put our goods together as a joint stock in trade, without either the one or the other being greatly the loser. I had secured the good opinion of my master, and it was perceivable by any one that he had more confidence in me than in any of his other slaves, and often treated me as the foreman of his people.

This aroused the indignation of my mistress, who, with all her ill qualities, retained a sort of selfish esteem for the slaves who had come with her from her father's estate. She seldom saw me without giving me her customary salutation of profanity; and she exceeded all other persons that I have ever known in the quickness and sarcasm of the jibes and jeers with which she seasoned her oaths. To form any fair conception of her volubility and scurrilous wit, it was necessary to hear her, more especially on Sunday morning or a rainy day, when the people were all loitering about the kitchens, which stood close round her dwelling. She treated my master with no more ceremony than she did me. Misery loves company, it is said, and I verily believe that my master and I felt a mutual attachment on account of our mutual sufferings.

CHAPTER XVIII.

The country I now lived in was new, and abounded with every sort of game common to a new settlement. Wages were high, and I could sometimes earn a dollar and a half a day by doing job work on Sunday. The price of a day's work here was a dollar. My master paid me regularly and fairly for all the work I did for him on Sunday, and I never went anywhere else to procure work. All his other hands were treated in the same way. He also gave me an old gun that had seen much hard service, for the stock was quite shattered to pieces, and the lock would not strike fire. I took my gun to a blacksmith in the neighbourhood, and he repaired the lock, so that my musket was as sure fire as any piece need be. I found upon trial, that though the stock and lock had been worn out, the barrel was none the worse for the service it had undergone.

I now, for the first time in my life, became hunter, in the proper sense of the word; and generally managed my affairs in such a way as to get the half of Saturday to myself. This I did by prevailing on my master to set my task for the week on Monday morning.

Saturday was appropriated to hunting, if I was not obliged to work all day, and I soon became pretty expert in the use of my gun. I made salt licks in the woods, to which the deer came, at night, and I shot them from a seat of clapboards that was placed on the branches of a tree. Rackoons abounded here, and were of a large size, and fat at all seasons. In the month of April I saw the ground thickly strewed with nuts, the growth of the last year. I now began to live well, notwithstanding the persecution that my mistress still directed against me, and to feel myself, in some measure, an independent man.

Serpents of various kinds swarmed in this country. I have killed more than twenty rattle-snakes in a day, and copper-heads were innumerable; but the snake that I most dreaded was the moccason, which is quite as venomous as the copper-head or rattle-snake, and much more active and malicious. Vipers and other poisonous reptiles were innumerable; and in the swamps was a monstrous serpent, though of rare occurrence, which was really dangerous on account of its prodigious size. This snake is of a brown colour, with ashy white spots distributed over its body. It lives by catching rabbits and squirrels, rackoons and other animals. I have no doubt that some of this species would attack and swallow children several years old. I once shot one of these snakes that was more than eight feet long, and as thick as the leg of an ordinary man. When coiled up it appeared as large as a small calf lying in its resting place. Panthers, wolves, and other beasts of prey, were common in the woods.

I had always observed that snakes congregate, either in large groups or in pairs; and that if one snake is killed, another is soon after seen near the same place. I one day killed an enormous rattle-snake in the cotton field near my master's house. This snake was full six feet in length, of a corresponding thickness, and had fangs an inch and three-quarters in length. When dead, I skinned it, and stretched the skin on a board. A few days after, having occasion to cross a fence near where I had killed the large snake, and jumping from the top of the fence upon the ground, without looking down, I alighted close beside another rattle-snake, quite as large as the one I had killed. This one was lying at full length, and I was surprised that it did not attempt to bite me, nor even to throw itself into coil. It only sounded its rattles, making a noise sufficiently loud to be heard a hundred yards. I killed this snake also and seeing it appear to be full of something that it had eaten, I ripped it open with my knife, and found the whole cavity of its body stuffed full of corn meal that it had eaten in the house where my master kept his stores, to which it had found access through some aperture in the logs of the house. The snake was so full of meal that it could not coil itself, and thus saved my life, for the bite of such a snake as this was, is almost certain death. I knew a white man some time afterwards, who was bitten by one of these large rattle-snakes in the hand, as he was trying to punch it to death with a stick in a hollow stump, and he died before he could be taken to his own house, which was little more than a mile from the place where he was bitten.

A neighbour of my master was one day hunting deer in the woods with hounds; and hearing one of his hounds cry out as if hurt by something, the gentlemen proceeded to the spot, and found his dog lying in the agonies of death, and a great rattle-snake near him. On examining the dog it was found that the snake had struck him with its fangs in the side, and cut a deep gash in the skin. The dog being heated with running, death ensued almost instantly.

I had a dog of my own which I had brought with me from Carolina, and which was an excellent hunting dog. He would tree rackoons and bears, and chase deer, and was so faithful, that I thought he would lose his life, if necessary, in my defence; but dogs, like men, have a certain limit, beyond which their friendship will not carry them, at least it was so with my dog.

Being in the woods one Sunday, at a place called the goose-pond, a shallow pool of water to which wild geese resorted, my dog came out of the cane to me, with his bristles raised, and showing by his conduct that he had seen something in the canes of which he was afraid. I had gone to the pond that for the purpose of cutting and putting into the water some sticks of a tree that grows in that part of Georgia, of which very good ropes can be made. The timber is cut and thrown into the water until the bark becomes soft and loose, and it is then peeled off, beaten, and split to pieces; and of this bark ropes can be made nearly equal to hempen ropes. I got a good deal of money by making ropes of this bark and selling them. At the time I speak of, I had my axe with me, but was without my gun. I endeavoured in vain to induce my dog to enter into the cane-brake, and started on my way home, my dog keeping a little in advance of me, and frequently looking back. I had not proceeded far before the cause of my dog's alarm became manifest. Looking behind me, I saw a huge panther creeping along the path after me, in the manner that a cat creeps when stealing upon her prey. I felt myself in danger and again endeavoured to urge my dog to attack the panther, but I could not prevail on him to place himself between me and the wild beast. I stood still for some time, and the panther lay down on the ground, still, however, looking attentively at me. When I again moved forward, the panther moved after me; and when I stopped and turned round, it stopped also. In this way I proceeded, alternately advancing and halting, with the panther sometimes within twenty steps of me, until I came in view of my master's clearing, when the panther turned off into the woods, and I saw it no more. I do not know whether this panther was in pursuit of me or my dog; but whether of the one or the other, it showed but little fear of both of us; and I believe that, if alone, it would not have hesitated to attack either of us. As soon as the panther disappeared I went home and told my master of my adventure. He sent immediately to the house of a gentleman who lived two miles distant, who came, and brought his dogs with him. These dogs, when joined to my master's made five in number. I went to the woods, and showed the place where the panther had left me, and the dogs immediately scented the trail. It was then late in the evening, and the chase was continued until near day-break the next morning, when the panther was forced to take a tree ten miles from my master's house. It was shot by my master with his rifle, and after it was dead, we measured it, from the end of the nose to the tip of the tail, and found the whole length to be eleven feet and ten inches.

In the fall of this year I went with my master to the Indian country, to purchase and bring to the settlement cattle and Indian horses. We travelled a hundred miles from the residence of my master, nearly west, before we came to any Indian village.

The country where the Indians lived was similar in soil and productions to that in which my master had settled; and I saw several fields of corn amongst the Indians of excellent quality, and well enclosed with substantial fences. I also saw amongst these people several log-houses, with square hewn logs. Some cotton was growing in small patches in the fields, but this plant was not extensively cultivated. Large herds of cattle were ranging in the woods, and cost their owners nothing for their keeping, except a small quantity of salt. These cattle were of the Spanish breed, generally speckled, but often of a dun or mouse colour, and sometimes of a leaden gray. They universally had long horns, and dark muzzles, and stood high on their legs, with elevated and bold fronts. When ranging in droves in the woods, they were the finest cattle in appearance that I ever saw. They make excellent working oxen, but their quarters are not so heavy and fleshy as those of the English cattle. The cows do not give large quantities of milk.

The Indian horses run at large in the woods like the cattle, and receive no feed from their owners, unless on some very extraordinary occasion. They are small, but very handsome little horses. I do not know that I ever saw one of these horses more than fourteen hands high; but they are very strong and active, and when brought upon the plantation, and broken to work, they are hardy and docile, and keep fat on very little food. The prevailing colour of these horses is black; but many of them are beautiful grays, with flowing manes and tails, and, of their size, are fine horses.

My master bought fifty horses, and more than a hundred of the cattle; and hired seven Indians, to help us to drive them into the settlement. We had only a path to travel in— no road having been opened to the Indian country, of width sufficient for wagons to pass upon it; and I was often surprised at the agility of the Indians, in riding the unbroken horses along this path, and through the cane-brakes, which lined it on either side, in pursuit of the cattle, when any of them attempted to leave the drove. With the horses we had but little trouble, after we had them once started on the path; but the cattle were much inclined to separate and wander in the woods, for several days after we set out from the Nation,—but the greatest trouble was experienced at the time we halted in the evening, for the night. Some of the cattle, and many of the horses, would wander off from the fire, to a great distance in the woods, if not prevented; and might attempt to return to the Indian country. To obviate this, as soon as the fire was kindled, and the Indians had taken their supper, they would take off into the woods in all directions, and, stationing themselves at the distance of about half a quarter of a mile from the fire, would set up such a horrible yelling and whooping, that the whole forest appeared to be full of demons, come to devour us and our drove too. This noise never failed to cause both horse and cattle to keep within the circle formed by the Indians; and I believe we did not lose a single beast on the whole journey.

My master kept many of the cattle, and several of the horses, which he used on the plantation, instead of mules. The residue he sold among the planters, and I believe the expedition yielded him a handsome profit in the end; it also afforded me an opportunity of seeing the Cherokee Indians in their own country, and of contrasting the immense difference that exists between man in a state of civilization and industry, and man in a state of barbarism and indolence.

Ever since I had been in the southern country, vast numbers of African negroes had been yearly imported; but this year the business ceased altogether, and I did not see any African who was landed in the United States after this date.

I shall here submit to the reader, the results of the observations I have made on the regulations of southern society. It is my opinion, that the white people in general, are not nearly so well informed in the southern states, as they are in those lying farther north. The cause of this may not be obvious to strangers; but to a man who has resided amongst the cotton plantations, it is quite plain.

There is a great scarcity of schools, throughout all the cotton country, that I have seen; because the white population is so thinly scattered over the country, and the families live so far apart, that it is not easy to get a sufficient number of children together to constitute a school. The young men of the country, who have received educations proper to qualify them for the profession of teachers, are too proud to submit to this kind of occupation; and strangers, who come from the north, will not engage in a service that is held in contempt, unless they can procure large salaries from individuals, or get a great number of pupils to attend their instructions, whose united contributions may amount, in the aggregate, to a large sum.

Great numbers of the young men of fortune are sent abroad to be educated: but thousands of the sons of land and slave-holders receive very little education, and pass their lives in ignorant idleness. The poor white children are not educated at all. It is my opinion, that the women are not better educated than the men.

A few of the great families live in a style of luxury and magnificence on their estates, that people in the north are not accustomed to witness; but this splendour is made up of crowds of slaves, employed as household servants, and a gaudy show of silver plate, rather than in good houses, or convenient furniture. Good beef and good mutton, such are seen in Philadelphia and New-York, are not known on the cotton plantations. Good butter is also a rarity; and, in the summer time, sweet flour, or sweet wheaten bread, is scarcely to be looked for. The flour is imported from the north, or west; and in the hot, damp climate of the southern summer, it cannot be kept from souring, more than four or five weeks.

The temper of my mistress grew worse daily—if that could grow worse, which was already as bad as it could be— and her enmity against me increased, the more she observed that my master confided in me. To enhance my misfortunes, the health of my master began, about this time, visibly to decline, and towards the latter end of the autumn of this year, he one day told me, that he believed he should not live long, as he already felt the symptoms of approaching decay and death.

This was a source of much anxiety and trouble to me; for I clearly foresaw, that if ever I fell under the unbridled dominion of my mistress, I should regret the worst period of my servitude in South Carolina. I was much afraid, as the winter came on, that my master might grow worse, and pass to the grave in the spring, for his disease was a consumption of the lungs; and it is well known, that the spring of the year, which brings joy, gladness, and vitality, to all creation, animate and inanimate, except the victim of consumption, is often the season that consigns him to the grave.

CHAPTER XIX.

We passed this winter in clearing land, after we had secured the crops of cotton and corn, and nothing happened on our plantation, to disturb the usual monotony of the life of a slave, except, that in the month of January, my master informed me, that he intended to go to Savannah for the purpose of purchasing groceries, and such other supplies as might be required on the plantation, in the following season; and that he intended to take down a load of cotton with our wagon and team; and that I must prepare to be the driver. This intelligence was not disagreeable to me, as the trip to Savannah would, in the first place, release me for a short time, from the tyranny of my mistress; and, in the second, would give me an opportunity of seeing a great deal of strange country. I derived a third advantage, in after times, from this journey; but which did not enter into my estimate of this affair, at that time.

My master had not yet erected a cotton-gin on his place— the land not being his own—and we hauled our cotton, in the seed, nearly three miles to be ginned, for which we had to give one-fourth to the owner of the gin.

When the time of my departure came, I loaded my wagon with ten bales of cotton, and set out with the same team of six mules that I had driven from South Carolina. Nothing of moment happened to me until the evening of the fourth day, when we were one hundred miles from home. My master stopped to-night (for he travelled with me on his horse) at the house of an old friend of his; and I heard my master, in conversation with this gentleman, (for such he certainly was) give me a very good character, and tell him, that I was the most faithful and trusty negro that he had ever owned. He also said that if he lived to see the expiration of the seven years for which he had leased me, he intended to buy me. He said much more of me; and I thought I heard him tell his friend something about my mistress, but this was spoken in a low tone of voice, and I could not distinctly understand it. When I was going away in the morning with my team, this gentleman came out to the wagon, and ordered one of his own slaves to help me to put the harness on my mules. At parting, he told me to stop at his house on my return, and stay all night; and said, I should always be welcome to the use of his kitchen, if it should ever be my lot to travel that way again.

I mention these trifles to show, that if there are hard and cruel masters in the south, there are also others of a contrary character. The slave-holders are neither more nor less than men, some of whom are good, and very many are bad. My master and this gentleman, were certainly of the number of the good; but the contrast between them and some others that I have seen, was, unhappily for many of the slaves, very great. I shall, hereafter, refer to this gentleman, at whose house I now was; and shall never name him without honour, nor think of him without gratitude.

As I travelled through the country with my team, my chief employment, beyond my duty of a teamster was to observe the condition of the slaves on the various plantations by which we passed on our journey, and to compare things in Georgia, as I now saw them, with similar things in Carolina, as I had heretofore seen them.

There is as much sameness amongst the cotton plantations, in Georgia, as there is amongst the various farms in New-York, or New-Jersey. He who has seen one cotton field, has seen all other cotton fields, bating the difference that naturally results from good and bad soils, or good and bad culture; but the contrast that prevails in the treatment of the slaves, on different plantations, is very remarkable. We travelled a road that was not well provided with public houses, and we frequently stopped for the night at the private dwellings of the planters; and I observed that my master was received as a visiter, and treated as a friend in the family, whilst I was always left at the road with my wagon, my master supplying me with money to buy food for myself and my mules.

It was my practice, when we remained all night at these gentlemen's houses, to go to the kitchen in the evening, after I had fed my mules and eaten my supper, and pass some time in conversation with the black people I might chance to find there. One evening, we halted before sundown, and I unhitched my mules at the road, about two hundred yards from the house of a planter, to which my master went to claim hospitality for himself.

After I had disposed of my team for the night, and taken my supper, I went as usual to see the people of colour in the kitchen, belonging to this plantation. The sun had just set when I reached the kitchen, and soon afterwards, a black boy came in and told the woman who was the only person in the kitchen when I came to it, that she must go down to the overseer's house. She immediately started, in obedience to this order, and not choosing to remain alone in a strange house, I concluded to follow the woman, and see the other people of this estate. When we reached the house of the overseer, the coloured people were coming in from the field, and with them came the overseer, and another man, better dressed than overseers usually are.

I stood at some distance from these gentlemen, not thinking it prudent to be too forward amongst strangers. The black people were all called together, and the overseer told them, that some one of them had stolen a fat hog from the pen, carried it to the woods, and there killed and dressed it; that he had that day found the place where the hog had been slaughtered, and that if they did not confess, and tell who the perpetrators of this theft were, they would all be whipped in the severest manner. To this threat, no other reply was made than a universal assertion of the innocence of the accused. They were all then ordered to lie down upon the ground, and expose their backs, to which the overseer applied the thong of his long whip, by turns, until he was weary. It was fortunate for these people, that they were more than twenty in number, which prevented the overseer from inflicting many lashes on any one of them.

When the whole number had received, each in turn, a share of the lash, the overseer returned to the man, to whom he had first applied the whip, and told him he was certain that he knew who stole the hog; and that if he did not tell who the thief was, he would whip him all night. He then again applied the whip to the back of this man, until the blood flowed copiously; but the sufferer hid his face in his hands, and said not a word. The other gentleman then asked the overseer, if he was confident this man had stolen the pig; and, receiving an affirmative answer, he said he would make the fellow confess the truth, if he would follow his directions. He then asked the overseer if he had ever tried cat-hauling, upon an obstinate negro; and was told that this punishment had been heard of, but never practised on this plantation.

A boy was then ordered to get up, run to the house, and bring a cat, which was soon produced. The cat, which was a large gray tom-cat, was then taken by the well-dressed gentleman, and placed upon the bare back of the prostrate black man, near the shoulder, and forcibly dragged by the tail down the back, and along the bare thighs of the sufferer. The cat sunk his nails into the flesh, and tore off pieces of the skin with his teeth. The man roared with the pain of this punishment, and would have rolled along the ground, had be not been held in his place by the force of four other slaves, each one of whom confined a hand or a foot. As soon as the cat was drawn from him, the man said he would tell who stole the hog, and confessed that he and several others, three of whom were then holding him, had stolen the hog—killed, dressed, and eaten it. In return for this confession, the overseer said he should have another touch of the cat, which was again drawn along his back, not as before, from the head downwards, but from below the hips to the head. The man was then permitted to rise, and each of those who had been named by him as a participator in stealing the hog, was compelled to lie down, and have the cat twice drawn along his back; first downwards, and then upwards. After the termination of this punishment, each of the sufferers was washed with salt water, by a black woman, and they were then all dismissed. This was the most excruciating punishment that I ever saw inflicted on black people, and, in my opinion, it is very dangerous; for the claws of the cat are poisonous, and wounds made by them are very subject to inflammation.

During all this time, I had remained at the distance of fifty yards from the place of punishment, fearing either to advance or retreat, lest I too, might excite the indignation of these sanguinary judges. After the business was over, and my feelings became a little more composed, I thought the voice or the gentleman, in good clothes, was familiar to me; but I could not recollect who he was, nor where I had heard his voice, until the gentlemen at length left this place, and went towards the great house, and as they passed me, I recognized in the companion of the overseer, my old master, the negro trader, who had bought me in Maryland, and brought me to Carolina.

I afterwards learned from my master, that this man had formerly been engaged in the African slave-trade, which he had given up some years before, for the safer and less arduous business of buying negroes in the north, and bringing them to the south, as articles of merchandise, in which he had acquired a very respectable fortune— had lately married in a wealthy family, in this part of the country, and was a great planter.

Two days after this, we reached Savannah, where my master sold his cotton, and purchased a wagon load of sugar, molasses, coffee, shoes, dry goods, and such articles as we stood in need of at home; and on the next day after I entered the city, I again left it, and directed my course up the country. In Savannah I saw many black men, who were slaves, and who yet acted as freemen so far, that they went out to work, where and with whom they pleased, received their own wages, and provided their own subsistence; but were obliged to pay a certain sum at the end of each week to their masters. One of these men told me, that he paid six dollars on every Saturday evening, to his master; and yet he was comfortably dressed, and appeared to live well. Savannah was a very busy place, and I saw vast quantities of cotton, piled up on the wharves; but the appearance of the town itself, was not much in favour of the people who lived in it.

On my way home I travelled for several days, by a road different from that which we had pursued in coming down; and at the distance of fifty or sixty miles from Savannah, I passed by the largest plantation that I had ever seen. I think I saw at least a thousand acres of cotton in one field, which was all as level as a bowling-green. There were, as I was told, three hundred and fifty hands at work in this field, picking the last of the cotton from the burs; and these were the most miserable looking slaves that I had seen in all my travels.

It was now the depth of winter, and although the weather was not cold, yet it was the winter of this climate; and a man who lives on the Savannah river a few years, will find himself almost as much oppressed with cold, in winter there, as he would be in the same season of the year, on the banks of the Potomac, if he had always resided there.

These people were, as far as I could see, totally without shoes; and there was no such garment as a hat of any kind amongst them. Each person had a coarse blanket, which had holes cut for the arms to pass through, and the top was drawn up round the neck, so as to form a sort of loose frock, tied before with strings. The arms, when the people were at work, were naked, and some of them had very little clothing of any kind, besides this blanket frock. The appearance of these people, afforded the most conclusive evidence that they were not eaters of pork; and that lent lasted with them throughout the year.

I again staid all night, as I went home, with the gentleman whom I have before noticed, as the friend of my master, who had left me soon after we quitted Savannah, and I saw him no more, until I reached home.

Soon after my return from Savannah, an affair of a very melancholy character took place in the neighbourhood of my master's plantation. About two miles from our residence, lived a gentleman who was a bachelor, and who had for his housekeeper a mulatto woman. The master was a young man, not more than twenty-five years old, and the housekeeper must have been at least forty. She had children grown up, one of whom had been sold by her master, the father of the bachelor, since I lived here, and carried away to the west. This woman had acquired a most unaccountable influence over her young master, who lived with her as his wife, and gave her the entire command of his house, and of every thing about it. Before he came to live where he now did, and whilst he still resided with his father, to whom the woman then belonged, the old gentleman perceiving the attachment of his son to this female, had sold her to a trader, who was on his way to the Mississippi river, in the absence of the young man; but when the latter returned home, and learned what had been done, he immediately set off in pursuit of the purchaser, overtook him somewhere in the Indian territory, and bought the woman of him, at an advanced price. He then brought her back, and put her, as his housekeeper, on the place where he now lived; left his father, and came to rejoice in person with the woman.

On a plantation adjoining that of the gentleman bachelor, lived a planter, who owned a young mulatto man, named Frank, not more than twenty-four or five years old, a very smart, as well as handsome fellow. Frank had become as much enamoured of this woman, who was old enough to have been his mother, as her master, the bachelor was; and she returned Frank's attachment to the prejudice of her owner. Frank was in the practice of visiting his mistress at night, a circumstance of which her master was suspicious; and he forbade Frank from coming to the house. This only heightened the flame that was burning in the bosoms of the lovers; and they resolved, after many and long deliberations, to destroy the master. She projected the plot, and furnished the means for the murder, by taking her master's gun from the place where he usually kept it, and giving it to Frank, who came to the house in the evening, when the gentleman was taking his supper alone.

Lucy always waited upon her master at his meals, and knowing his usual place of sitting, had made a hole between two of the logs of the house, towards which, she knew his back would be at supper. At a given signal, Frank came quietly up to the house, levelled the gun through the hole prepared for him, and discharged a load of buck-shot between the shoulders of the unsuspecting master, who sprang from his seat and fell dead beside the table. This murder was not known in the neighbourhood until the next morning, when the woman herself went to a house on an adjoining plantation, and told it.

The murdered gentleman had several other slaves, none of whom were at home at the time of his death, except one man; and he was so terrified that he was afraid to run and alarm the neighbourhood. I knew this man well, and believe he was afraid of the woman and her accomplice. I never had any doubt of his innocence, though he suffered a punishment, upon no other evidence than mere suspicion, far more terrible than any ordinary form of death.

As soon as the murder was known to the neighbouring gentlemen, they hastened to visit the dead body, and were no less expeditious in instituting inquiries after those who had done the bloody deed. My master was amongst the first who arrived at the house of the deceased; and in a short time, half the slaves of the neighbouring plantations were arrested, and brought to the late dwelling of the dead man. For my own part, from the moment I heard of the murder, I had no doubt of its author.

Silence is a great virtue when it is dangerous to speak; and I had long since determined never to advance opinions, uncalled for, in controversies between the white people and the slaves. Many witnesses were examined by a justice of the peace, before the coroner arrived, but after the coming of the latter, a jury was called; and more than half a day was spent in asking questions of various black people, without the disclosure of any circumstance, which tended to fix the guilt of the murder upon any one. My master, who was present all this time, at last desired them to examine me, if it was thought that my testimony could be of any service in the matter, as he wished me to go home to attend to my work. I was sworn on the testament to tell the whole truth; and stated at the commencement of my testimony, that I believed Frank and Lucy to be the murderers, and proceeded to assign the reasons upon which my opinion was founded. Frank had not been present at this examination, and Lucy who had been sworn, had said she knew nothing of the matter; that at the time her master was shot, she had gone into the kitchen for some milk for his supper, and that on hearing the gun, she had come into the room, at the moment he fell to the floor and expired; but when she opened the door and looked out, she could neither hear nor see any one.

When Frank was brought in and made to touch the dead body, which he was compelled to do, because some said that if he was the murderer, the corpse would bleed at his touch, he trembled so much, that I thought he would fall; but no blood issued from the wound of the dead man. This compulsory touching of the dead had, however, in this instance, a much more powerful effect, in the conviction of the criminal, than the flowing of any quantity of blood could have had; for as soon as Frank had withdrawn his hand from the touch of the dead, the coroner asked him, in a peremptory tone, as conscious of the fact, why he had done this. Frank was so confounded with fear, and overwhelmed by this interrogatory, that he lost all self-possession, and cried out in a voice of despair, that Lucy had made him do it.

Lucy, who had left the room when Frank was brought in, was now recalled, and confronted with her partner in guilt; but nothing could wring a word of confession from her. She persisted, that if Frank had murdered her master, he had done it of his own accord, and without her knowledge or advice. Some one now, for the first time, thought of making search for the gun of the dead man, which was not found in the place where he usually had kept it. Frank said he had committed the crime with this gun, which had been placed in his hands by Lucy. Frank, Lucy, and Billy, a black man, against whom there was no evidence, nor cause of suspicion, except that he was in the kitchen at the time of the murder, were committed to prison in a new log-house on an adjoining plantation, closely confined in irons, and kept there a little more than two weeks, when they were all tried before some gentlemen of the neighbourhood, who held a court for that purpose. Lucy and Frank were condemned to be hung; but Billy was found not guilty; although he was not released, but kept in confinement until the execution of his companions, which took place ten days after the trial.

On the morning of the execution, my master told me, and all the rest of the people, that we must go to the *hanging*, as it was termed by him as well as others. The place of punishment was only two miles from my master's residence, and I was there in time to get a good stand, near the gallows' tree, by which I was enabled to see all the proceedings connected with this solemn affair. It was estimated by my master, that there were at least fifteen thousand people present at this scene, more than half of whom were blacks; all the masters, for a great distance round the country, having permitted, or compelled, their people to come to this *hanging*.

Billy was brought to the gallows with Lucy and Frank, but was permitted to walk beside the cart in which they rode. Under the gallows, after the rope was around her neck, Lucy confessed that the murder had been designed by her, in the first place, and that Frank had only perpetrated it at her instance. She said she had at first intended to apply to Billy to assist her in the undertaking, but had afterwards communicated her designs to Frank, who offered to shoot her master, if she would supply him with a gun, and let no other person be in the secret.

A long sermon was preached by a white man under the gallows, which was only the limb of a tree, and afterwards an exhortation was delivered by a black man. The two convicts were hung together, and after they were quite dead, a consultation was held among the gentlemen as to the future disposition of Billy, who, having been in the house when his master was murdered, and not having given immediate information of the fact, was held to be guilty of concealing the death, and was accordingly sentenced to receive five hundred lashes. I was in the branches of a tree close by the place where the court was held, and distinctly heard its proceedings and judgment. Some went to the woods to cut hickories, whilst others stripped Billy and tied him to a tree. More than twenty long switches, some of them six or seven feet in length, had been procured, and two men applied the rods at the same time, one standing on each side of the culprit, one of them using his left hand.

I had often seen black men whipped, and had always, when the lash was applied with great severity, heard the sufferer cry out and beg for mercy; but in this case, the pain inflicted by the double blows of the hickory was so intense, that Billy never uttered so much as a groan; and I do not believe he breathed for the space of two minutes after he received the first strokes. He shrank his body close to the trunk of the tree, around which his arm, and legs were lashed, drew his shoulders up to his head like a dying man, and trembled, or rather shivered, in all his members. The blood flowed from the commencement, and in a few minutes lay in small puddles at the root of the tree. I saw flakes of flesh as long as my finger fall out of the gashes in his back; and I believe he was insensible during all the time that he was receiving the last two hundred lashes. When the whole five hundred lashes had been counted by the person appointed to perform this duty, the half dead body was unbound and laid in the shade of the tree upon which I sat. The gentlemen who had done the whipping, eight or ten in number, being joined by their friends, then came under the tree and drank punch until their dinner was made ready, under a booth of green boughs at a short distance.

After dinner, Billy, who had been groaning on the ground where he was laid, was taken up, placed in the cart in which Lucy and Frank had been brought to the gallows, and conveyed to the dwelling of his late master, where he was confined to the house and his bed more than three months, and was never worth much afterwards while I remained in Georgia.

Lucy and Frank, after they had been half an hour upon the gallows, were cut down, and suffered to drop into a deep hole that had been dug under them whilst they were suspended. As they fell, so the earth was thrown upon them, and the grave closed over them for ever.

They were hung on Thursday, and the vast assemblage of people that had convened to witness their death did not leave the place altogether until the next Monday morning. Wagons, carts, and carriages had been brought upon the ground; booths and tents erected for the convenience and accommodation of the multitude; and the terrible spectacles that I have just described were succeeded by music, dancing, trading in horses, gambling, drinking, fighting, and every other species of amusement and excess to which the southern people are addicted.

I had to work in the day-time, but went every night to witness this funereal carnival, the numbers that joined in which appeared to increase, rather than diminish, during the Friday and Saturday that followed the execution. It was not until Sunday afternoon that the crowd began sensibly to diminish; and on Monday morning, after breakfast time, the last wagons left the ground, now trampled into dust as dry and as light as ashes, and the grave of the murderers was left to the solitude of the woods.

Certainly those who were hanged well deserved their punishment; but it was a very arbitrary exercise of power to whip a man until he was insensible because he did not prevent a murder which was committed without his knowledge; and I could not understand the right of punishing him, because he was so weak or timorous as to refrain from the disclosure of the crime the moment it came to his knowledge.

It is necessary for the southern people to be vigilant in guarding the moral condition of their slaves, and even to punish the intention to commit crimes, when that intention can be clearly proved; for such is the natural relation of master and slave, in by far the greater number of cases, that no cordiality of feeling can ever exist between them; and the sentiments that bind together the different members of society in a state of freedom and social equality, being absent, the master must resort to principles of physical restraint, and rules of mental coercion, unknown in another and a different condition of the social compact.

It is a mistake to suppose that the southern planters could ever retain their property, or live amongst their slaves, if those slaves were not kept in terror of the punishment that would follow acts of violence disorder. There is no difference between the feelings of the different races of men, so far as their personal rights are concerned. The black man is as anxious to possess and to enjoy liberty as the white one would be, were he deprived of this inestimable blessing. It is not for me to say that the one is as well qualified for the enjoyment of liberty as the other. Low ignorance, moral degradation of character, and mental depravity, are inseparable companions; and in the breast of an ignorant man, the passions of envy and revenge hold unbridled dominion.

It was in the month of April that I witnessed the painful spectacle of two fellow-creatures being launched into the abyss of eternity, and a third, being tortured beyond the sufferings of mere death, not for his crimes, but as a terror to others; and this, not to deter others from the commission of crimes but to stimulate them to a more active and devoted performance of their duties to their owners. My spirits had not recovered from the depression produced by that scene, in which my feelings had been awakened in the cause of others, when I was called to a nearer and more immediate apprehension of sufferings, which, I now too clearly saw, were in preparation for myself.

My master's health became worse continually, and I expected he would not survive this summer. In this, however, I was disappointed; but he was so ill that he was seldom able to come to the field, and paid but little attention to his plantation, or the culture of his crops. He left the care of the cotton field to me after the month of June, and was not again out on the plantation before the following October; when he one day came out on a little Indian pony that he had used as his hackney, before he was so far reduced as to decline the practice of riding. I suffered very much this summer for want of good and substantial provisions, my master being no longer able to supply me, with his usual liberality, from his own meat house. I was obliged to lay out nearly all my other earnings, in the course of the summer, for bacon, to enable me to bear the hardship and toil to which I was exposed. My master often sent for me to come to the house, and talked to me in a very kind manner; and I believe that no hired overseer could have carried on the business more industriously than I did, until the crop was secured the next winter.

Soon after my master was in the field, in October, he sent for me to come to him one day, and gave me, on parting, a pretty good great coat of strong drab cloth, almost new, which he said would be of service to me in the coming winter. He also gave me at the same time a pair of boots which he had worn half out, but the legs of which were quite good. This great coat and these boots were afterwards of great service to me.

As the winter came on my master grew worse, and though he still continued to walk about the house in good weather, it was manifest that he was approaching the close of his earthly existence. I worked very hard this winter. The crop of cotton was heavy, and we did not get it all out of the field until some time after Christmas, which compelled me to work hard myself, and cause my fellow-slaves to work hard too, in clearing the land that my master was bound to clear every year on this place. He desired me to get as much of the land cleared in time for cotton as I could, and to plant the rest with corn when cleared off.

As I was now entrusted with the entire superintendence of the plantation by my master, who never left his house, it became necessary for me to assume the authority of an overseer of my fellow-slaves, and I not unfrequently found it proper to punish them with stripes to compel them to perform their work. At first I felt much repugnance against the use of the hickory, the only instrument with which I punished offenders, but the longer I was accustomed to this practice, the more familiar and less offensive it became to me;

and I believe that a few years of perseverance and experience would have made me as inveterate a negro-driver as any in Georgia, though I feel conscious that I never should have become so hardened as to strip a person for the purpose of whipping, nor should I ever have consented to compel people to work without a sufficiency of good food, if I had it in my power to supply them with enough of this first of comforts.

In the month of February, my master became so weak, and his cough was so distressing, that he took to his bed, from which he never again departed, save only once, before the time when he was removed to be wrapped in his winding-sheet. In the month of March, two of the brothers of my mistress came to see her, and remained with her until after the death of my master.

When they had been with their sister about three weeks, they came to the kitchen one day when I had come in for my dinner, and told me that they were going to whip me. I asked them what they were going to whip me for? to which they replied, that they thought a good whipping would be good for me, and that at any rate, I must prepare to take it. My mistress now joined us, and after swearing at me in the most furious manner, for a space of several minutes, and bestowing upon me a multitude of the coarsest epithets, told me that she had long owed me a whipping, and that I should now get it.

She then ordered me to take off my shirt, (the only garment I had on, except a pair of old tow linen trowsers,) and the two brothers backed the command of their sister, the one by presenting a pistol at my breast, and the other by drawing a large club over his head in the attitude of striking me. Resistance was vain, and I was forced to yield. My shirt being off, I was tied by the hands with a stout bed-cord, and being led to a tree, called the Pride of China, that grew in the yard, my hands were drawn by the rope, being passed over a limb, until my feet no longer touched the ground. Being thus suspended in the air by the rope, and my whole weight hanging on my wrists, I was unable to move any part of my person, except my feet and legs. I had never been whipped since I was a boy, and felt the injustice of the present proceeding with the utmost keenness; but neither justice nor my feelings had any influence upon the hearts of my mistress and her brothers, two men as cruel in temper and as savage in manners as herself.

The first strokes of the hickory produced a sensation that I can only liken to streams of scalding water, running along my back; but after a hundred, or hundred and fifty lashes had been showered upon me, the pain became less acute and piercing, but was succeeded by a dead and painful aching, which seemed to extend to my very backbone.

As I hung by the rope, the moving of my legs sometimes caused me to turn round, and soon after they began to beat me I saw the pale and death-like figure of my master standing at the door, when my face was turned toward the house, and heard him, in a faint voice, scarcely louder than a strong breathing, commanding his brothers-in-law to let me go. These commands were disregarded, until I had received full three hundred lashes; and doubtlessly more would have been inflicted upon me, had not my master, with an effort beyond his strength, by the aid of a stick on which he supported himself, made his way to me, and placing his skeleton form beside me as I hung, told his brothers-in-law that if they struck another stroke, he would send for a lawyer and have them both prosecuted at law. This interposition stopped the progress of my punishment, and after cutting me down, they carried my master again into the house. I was yet able to walk, and went into the kitchen, whither my mistress followed, and compelled me to submit to be washed in brine by a black woman, who acted as her cook. I was then permitted to put my shirt on, and to go to my bed.

This was Saturday, and on the next day, when I awoke late in the morning, I found myself unable to turn over or to rise. I felt too indignant at the barbarity with which I had been treated to call for help from any one, and lay in my bed made of corn husks until after twelve o'clock, when my mistress came to me and asked me how I was. A slave must not manifest feelings of resentment, and I answered with humility, that I was very sore and unable to get up. She then called a man and a woman, who came and raised me up; but I now found that my shirt was as fast to my back as if it had grown there. The blood and bruised flesh having become incorporated with the substance of the linen, it formed only the outer coat of the great scab that covered my back.

After I was down stairs, my mistress had me washed in warm water, and warm grease was rubbed over my back and sides, until the shirt was saturated with oil, and becoming soft, was at length separated from my back. My mistress then had my back washed and greased, and put upon me one of my master's old linen shirts. She had become alarmed, and was fearful either that I should die, or would not be able to work again for a long time. As it was, she lost a month of my labour at this time, and in the end, she lost myself, in consequence of this whipping.

As soon as I was able to walk, my master sent for me to come to his bed-side, and told me that he was very sorrow for what had happened; that it was not his fault, and that if he had been well I should never have been touched. Tears came in his eyes as he talked to me, and said that as he could not live long, he hoped I would continue faithful to him whilst he did live. This I promised to do, for I really loved my master; but I had already determined, that as soon as he was in his grave, I would attempt to escape from Georgia and the cotton country, if my life should be the forfeiture of the attempt.

As soon as I had recovered of my wounds, I again went to work, not in my former situation of superintendent of my master's plantation, for this place was now occupied by one of the brothers of my mistress, but in the woods, where my mistress had determined to clear a new field. After this time, I did nothing but grub and clear land, while I remained in Georgia, but I was always making preparations for my departure from that country.

My master was an officer of militia, and had a sword which he wore on parade days, and at other times he hung it up in the room where he slept. I conceived an idea that this sword would be of service to me in the long journey that I intended to undertake. One evening, when I had gone in to see my master, and had remained standing at his bed-side some time, he closed his eyes as if going to sleep, and it being twilight, I slipped the sword from the place where it hung, and dropped it out of the window. I knew my master could never need this weapon again, but yet I felt some compunction of conscience at the thought of robbing so good a man. When I left the room, I took up the sword, and afterwards secreted it in a hollow tree in the woods, near the place at which I worked daily.

CHAPTER XX.

My master died in the month of May, and I followed him to his grave with a heavy heart, for I felt that I had lost the only friend I had in the world who possessed at once the power and the inclination to protect me against the tyranny and oppression to which slaves on a cotton plantation are subject.

Had he lived, I should have remained with him, and never have left him, for he had promised to purchase the residue of my time of my owners in Carolina; but when he was gone, I felt the parting of the last tie that bound me to the place where I then was, and my heart yearned for my wife and children, from whom I had now been separated more than four years.

I held my life in small estimation, if it was to be worn out under the dominion of my mistress and her brothers, though since the death of my master she had greatly meliorated my condition by giving me frequent allowances of meat and other necessaries. I believe she entertained some vague apprehensions that I might run away, and betake myself to the woods for a living, perhaps go to the Indians; but I do not think she ever suspected that I would hazard the untried undertaking of attempting to make my way back to Maryland. My purpose was fixed, and now nothing could shake it. I only waited for a proper season of the year to commence my toilsome and dangerous journey. As I must of necessity procure my own subsistence on my march, it behoved me to pay regard to the time at which I took it up.

I furnished myself with a fire-box, as it is called, that is, a tin case containing flints, steel, and tinder, this I considered indispensable. I took the great coat that my master had given me, and with a coarse needle and thread quilted a scabbard of old cloth in one side of it, in which I could put my sword and carry it with safety. I also procured a small bag of linen that held more than a peck. This bag I filled with the meal of parched corn, grinding the corn after it was parched in the wood, where I worked at the mill at night. These operations, except the grinding of the corn, I carried on in a small conical cabin that I had built in the woods. The boots that my master gave me, I had repaired by a Spaniard who lived in the neighbourhood, and followed the business of a cobbler.

Before the first of August I had all my preparations completed, and had matured them with so much secrecy, that no one in the country, white or black, suspected me of entertaining any extraordinary design. I only waited for the corn to be ripe, and fit to be roasted, which time I had fixed as the period of my departure. I watched the progress of the corn daily, and on the eighth of August I perceived, on examining my mistress' field, that nearly half of the ears were so far grown, that by roasting them, a man could easily subsist himself; and as I knew that this corn had been planted later than the most of the corn in the country, I resolved to take leave of the plantation and its tenants, for ever, on the next day.

I had a faithful dog, called Trueman, and this poor animal had been my constant companion for more than four years, without ever showing cowardice or infidelity, but once, and that was when the panther followed us from the woods. I was accordingly anxious to bring my dog with me; but as I knew the success of my undertaking depended on secrecy and silence, I thought it safest to abandon my last friend, and engage in my perilous enterprise alone. On the morning of the ninth, I went to work as usual, carrying my dinner with me, and worked diligently at grubbing until about one o'clock in the day. I now sat down and took my last dinner as the slave of my mistress, dividing the contents of my basket with my dog. After I had finished, I tied my dog with a rope to a small tree; I set my gun against it, for I thought I should be better without the gun than with it; tied my knapsack with my bag of meal on my shoulders, and then turned to take a last farewell of my poor dog, that stood by the tree to which he was bound, looking wistfully at me. When I approached him, he licked my hands, and then rising on his hind feet, and placing his fore paws on my breast, he uttered a long howl, which thrilled through my heart, as if he had said, "My master, do not leave me behind you." All the affection that the poor animal had testified for me in the course of his life, now rose fresh in my memory. I recollected that he had always been ready to lay down his life for me; that when I was tied and bound to the tree to be whipped, they were forced to compel me to order my dog to be quiet, to prevent him from attacking my executioner in my defence; and even when he fled from the panther, he had not left me, only advancing a few feet before me, and beckoning me to fly from an enemy whose strength was too great for us to contend against with hope of success; and I now felt assured, that had the panther attacked me, my dog would have conquered at my side, or have died in defending me. This was the first time that I had ever tied him. I had often left him for a whole day to guard my coat, my basket, or my gun, which he never deserted; and he now seemed to feel that I charge him with ingratitude and infidelity, when I bound him to a charge which I had never known him to forsake.

As I was now leaving my dog for ever, I talked to him as to a creature that understood language, and was sensible of the dangers I was going to meet.

"Poor Trueman, faithful Trueman, fare thee well. Thou hast been an honest dog, and sure friend to thy master in all his shades of fortune. When my basket was well filled, how cheerfully we have partaken together of its contents. I did not then upbraid thee, that thou atest in idleness the proceeds of my labour, for I knew that thy heart was devoted to thy protector. In the day of my adversity, when all the world had forsaken me, when my master was dead, and I had no friend to protect me, still, poor Trueman, thou wert the same. Thou laidest thyself down at my feet when the world had united to oppress me. How often, when I was sick, and the fever raged in my veins, didst thou come at the going down of the sun, and lick my feet in token of thy faith; and how patiently didst thou watch with thy poor master through the long and lonely night.

"When I had no crumbs in my basket to give thee, nor crust in my pocket to divide with thee, thy faithful heart failed not; and a glance from the eye of thy hungry master filled thee with gratitude and joy. Poor dog, I must bid thee farewell. To-morrow they will come and release thee. Perhaps they will hate thee for my sake, and persecute thee as they have persecuted me; but I leave thee my gun to secure thee protection at the hands of those who will be the arbiters of thy fate when I am gone. It is all the legacy I can give thee; and surely they will not kill so good a dog when they see him possessed of so true a gun. Man is selfish and heartless— the richest of them all are as wretched slaves as I am, and are only minions of fear and avarice. Could pride and ambition witness thy fidelity and gratitude to thy forsaken master, and learn humility from thy example, how many tears would be wiped from the eyes of sorrow. Follow the new master who shall possess my gun, and may he be as kind to thee as thou hast been faithful to me."

I now took to the forest, keeping as nearly as I could, a north course all the afternoon. Night overtook me, before I reached any watercourse, or any other object worthy of being noticed; and I lay down and slept soundly, without kindling a fire, or eating any thing. I was awake before day, and as soon as there was light enough to enable me to see my way, I resumed my journey and walked on, until about eight o'clock, when I came to a river, which I knew must be the Appalachie. I sat down on the bank of the river, opened my bag of meal, and made my breakfast of a part of its contents. I used my meal very sparingly, it being the most valuable treasure that I now possessed; though I had in my pocket three Spanish dollars; but in my situation this money could not avail me any thing, as I was resolved not to show myself to any person, either white or black. After taking my breakfast, I prepared to cross the river, which was here about a hundred yards wide, with a sluggish and deep current. The morning was sultry, and the thickets along the margin of the river teemed with insects and reptiles. By sounding the river with a pole, I found the stream too deep to be waded, and I therefore prepared to swim it. For this purpose, I stripped myself, and bound my clothes on the top of my knapsack, and my bag of meal on the top of my clothes; then drawing my knapsack close up to my head, I threw myself into the river. In my youth I had learned to swim in the Patuxent, and have seldom met with any person who was more at ease in deep water than myself. I kept a straight line from the place of my entrance into the Appalchie, to the opposite side, and when I had reached it, stepped on the margin of the land, and turned round to view the place from which I had set out on my aquatic passage; but my eye was arrested by an object nearer to me than the opposite shore. Within twenty feet of me, in the very line that I had pursued in crossing the river, a large alligator was moving in full pursuit of me, with his nose just above the surface, in the position that creature takes when he gives chase to his intended prey in the water. The alligator can swim more than twice as fast as a man, for he can overtake young ducks on the water; and had I been ten seconds longer in the river, I should have been dragged to the bottom, and never again been heard of.

Seeing that I had gained the shore, my pursuer turned, made two or three circles in the water close by me, and then disappeared.

I received this admonition as a warning of the dangers that I must encounter in my journey to the north. After adjusting my clothes, I again took to the woods, and bore a little to the east of north; it now being my determination to turn down the country, so as to gain the line of the roads by which I had come to the south. I travelled all day in the woods; but a short time before sundown, came within view of an opening in the forest, which I took to be cleared fields, but upon a closer examination, finding no fences or other enclosures around it, I advanced into it and found it to be an open savannah, with a small stream of water creeping slowly through it. At the lower side of the open space, were the remains of an old beaver dam, the central part of which had been broken away by the current of the stream, at the time of some flood. Around the margin of this former pond, I observed several decayed beaver lodges, and numerous stumps of small trees, that had been cut down for the food or fortifications of this industrious little nation, which had fled at the approach of the white man, and all its people were now, like me, seeking refuge in the deepest solitudes of the forest, from the glance of every human eye. As it was growing late, and I believed I must now be near the settlements, I determined to encamp for the night, beside this old beaver dam. I again took my supper from my bag of meal, and made my bed for the night, amongst the canes that grew in the place. This night I slept but little: for it seemed as if all the owls in the country had assembled in my neighbourhood to perform a grand musical concert. Their hooting and chattering commenced soon after dark, and continued until the dawn of day. In all parts of the southern country, the owls are very numerous, especially along the margins of streams, and in the low grounds, with which the waters are universally bordered; but since I had been in the country, although I had passed many nights in the woods, at all seasons of the year, I had never before heard so clamorous and deafening a chorus of nocturnal music. With the coming of morning, I arose from my couch, and proceeded warily along the woods, keeping a continual lookout for plantations, and listening attentively to every noise that I heard in the trees, or amongst the cane-brakes. When the sun had been up two or three hours, I saw an appearance of blue sky at a distance, through the trees, which proved that the forest had been removed from a spot somewhere before me, and at no great distance from me; and, as I cautiously advanced, I heard the voices of people in loud conversation. Sitting down amongst the palmetto plants, that grew around me in great numbers, I soon perceived that the people whose conversation I heard, were coming nearer to me. I now heard the sound of horses' feet, and immediately afterwards, saw two men on horseback, with rifles on their shoulders, riding through the woods, and moving on a line that led them past me, at a distance of about fifty or sixty yards. Perceiving that these men were equipped as hunters, I remained almost breathless, for the purpose of hearing their conversation. When they came so near that I could distinguish their words, they were talking of the best place to take a stand, for the purpose of seeing the deer; from which I inferred, that they had sent men to some other point, for the purpose of rousing the deer with dogs. After they had passed that point of their way that was nearest to me, and were beginning to recede from me, one of them asked the other, if he had heard that a negro had run away the day before yesterday, in Morgan county; to which his companion answered in the negative. The first then said, he had seen an advertisement at the store, which offered a hundred dollars reward for the runaway, whose name was Charles.

The conversation of these horsemen was now interrupted by the cry of hounds, at a distance in the woods, and heightening the speed of their horses, they were soon out of my sight and hearing.

Information of the state of the country through which I was travelling, was of the highest value to me; and nothing could more nearly interest me than a knowledge of the fact, that my flight was known to the white people, who resided round about, and before me. It was now necessary for me to become doubly vigilant, and to concert with myself measures of the highest moment.

The first resolution that I took was, that I would travel no more in the day-time. This was the season of hunting deer, and knowing that the hunters were under the necessity of being as silent as possible in the woods, I saw at a glance that they would be at least as likely to discover me in the forest, before I could see them, as I should be to see them, before I myself could be seen.

I was now very hungry, but exceedingly loath to make any further breaches on my bag of meal, except in extreme necessity. Feeling confident that there was a plantation within a few rods of me, I was anxious to have a view of it, in hope that I might find a corn-field upon it, from which I could obtain a supply of roasting ears. Fearful to stand upright, I crept along through the low ground, where I then was, at times raising myself to my knees, for the purpose of obtaining a better view of things about me. In this way I advanced until I came in view of a high fence, and beyond this saw cotton, tall and flourishing, but no sign of corn. I crept up close to the fence, where I found the trunk of a large tree, that had been felled in clearing the field. Standing upon this, and looking over the plantation, I saw the tassels of corn, at the distance of half a mile, growing in a field which was bordered on one side by the wood, in which I stood.

It was now nine or ten o'clock in the morning, and as I had slept but little the night before, I crept into the bushes, great numbers of which grew in and about the top of the fallen tree, and, hungry as I was, fell asleep. When I awoke, it appeared to me from the position of the sun, which I had carefully noted, before I lay down, to be about one or two o'clock. As this was the time of the day, when the heat is most oppressive, and when every one was most likely to be absent from the forest, I again moved, and taking a circuitous route at some distance from the fields, reached the fence opposite the corn-field, without having met with any thing to alarm me. Having cautiously examined every thing around me, as well by the eye as by the ear, and finding all quiet, I ventured to cross the fence and pluck from the standing stalks, about a dozen good ears of corn, with which I stole back to the thicket in safety. This corn was of no use to me without fire to roast it, and it was equally dangerous to kindle fire by night, as by day, the light at one time, and the smoke at another, might betray me to those who I knew were ever ready to pursue and arrest me. "Hunger eats through stone walls," says the proverb; and an empty stomach is a petitioner, whose solicitations cannot be refused, if there is any thing to satisfy them with.

Having regained the woods in safety, I ventured to go as far as the side of a swamp, which I knew to be at the distance of two or three hundred yards, by the appearance of the timber. When in the swamp, I felt pretty secure, but determined that I would never again attempt to travel in the neighbourhood of a plantation in the daytime.

When in the swamp a quarter of a mile, I collected some dry wood, and lighted it with the aid of my tinder-box, flint, and steel. This was the first fire that I kindled on my journey, and I was careful to burn none but dry wood, to prevent the formation of smoke. Here I roasted my corn, and ate as much of it as I could. After my dinner, I lay down and slept for three or four hours. When I awoke, the sun was scarcely visible through the tree tops. It was evening, and prudence required me to leave the swamp before dark, lest I should not be able to find my way out.

Approaching the edge of the swamp, I watched the going down of the sun, and noted the stars as they appeared in the heavens. I had long since learned to distinguish the north-star, from all the other small luminaries of the night; and the seven pointers were familiar to me. These heavenly bodies were all the guides I had to direct me on my way, and as soon as the night had set in, I commenced my march through the woods, bearing as nearly due east as I could.

I took this course for the purpose of getting down the country, as far as the road leading from Augusta to Morgan County, with the intention of pursuing the route by which I had come out from South Carolina; deeming it more safe to travel the high road by night, than to attempt to make my way at random over the country, guided only by the stars. I travelled all night, keeping the north-star on my left hand as nearly as I could, and passing many plantations, taking care to keep at a great distance from the houses. I think I travelled at least twenty-five miles to-night, without passing any road that appeared so wide, or so much beaten, as that which I had travelled when I came from South Carolina. This night I passed through a peach orchard, laden with fine ripe fruit, with which I filled my pockets and hat; and before day, in crossing a corn-field, I pulled a supply of roasting-ears, with which and my peaches, I retired at break of day to a large wood, into which I travelled more than a mile before I halted. Here, in the midst of a thicket of high whortleberry bushes, I encamped for the day. I made my breakfast upon roasted corn and peaches, and then lay down and slept, unmolested, until after twelve o'clock, when I awoke and rose up for the purpose of taking a better view of my quarters; but I was scarcely on my feet, when I was attacked by a swarm of hornets, that issued from a large nest that hung on the limb of a tree, within twenty or thirty feet of me.

I knew that the best means of making peace with my hostile neighbours, was to lie down with my face to the ground; and this attitude I quickly took, not however before I had been stung by several of my assailants, which kept humming through the air about me for a long time, and prevented me from leaving this spot until after sundown, and after they had retired to rest for the night. I now commenced the attack on my part, and taking a handful of dry leaves, approached the nest, which was full as large as a half bushel, and thrusting the leaves into the hole at the bottom of the nest, through which its tenants passed in and out, secured the whole garrison prisoners in their own citadel. I now cut off the branch upon which the nest hung, and threw it, with its contents, into my evening fire, over which I roasted a supply of corn, for my night's journey.

Commencing my march this evening, soon after nightfall, I travelled until about one o'clock in the morning, as nearly as I could estimate the time, by the appearance of the stars, when I came upon a road, which from its width, and beaten appearance, I took to be the road leading to Augusta, and determined to pursue it.

I travelled on this road until I saw the appearance of daylight, when I turned into the woods, and went full a mile before I ventured to stop for the day. I concealed myself to-day in a thicket of young pine trees, that had sprung up round about an old pen of logs, which had formerly been used, either as a wolf or turkey trap. In this retreat nothing disturbed me this day, and at dark I again returned to the road, which I travelled in silence, treading as lightly as possible with my feet, and listening most attentively to every sound that I heard. After being on the road more than an hour, I heard the sound of the feet of horses, and immediately stepped aside, and took my place behind the trunk of a large tree. Within a minute or two, several horses with men on them, passed me. The men were talking to each other, and one of them asked another, in my hearing, if it was not about five miles to the Oconee. The reply was too low to be understood by me; but I was now satisfied that I was on the high road, leading down the country, on the Savannah side of Oconee.

Waiting until these horsemen were out of hearing, I followed them at a brisk walk, and within less than on hour, came to the side of a river, the width of which I could not ascertain, by reason of the darkness of the night, some fog having risen from the water.

I had no doubt that this stream was the Oconee; and as I had heretofore forded that river with a wagon and team, I procured a long stick from the shore, and entered the river with all my clothes on me, except my great coat and pantaloons, which I carried on my back. The river proved shallow, not being more than four feet deep in the deepest part; and I had proceeded in safety beyond the middle of the stream, when I heard the noise produced by horses' feet in front of me, and within two or three minutes several horsemen rode into the river directly before me, and advanced towards me. I now stooped down into the water, so as to leave nothing but my head, and the upper part of my pack above its surface, and waited the passage of the strangers, who, after riding into the river until the water washed the bellies of their horses, stopped to permit the animals to drink; two of them being, at this time, not more than ten yards from me. Here they entered into conversation with each other, and one said, it was his opinion that "that fellow had not come this way at all." The other then asked what his name was, and the first replied that he was called Charles, in the advertisement, but that he would no doubt call himself by some other name; as runaway negroes always took some false name, and assumed a false character. I now knew that I was within a few feet of a party, who were patrolling the country in search of me, and that nothing could save me from falling into their hands, but the obscurity produced by the fog.

There were no clouds, and if the fog had not been in the air, they must have perceived my head, on the smooth surface of the water, and have known that it was no stump or log of wood. After a few minutes of pause, these gentlemen all rode on to the side of the river from which I had come, and in a short time were out of hearing.

Notwithstanding they were gone, I remained in the water full a quarter of an hour, until I was certain that no other persons were moving along the road near me. These were the same gentlemen who had passed me, early in the night, and from whom I learned the distance to the river. From these people I had gained intelligence, which I considered of much value to me. It was now certain, that the whole country had been advised of my flight; but it was equally certain that no one had any knowledge of the course I had taken, nor of the point I was endeavouring to reach. To prevent any one from acquiring a knowledge of my route, was a primary object with me; and I determined from this moment, so to regulate my movements, as to wrap my very existence, in a veil of impenetrable secrecy. After leaving the river one or two miles, I turned aside from the road, and wrung the water from my clothes, which were all wet. This occupied some time, and after being again equipped for my journey, I made all haste to gain as much distance this night, as possible. The fog extended only a few miles from the river, and from the top of an eminence which I gained, an hour after wringing my clothes, the stars were distinctly visible. Here I discovered that the road I was travelling bore nearly east, and was not likely to take me to the Savannah river, for a long time. Nevertheless, I travelled hard until daylight appeared before me, which was my signal for turning into the woods, and seeking a place of safety for the day.

The country in which I now was, appeared high and dry, without any swamps or low grounds, in which an asylum might be found; I therefore determined to go to the top of a hill, that extended on my right for some distance either way. The summit of this ridge was gained before there was enough of daylight to enable me to see objects clearly; but, as soon as a view of the place could be had, I discovered, that it was a thicket of pine trees; and that the road which I had left, led through a plantation that lay within sight: the house and other buildings on which, appeared to be such as I had before seen; but I could not at once recollect where, or at what time I had seen them.

Going to an open space in the thicket, from which I could scan the plantation at leisure, I became satisfied, after the sun had risen, and thrown his light upon the earth, that this was no other than the residence of the gentleman, who had so kindly entertained my master and me, as we went to, and returned from, Savannah with the wagon. I now remembered that this gentleman was the friend of my late master, and that he had told me, to come and see him if ever I passed this way again; but I knew that he was a slave-holder and a planter; and that when he gave me liberty to visit his plantation, he expected that my visits would always be the visits of a slave, and not the clandestine calls of a runaway negro.

It seemed to me, that this gentleman was too benevolent a man, to arrest and send me back to my cruel mistress; and yet, how could I expect, or even hope, that a cotton planter would see a runaway slave on his premises, and not cause him to be taken up, and sent home? Failing to seize a runaway slave, when he has him in his power, is held to be one of the most dishounorable acts, to which a southern planter can subject himself. Nor should the people of the north be surprised at this. Slaves are regarded, in the south, as the most precious of all earthly possessions; and at the same time, as a precarious and hazardous kind of property, in the enjoyment of which the master is not safe. The planters may well be compared to the inhabitants of a national frontier, which is exposed to the inroads of hostile invading tribes. Where all are in like danger, and subject to like fears, it is expected that all will be governed by like sentiments, and act upon like principles.

I stood and looked at the house of this good planter, for more than an hour after the sun had risen, and saw all the movements which usually take place on a cotton plantation in the morning. Long before the sun was up, the overseer had proceeded to the field, at the head of the hands; the black women who attended to the cattle, and milked the cows, had gone to the cow-pen with their pails; and the smoke ascended from the chimney of the kitchen, before the doors of the great house were opened, or any of the members of the family were seen abroad. At length, two young ladies opened the door, and stood in the freshness of the morning air. These were soon joined by a brother; and at last, I saw the gentleman himself leave the house, and walk towards the stables, that stood at some distance from the house, on my left. I think even now, that it was a foolish resolution that emboldened me to show myself to this gentleman. It was like throwing one's self in the way of a lion who is known sometimes to spare those whom he might destroy; but I resolved to go and meet this planter at his stables, and tell him my whole story. Issuing from the woods, I crossed the fields unperceived by the people at the house, and going directly to the stables, presented myself to then, proprietor, as he stood looking at a fine horse, in one of the yards. At first, he did not know me, and asked me whose man I was. I then asked him if he did not remember me; and named the time when I had been at his house. I then told at once, that I was a runaway: that my master was dead, and my mistress so cruel, that I could not live with her: not omitting to show the scars on my back, and to give a full account of the manner in which they had been made. The gentleman stood and looked at me more than a minute, without uttering a word, and then said, "Charles, I will not betray you, but you must not stay here. It must not be known that you were on this plantation, and that I saw and conversed with you. However, as I suppose you are hungry, you may go to the kitchen and get your breakfast with my house servants."

He then set off for the house, and I followed, but turning into the kitchen, as he ordered me, I was soon supplied with a good breakfast of cold meat, warm bread, and as much new butter-milk as I chose to drink. Before I sat down to breakfast, the lady of the house came into the kitchen, with her two daughters, and gave me a dram of peach brandy. I drank this brandy, and was very thankful for it; but I am fully convinced now that it did me much more harm than good; and that this part of the kindness of this most excellent family, was altogether misplaced.

Whilst I was taking my breakfast, a black man came into the kitchen, and gave me a dollar that he said his master had sent me, at the same time laying on the table before me a package of bread and meat, weighing at least ten pounds, wrapped up in a cloth. On delivering these things, the black man told me that his master desired me to quit his premises as soon as I had finished my breakfast.

This injunction I obeyed; and within less than an hour after I entered this truly hospitable house, I quitted it forever, but not without leaving behind me my holiest blessings upon the heads of its inhabitants. It was yet early in the morning when I regained the woods on the opposite side of the plantation, from that by which I had entered it.

CHAPTER XXI.

I could not believe it possible that the white people whom I had just left, would give information of the route I had taken; but as it was possible that all who dwelt on this plantation might not be so pure of heart as were they who possessed it, I thought it prudent to travel some distance in the woods, before I stopped for the day, notwithstanding the risk of moving about in the open light. For the purpose of precluding the possibility of being betrayed, I now determined to quit this road, and travel altogether in the woods, or through open fields, for two or three nights, guiding my march by the stars. In pursuance of this resolution, I bore away to the left of the high road, and travelled five or six miles before I stopped, going round all the fields that I saw in my way, and keeping them at a good distance from me.

In the afternoon of this day, it rained, and I had no other shelter than the boughs and leaves of a large magnolia tree; but this kept me tolerably dry, and as it cleared away in the evening, I was able to continue my journey by starlight. I have no definite idea of the distance that I travelled in the course of this and the two succeeding nights, as I had no road to guide me, and was much perplexed by the plantations and houses, the latter of which I most carefully eschewed; but on the third night after this, I encountered a danger, which was very nearly fatal to me.

At the time of which I now speak, the moon having changed lately, shone until about eleven o'clock. I had been on my way two or three hours this evening, and all the world seemed to be quiet, when I entered a plantation that lay quite across my way. In passing through these fields, I at last saw the houses, and other improvements, and about a hundred yards from the house, a peach orchard, which I could distinguish by the faint light of the moon. This orchard was but little out of my way, and a quarter of a mile, as nearly as I could judge, from the woods. I resolved to examine these peach trees, and see what fruit was on them. Coming amongst them, I found the fruit of the kind called Indian peaches, in Georgia.

These Indian peaches are much the largest and finest peaches that I have ever seen, one of them oftentimes being as large as a common quince. I had filled all my pockets, and was filling my handkerchief with this delicious fruit, which is of deep red, when I heard the loud growl of a dog toward the house, the roof of which I could see. I stood as still as a stone, but yet the dog growled on, and at length barked out. I presume he smelled me, for he could not hear me, In a short time I found that the dog was coming towards me, and I then started and ran as fast as I could for the woods. He now barked louder, and was followed by another dog, both making a terrible noise. I was then pretty light of foot, and was already close by the woods when the first dog overtook me. I carried a good stick in my hand, and with this I kept the dogs at bay, until I gained the fence, and escaped into the woods; but now I heard the shouts of men encouraging the dogs, both of which were now up with me, and the men were coming as fast as they could. The dogs would not permit me to run, and unless I could make free use of my heels, it was clear that I must be taken in a few minutes. I now thought of my master's sword, which I had not removed from its quilted scabbard, in my great coat, since I commenced my journey. I snatched it from its sheath, and, at a single cut, laid open the head of the largest and fiercest of the dogs, from his neck to his nose. He gave a loud yell and fell dead on the ground. The other dog, seeing the fate of his companion, leaped the fence, and escaped into the field, where he stopped, and like a cowardly cur, set up a clamorous barking at the enemy he was afraid to look in the face. I thought this no time to wait to ascertain what the men would say, when they came to their dead dog, but made the best of my way through the woods and did not stop to look behind me, for more than an hour. In my battle with the dogs, I lost all my peaches, except a few that remained in my pockets; and in running through the woods I tore my clothes very badly, a disaster not easily repaired in my situation; but I had proved the solidity of my own judgment in putting up my sword as a part of my travelling equipage.

I now considered it necessary to travel as fast as possible, and get as far as I could before day, from the late battle-ground, and certainly I lost no time; but from the occurrences of the next day, I am of opinion, that I had not continued in a straight line all night, but that I must have travelled in a circular or zigzag route. When a man is greatly alarmed, and in a strange country, he is not able to note courses, or calculate distances, very accurately.

Daylight made its appearance, when I was moving to the south, for the daybreak was on my left hand; but I immediately stopped, went into a thicket of low white oak bushes, and lay down to rest myself, for I was very weary, and soon fell asleep, and did not awake until it

was ten or eleven o'clock. Before I fell asleep, I noted the course of
the rising sun, from the place where I lay, in pursuance of a rule that
I had established; for by this means I could tell the time of day at any
hour, within a short period of time, by taking the bearing of the sun
in the heavens, from where I lay, and then comparing it with the
place of his rising.

When I awoke to-day, I felt hungry, and after eating my breakfast,
again lay down, but, felt an unusual sense of disquietude and alarm.
It seemed to me that this was not a safe place to lie in, although it
looked as well as any other spot, that I could see. I rose and looked
for a more secure retreat, but not seeing any, lay down again—still I
was uneasy, and could not lie still. Finally I determined to get up,
and remove to the side of a large and long black log, that lay at the
distance of seventy or eighty yards from me. I went to the log and
lay down by it, placing my bundle under my head, with the
intention of going to sleep again, if I could; but I had not been here
more than fifteen or twenty minutes, when I heard the noise of men's
voices, and soon after the tramping of horses on the ground. I lay
with my back to the log in such a position, that I could see the place
where I had been in the bushes. I saw two dogs go into this little
thicket, and three horsemen rode over the very spot where I had lain
when asleep in the morning, and immediately horses and voices
were at my back, around me, and over me. Two horses jumped over
the log by the side of which I lay, one about ten feet from my feet,
and the other within two yards from my head. The horses both saw
me, took fright, and started to run; but fortunately their riders, who
were probably looking for me in the tops of the trees, or expecting to
see me start before them in the woods, and run for my life, did not
see me, and attributed the alarm of their horses to the black
appearance of the log, for I heard one of them say—"Our horses are
afraid of black logs—I wonder how they would stand the sight of the
negro, if we should meet him."

There must have been in the troop, at least twenty horsemen; and the
number of dogs was greater than I could count, as, they ran in the
woods. I knew, that all these men and dogs were in search of me,
and that if they could find me, I should be hunted down like a wild
beast. The dogs that had gone into the thicket where I had been,
fortunately for me, had not been trained to hunt negroes in the
woods, and were probably brought out for the purpose of being
trained. Doubtless, if some of the kept dogs, as they are called, of
which there were certainly several in this large pack, had happened

to go into that thicket, instead of those that did go there, my race would soon have been run.

I lay still by the side of the log for a long time after the horses, dogs, and men, had ceased to trouble the woods with their noise; if it can be said that a man lies still, who is trembling in every joint, nerve, and muscle, like a dog lying upon a cake of ice; and when I arose and turned round, I found myself so completely bereft of understanding, that I could not tell south from north, nor east from west. I could not even distinguish the thicket of bushes, from which I had removed to come to this place, from the other bushes of the woods. I remained here all day, and at night it appeared to me, that the sun set in the south-east. After sundown, the moon appeared to my distempered judgment, to stand due north from me; and all the stars were out of their places. Fortunately I had sense enough remaining to know, that it would not be safe for me to attempt to travel, until my brain had been restored to its ordinary stability; which did not take place until the third morning after my fright. The three days that I passed in this place, I reckon the most unhappy of my life; for surely it is the height of human misery, to be oppressed with alienation of mind, and to be conscious of the affliction.

Distracted as I was, I had determined never to quit this wood, and voluntarily return to slavery; and the joy I felt on the third morning, when I saw the sun rise in his proper place in the heavens; the black log, the thicket of bushes, and all other things resume the positions in which I found them, may be imagined by those who have been saved from apparently hopeless shipwreck on a barren rock, in the midst of the ocean; but cannot be described by any but a poetic pen.

I spent this day in making short excursions through the woods, for the purpose of ascertaining whether any road was near to me or not; and in the afternoon I came to one, about a mile from my camp, which was broad, and had the appearance of being much travelled. It appeared to me to lead to the north.

Awhile before sundown, I brought my bundle to this road, and lay down quietly to await the approach of night. When it was quite dark, except the light of the moon, which was now brilliant, I took to this road, and travelled all night, without hearing or seeing any person, and on the succeeding night, about two o'clock in the morning, I came to the margin of a river, so wide that I could not see across it; but the fog was so dense at this time, that I could not have seen across a river of very moderate width. I procured a long pole, and sounded the depth of the water, which I found not very deep; but as I could not see the opposite shore, was afraid to attempt to ford the stream.

In this dilemma, I turned back from the river, and went more than a mile to gain the cover of a small wood, where I might pass the day in safety, and wait a favourable moment for obtaining a view of the river, preparatory to crossing it. I lay all day in full view of the high road, and saw, at least, a hundred people pass; from which I inferred, that the country was populous about me. In the evening as soon as it was dark, I left my retreat, and returned to the river side. The atmosphere was now clear, and the river seemed to be at least a quarter of a mile in width; and whilst I was divesting myself of my clothes, preparatory to entering the water, happening to look down the shore, I saw a canoe, with its head drawn high on the beach. On reaching the canoe, I found that it was secured to the trunk of a tree by a lock and chain; but after many efforts, I broke the lock and launched the canoe into the river. The paddles had been removed, but with the aid of my sounding-pole, I managed to conduct the canoe across the water.

I was now once more in South Carolina, where I knew it was necessary for me to be even more watchful than I had been in Georgia. I do not know where I crossed the Savannah river, but I think it must have been only a few miles above the town of Augusta.

After gaining the Carolina shore, I took an observation of the rising moon and of such stars as I was acquainted with, and hastened to get away from the river, from which I knew that heavy fogs rose every night, at this season of the year, obscuring the heavens for many miles on either side. I travelled this night at least twenty miles, and provided myself with a supply of corn, which was now hard, from a field at the side of the road. At daybreak I turned into the woods, and went to the top of a hill on my left, where the ground was overgrown by the species of pine-tree called spruce in the south. I here kindled a fire, and parched corn for my breakfast.

In the afternoon of this day the weather became cloudy, and before dark the rain fell copiously, and continued through the night, with the wind high. I took shelter under a large stooping tree that was decayed and hollow on the lower side, and kept me dry until the morning. When daylight appeared, I could see that the country around me was well inhabited, and that the forest in which I lay was surrounded by plantations, at the distance of one or two miles from me. I did not consider this a safe position, and waited anxiously for night, to enable me to change my quarters. The weather was foul throughout the day; and when night returned, it was so dark that I could not see a large tree three feet before me. Waiting until the moon rose, I made my way back to the road, but had not proceeded more than two or three miles on my way, when I came to a place where the road forked, and the two roads led away almost at right angles from each other. It was so cloudy that I could not see the place of the moon in the heavens, and I knew not which of these roads to take. To go wrong was worse than to stand still, and I therefore determined to look out for some spot in which I could hide myself, and remain in this neighbourhood until the clearing up of the weather. Taking the right hand road, I followed its course until I saw at the distance, as I computed it in the night, of two miles from me a large forest which covered elevated ground. I gained it by the shortest route across some cotton fields. Going several hundred yards into this wood, I attempted to kindle a fire, in which I failed, every combustible substance being wet. This compelled me to pass the night as well as I could amongst the damp bushes and trees that overhung me. When day came, I went farther into the woods, and on the top of the highest ground that I could see, established my camp, by cutting bushes with my knife, and erecting a sort of rude booth.

It was now, by my computation, about the twenty-fifth of August, and I remained here eleven days without seeing one clear night; and in all this time the sun never shone for half a day at once. I procured my subsistence while here from a field of corn which I discovered at the distance of a mile and a half from my camp. This was the first time that I was weather-bound, and my patience had been worn out and renewed repeatedly before the return of the clear weather; but one afternoon I perceived the trees to be much agitated by the wind, the clouds appeared high, and were driven with velocity over my head. I saw the clear sky appear in all its beauty, in the northwest.

Before sundown the wind was high, the sun shone in full splendour, and a few fleecy clouds, careering high in the upper vault of heaven, gave assurance that the rains were over and gone.

At nightfall I returned to the forks of the road, and after much observation, finally concluded to follow the right hand road, in which I am satisfied that I committed a great error. Nothing worthy of notice occurred for several days after this. As I was now in a thickly-peopled country, I never moved until long after night, and was cautious never to permit daylight to find me on the road; but I observed that the north-star was always on my left hand. My object was to reach the neighbourhood of Columbia, and get upon the road which I had travelled and seen years before in coming to the south; but the road I was now on must have been the great Charleston road, leading down the country, and not across the courses of the rivers. So many people travelled this road, as well by night as by day, that my progress was very slow; and in some of the nights I did not travel more than eight miles. At the end of a week, after leaving the forks, I found myself in a flat, sandy, poor country; and as I had not met with any river on this road, I now concluded that I was on the way to the sea-board instead of Columbia. In my perplexity, I resolved to try to get information concerning the country I was in, by placing myself in some obscure place in the side of the road, and listening to the conversation of travellers as they passed me. For this purpose I chose the corner of a cotton field, around which the road turned, and led along the fence for some distance. Passing the day in the woods among the pine-trees I came to this corner in the evening, and lying down within the field, waited patiently the coming of travellers, that I might hear their conversation, and endeavour to learn from that which they said, the name at least of some place in this neighbourhood. On the first and second evenings that I lay here, I gleaned nothing from the passengers that I thought could be of service to me; but on the third night, about ten o'clock, several wagons drawn by mules passed me, and I heard one of the drivers call to another and tell him that it was sixty miles to Charleston; and that they should be able to reach the river to-morrow. I could not at first imagine what river this could be; but another of the wagoners enquired how far it was to the Edisto, to which it was replied by some one, that it was near thirty miles. I now perceived that I had mistaken my course; and was as completely lost as a wild goose in cloudy weather.

Not knowing what to do, I retraced the road that had led me to this place for several nights, hoping that something would happen from which I might learn the route to Columbia; but I gained no information that could avail me anything. At length I determined to quit this road altogether, travel by the north-star for two or three weeks, and after that to trust to Providence to guide me to some road that might lead me back to Maryland. Having turned my face due north, I made my way pretty well for the first night; but on the second, the fog was so dense that no stars could be seen. This compelled me to remain in my camp, which I had pitched in a swamp. In this place I remained more than a week, waiting for clear nights; but now the equinoctial storm came on, and raged with a fury which I had never before witnessed in this annual gale; at least it had never before appeared so violent to me, because, perhaps, I had never been exposed to its blasts, without the shelter of a house of some kind. This storm continued four days; and no wolf ever lay closer in his lair, or moved out with more stealthy caution than I did during this time. My subsistence was drawn from a small corn-field at the edge of the swamp in which I lay.

After the storm was over, the weather became calm and clear, and I fell into a road which appeared to run nearly north-west. Following the course of this road by short marches, because I was obliged to start late at night and stop before day, I came on the first day, or rather night, of October, by my calender, to a broad and well-frequented road that crossed mine at nearly right angles. These roads crossed in the middle of a plantation, and I took to the right hand along this great road, and pursued it in the same cautious and slow manner that I had travelled for the last month.

When the day came I took refuge in the woods as usual, choosing the highest piece of ground that I could find in the neighbourhood. No part of this country was very high, but I thought people who visited these woods, would be less inclined to walk to the tops of the hills, than to keep their course along the low grounds.

I had lately crossed many small streams; but on the second night of my journey on this road, came to a narrow but deep river, and after the most careful search, no boat or craft of any kind could be found on my side. A large flat, with two or three canoes, lay on the opposite side, but they were as much out of my reach as if they had never been made. There was no alternative but swimming this stream, and I made the transit in less than three minutes, carrying my packages on my back.

I had as yet fallen in with no considerable towns, and whenever I had seen a house near the road, or one of the small hamlets of the south in my way, I had gone round by the woods or fields, so as to avoid the inhabitants; but on the fourth night after swimming the small river, I came in sight of a considerable village, with lights burning and shining through many of the windows. I knew the danger of passing a town, on account of the patrols with which all southern towns are provided, and making a long circuit to the right, so as totally to avoid this village, I came to the banks of a broad river, which, upon further examination, I found flowing past the village, and near its border. This compelled me to go back, and attempt to turn the village on the left, which was performed by wandering a long time in swamps and pine woods.

It was break of day when I regained the road beyond the village, and returning to the swamps from which I had first issued, I passed the day under their cover. On the following night, after regaining the road, I soon found myself in a country almost entirely clear of timber, and abounding in fields of cotton and corn.

The houses were numerous, and the barking of dogs was incessant. I felt that I was in the midst of dangers, and that I was entering a region very different from those tracts of country though which I had lately passed, where the gloom of the wilderness was only broken by solitary plantations or lonely huts. I had no doubt that I was in the neighbourhood of some town, but of its name, and the part of the country in which it was located, I was ignorant. I at length found that I was receding from the woods altogether, and entering a champaign country, in the midst of which I now perceived a town of considerable magnitude, the inhabitants of which were entirely silent, and the town itself presented the appearance of total solitude. The country around was so open, that I despaired of turning so large a place as this was, and again finding the road I travelled I therefore determined to risk all consequences, and attempt to pass this town under cover of darkness.

Keeping straight forward, I came unexpectedly to a broad river, which I now saw running between me and the town. I took it for granted that there must be a ferry at this place, and on examining the shore, found several small boats fastened only with ropes to a large scow. One of these boats I seized, and was quickly on the opposite shore of the river. I entered the village and proceeded to its centre, without seeing so much as a rat in motion. Finding, myself in an open space I stopped to examine the streets, and upon looking at the houses around me, I at once recognized the jail of Columbia, and the tavern in which I had lodged on the night after I was sold.

This discovery made me feel almost at home, with my wife and children. I remembered the streets by which I had come from the country to the jail, and was quickly at the extremity of the town, marching towards the residence of the paltry planter, at whose house I had lodged on my way south. It was late at night, when I left Columbia, and it was necessary for me to make all speed, and get as far as possible from that place before day. I ran rather than walked, until the appearance of dawn, when I left the road and took shelter in the pine woods, with which this part of the country abounds.

I had now been travelling almost two months, and was still so near the place from which I first departed, that I could easily have walked to it in a week, by daylight; but I hoped, that as I was now on a road with which I was acquainted, and in a country through which I had travelled before, that my future progress would be more rapid, and that I should be able to surmount, without difficulty, many of the obstacles that had hitherto embarrassed me so greatly.

It was now in my power to avail myself of the knowledge I had formerly acquired, of the customs of South Carolina. The patrol are very rigid in the execution of the authority, with which they are invested; but I never had much difficulty with these officers, anywhere. From dark until ten or eleven o'clock at night, the patrol are watchful, and always traversing the country in quest of negroes, but towards midnight these gentlemen grow cold, or sleepy, or weary, and generally betake themselves to some house, where they can procure a comfortable fire.

I now established, as a rule of my future conduct, to remain in my hiding place until after ten o'clock, according to my computation of time; and this night I did not come to the road, until I supposed it to be within an hour of midnight, and it was well for me that I practised so much caution, for when within two or three hundred yards of the road, I heard people conversing. After standing some minutes in the woods, and listening to the voices at the road, the people separated, and a party took each end of the road, and galloped away upon their horses. These people were certainly a band of patrollers, who were watching this road, and had just separated to return home for the night. After the horsemen were quite out of hearing, I came to the road, and walked as fast as I could for hours, and again came into the lane leading to the house, where I had first remained a few days, in Carolina. Turning away from the road I passed through this plantation, near the old cotton-gin house, in which I had formerly lodged, and perceived that every thing on this plantation was nearly as it was when I left it. Two or three miles from this place I again left the road, and sought a place of concealment, and from this time until I reached Maryland, I never remained in the road until daylight but once, and I paid dearly then for my temerity.

I was now in an open, thickly-peopled country, in comparison with many other tracts through which I had passed; and this circumstance compelled me to observe the greater caution. As nearly as possible, I confined my travelling within the hours of midnight and three o'clock in the morning. Parties of patrollers were heard by me almost every morning, before day. These people sometimes moved directly along the roads, but more frequently lay in wait near the side of the road, ready to pounce upon any runaway slave that might chance to pass; but I knew by former experience that they never lay out all night, except in times of apprehended danger; and the country appearing at this time to be quiet, I felt but little apprehension of falling in with these policemen, within my travelling hours.

There was now plenty of corn in the fields, and sweet potatoes had not yet been dug. There was no scarcity of provisions with me, and my health was good, and my strength unimpaired. For more than two weeks, I pursued the road that had led me from Columbia, believing I was on my way to Camden. Many small streams crossed my way, but none of them were large enough to oblige me to swim in crossing them.

CHAPTER XXII.

On the twenty-fourth of October, according to my computation, in a dark night, I came to a river, which appeared to be both broad and deep. Sounding its depth with a pole, I found it too deep to be forded, and after the most careful search along the shore, no boat could be discovered. This place appeared altogether strange to me, and I began to fear that I was again lost. Confident that I had never before been where I now found myself, and ignorant of the other side of the stream, I thought it best not to attempt to cross this water until I was better informed of the country through which it flowed. A thick wood bordered the road on my left, and gave me shelter until daylight. Ascending a tree at sunrise, that overlooked the stream, which appeared to be more than a mile in width, I perceived on the opposite shore a house, and one large, and several small boats in the river. I remained in this tree the greater part of the day, and saw several persons cross the river, some of whom had horses; but in the evening the boats were all taken back to the place at which I had seen them in the morning. The river was so broad, that I felt some fear of failing in the attempt to swim it; but seeing no prospect of procuring a boat to transport me, I resolved to attempt the navigation as soon as it was dark. About nine o'clock at night, having equipped myself in the best manner I was able, I undertook this hazardous navigation, and succeeded in gaining the farther shore of the river, in about an hour, with all my things in safety. On the previous day I had noted the bearing of the road, as it led from the river, and in the middle of the night I again resumed my journey, in a state of perplexity bordering upon desperation; for it was now evident that this was not the road by which we had travelled when we came to the southern country, and on which hand to turn to reach the right way, I knew not.

After travelling five or six miles on this road, and having the north-star in view all the time, I became satisfied that my course lay northwest, and that I was consequently going out of my way; and to heighten my anxiety, I had not tasted any animal food since I crossed the Savannah river—a sensation of hunger harrassed me constantly; but fortune, which had been so long adverse to me, and had led me so often astray, had now a little favour in store for me. The leaves were already fallen from some of the more tender trees, and near the road I this night perceived a persimmon tree, well laden with fruit, and whilst gathering the fallen persimmons under the tree, a noise over head arrested my attention. This noise was caused by a large opossum, which was on the tree gathering fruit like myself. With a long stick the animal was brought to the ground, and it proved to be very fat, weighing at least ten pounds. With such a luxury as this in my possession, I could not think of travelling far without tasting it, and accordingly halted about a mile from the persimmon tree, on a rising ground in a thick wood, where I killed my opossum, and took off its skin, a circumstance that I much regretted, for with the skin I took at least a pound of fine fat. Had I possessed the means of scalding my game, and dressing it like a pig, it would have afforded me provision for a week; but as it was, I made a large fire and roasted my prize before it, losing all the oil that ran out in the operation, for want of a dripping-pan to catch it. It was daylight when my meat was ready for the table, and a very sumptuous breakfast it yielded me.

Since leaving Columbia, I had followed as nearly as the course of the roads permitted, the index of the north-star; which, I supposed, would lead me on the most direct route to Maryland; but I now became convinced, that this star was leading me away from the line by which I had approached the cotton country.

I slept none this day, but passed the whole time, from breakfast until night, in considering the means of regaining my lost way. From the aspect of the country I arrived at the conclusion, that I was not near the sea-coast; for there were no swamps in all this region; the land lay rather high and rolling, and oak timber abounded.

At the return of night, I resumed my journey earlier than usual: paying no regard to the roads, but keeping the north-star on my left hand, as nearly as I could. This night I killed a rabbit, which had leaped from the bushes before me, by throwing my walking stick at it. It was roasted at my stopping place in the morning, and was very good.

I pursued the same course, keeping the north-star on my left hand for three nights; intending to get as far east as the road leading from Columbia to Richmond, in Virginia; but as my line of march lay almost continually in the woods, I made but little progress; and on the third day, the weather became cloudy, so that I could not see the stars. This again compelled me to lie by, until the return of fair weather.

On the second day, after I had stopped this time, the sun shone out bright in the morning, and continued to shed a glorious light during the day; but in the evening, the heavens became overcast with clouds; and the night that followed was so dark, that I did not attempt to travel. This state of the weather continued more than a week: obliging me to remain stationary all this time. These cloudy nights were succeeded by a brisk wind from the north-west, accompanied by fine clear nights, in which I made the best of my way towards the north-east, pursuing my course across the country without regard to roads, forests, or streams of water: crossing many of the latter, none of which were deep, but some of them were extremely muddy. One night I became entangled in a thick and deep swamp; the trees that grew in which, were so tall, and stood so close together, that the interlocking of their boughs, and the deep foliage in which the were clad, prevented me from seeing the stars. Wandering there for several hours, most of the time with mud and water over my knees, and frequently wading in stagnant pools, with deep slimy bottoms, I became totally lost, and was incapable of seeing the least appearance of fast land. At length, giving up all hope of extricating from this abyss of mud, water, brambles, and fallen timber, I scrambled on a large tussock, and sat down to await the coming of day, with the intention of going to the nearest high land, as soon as the sun should be up. The nights were now becoming cool, and though I did not see any frost in the swamp where I was in the morning, I have no doubt, that hoar frost was seen in the dry and open country. After daylight I found myself as much perplexed as I was at midnight. No shore was to be seen; and in every direction there was the same deep, dreary, black solitude. To add to my misfortune, the morning proved cloudly, and when the sun was up, I could not tell the east from the west. After waiting several hours for a sight of the sun, and failing to obtain it, I set out in search of a running stream of water, intending to strike off at right angels, with the course of the current, and endeavour to reach the dry ground by this means: but after wandering about, through tangled bushes, briars, and vines clambering over fallen tree-tops, and wading through fens overgrown with saw grass, for two or three hours, I sat down in despair of finding any guide to conduct me from this detestable place.

My bag of meal that I took with me at the commencement of my journey, was long since gone; and the only provisions that I now possessed, were a few grains of parched corn, and near a pint of chestnuts that I had picked up under a tree the day before I entered the swamp. The chestnut-tree was full of nuts, but I was afraid to throw sticks or to shake the tree, lest hunters or other persons hearing the noise, might be drawn to the place.

About ten o'clock I sat down under a large cypress tree, upon a decaying log of the same timber, to make my breakfast on a few grains of parched corn. Near me was an open space without trees, but filled with water that seemed to be deep, for no grass grew in it, except a small quantity near the shore. The water was on my left hand, and as I sat cracking my corn, my attention was attracted by the playful gambols of two squirrels that were running and chasing each other on the boughs of some trees near me. Half pleased with the joyous movements of the little animals, and half covetous of their carcasses, to roast and devour them, I paid no attention to a succession of sounds on my left, which I thought proceeded from the movement of frogs at the edge of the water, until the breaking of a stick near me caused me to turn my head, when I discovered that I had other neighbours than spring-frogs.

A monstrous alligator had left the water, and was crawling over the mud, with his eyes fixed upon me. He was now within fifteen feet of me, and in a moment more, if he had not broken the stick with his weight, I should have become his prey. He could easily have knocked me down with a blow of his tail; and if his jaws had once been closed on a leg or an arm, he would have dragged me into the water, spite of any resistance that I could have made.

At the sight of him, I sprang to my feet, and running to the other end of the fallen tree on which I sat, and being there out of danger; had an opportunity of viewing the motions of the alligator at leisure. Finding me out of his reach, he raised his trunk from the ground, elevated his snout, and gave a wistful look, the import of which I well understood; then turning slowly round, he retreated to the water, and sank from my vision.

I was much alarmed by this adventure with the alligator, for had I fallen in with this huge reptile in the night-time, I should have had no chance of escape from his tusks.

The whole day was spent in the swamp, not in travelling from place to place, but in waking for the sun to shine, to enable me to obtain a knowledge of the various points of the heavens. The day was succeeded by a night of unbroken darkness; and it was late in the evening of the second day before I saw the sun. It being then too late to attempt to extricate myself from the swamp for that day, I was obliged to pass another night in the lodge that I had formed for myself in the thick boughs of a fallen cypress tree, which elevated me several feet from the ground, where I believed the alligator could not reach me, if he should come in pursuit of me.

On the morning of the third day, the sun rose beautifully clear, and at sight of him I set off for the east. It must have been five miles from the place where I lay to the dry land on the east of the swamp; for with all the exertion that fear and hunger compelled me to make, it was two or three o'clock in the afternoon when I reached the shore, after swimming in several places, and suffering the loss of a very valuable part of my clothes, which were torn off by the briars and snags. On coming to high ground I found myself in the woods, and hungry as I was, lay down to await the coming of night, lest some one should see me moving through the forest in daylight.

When night came on, I resumed my journey by the stars, which were visible, and marched several miles before coming to a plantation. The first that I came to was a cotton field; and after much search, I found no corn nor grain of any kind on this place, and was compelled to continue on my way.

Two or three miles further on, I was more fortunate, and found a field of corn which had been gathered from the stalks and thrown in heaps along the ground. Filling my little bag, which I still kept, with this corn, I retreated a mile or two in the woods, and striking fire, encamped for the purpose of parching and eating it. After despatching my meal, I lay down beside the fire and fell into a sound sleep, from which I did not awake until long after sunrise; but on rising and looking around me, I found that my lodge was within less than a hundred yards of a new house that people were building in the woods, and upon which men were now at work. Dropping instantly to the ground, I crawled away through the woods, until being out of sight of the house, I ventured to rise and escape on my feet. After I lay down in the night, my fire had died away, and emitted no smoke; this circumstance saved me. This affair made me more cautious as to my future conduct.

Hiding in the woods until night again came on, I continued my course eastward, and some time after midnight came upon a wide, well beaten road, one end of which led, at this place, a little to the left of the north-star, which I could plainly see. Here I deliberated a long time, whether to take this road, or continue my course across the country by the stars; but at last resolved to follow the road, more from a desire to get out of the woods, than from a conviction that it would lead me in the right way. In the course of this night I saw but few plantations, but was so fortunate as to see a ground-hog crossing the road before me. This animal I killed with my stick, and carried it until morning.

At the approach of daylight, turning away to the right, I gained the top of an eminence, from which I could see through the woods for some distance around me. Here I kindled a fire and roasted my ground-hog, which afforded me a most grateful repast, after my late fasting and severe toils. According to custom, my meal being over, I betook myself to sleep, and did not awake until the afternoon; when descending a few rods down the hill, and standing still to take a survey of the woods around me, I saw, at the distance of half a mile from me, a man moving slowly about in the forest, and apparently watching, like myself, to see if any one was in view. Looking at this man attentively, I saw that he was a black, and that he did not move more than a few rods from the same spot where I first saw him. Curiosity impelled me to know more of the condition of my neighbour; and descending quite to the foot of the hill, I perceived that he had a covert of boughs of trees, under which I saw him pass, and after some time return again from his retreat. Examining the appearance of things carefully, I became satisfied that the stranger was, like myself, a negro slave, and I determined, without more ceremony, to go and speak to him, for I felt no fear of being betrayed by one as badly off in the world as myself.

When this man first saw me, at the distance of a hundred yards from him, he manifested great agitation, and at once seemed disposed to run from me; but when I called to him, and told him not to be afraid, he became more assured, and waited for me to come close to him. I found him to be a dark mulatto, small and slender in person, and lame in one leg. He had been well bred, and possessed good manners and fine address. I told him I was travelling, and presumed this was not his dwelling place. Upon which he informed me that he was a native of Kent county, in the state of Delaware, and had been brought up as a house-servant by his master, who, on his death-bed, had made his will, and directed him to be set free by his executors, at the age of twenty-five, and that in the meantime he would be hired out as a servant to some person who should treat him well. Soon after the death of his master, the executors hired him to a man in Wilmington, who employed him as a waiter in his house for three or four months, and then took him to a small town called Newport, and sold him to a man who took him immediately to Baltimore, where he was again sold or transferred to another man, who brought him to South Carolina, and sold him to a cotton planter, with whom he had lived more than two years, and had run away three weeks before the time I saw him, with the intention of returning to Delaware.

That being lame, and becoming fatigued by travelling, he had stopped here and made this shelter of boughs and bark of trees, under which he had, remained more than a week before I met him. He invited me to go into his camp, as he termed it, where he had an old skillet, more than a bushel of potatoes, and several fowls, all of which he said he had purloined from the plantations in the neighbourhood.

This encampment was in a level open wood, and it appeared surprising to me that its occupant had not been discovered and conveyed back to his master before this time. I told him that I thought he ran great risk of being taken up by remaining here, and advised him to break up his lodge immediately, and pursue his journey, travelling only in the night time. He then proposed to join me, and travel in company with me; but this I declined, because of his lameness and great want of discretion, though I did not assign these reasons to him.

I remained with this man two or three hours, and ate dinner of fowls dressed after his rude fashion. Before leaving him, I pressed upon him the necessity of immediately quitting the position he then occupied; but he said he intended to remain there a few days longer, unless I would take him with me.

On quitting my new acquaintance, I thought it prudent to change my place of abode for the residue of this day, and removed along the top of the hill that I occupied at least two miles, and concealed myself in a thicket until night, when returning to the road I had left in the morning, and travelling hard all night, I came to a large stream of water just at the break of day. As it was too late to pass the river with safety this morning, at this ford, I went half a mile higher, and swam across the stream in open daylight, at a place where both sides of the water were skirted with woods. I had several large potatoes that had been given to me by the man at his camp in the woods, and these constituted my rations for this day.

At the rising and setting of the sun, I took the bearing of the road by the course of the stream I that I had crossed, and found that I was travelling to the northwest, instead of the north or northeast, to one of which latter points I wished to direct my march.

Having perceived the country in which I now was to be thickly peopled, I remained in my resting place until late at night, when returning to the road, and crossing it, I took once more to the woods, with the stars for my guides, and steered for the northeast.

This was a fortunate night for me in all respects. The atmosphere was clear, the ground was high, dry, and free from thickets. In the course of the night I passed several corn fields, with the corn still remaining in them, and passed a potato lot, in which large quantities of fine potatoes were dug out of the ground, and lay in heaps covered with vines; but my most signal good luck occurred just before day, when passing under a dog-wood tree, and hearing a noise in the branches above me, I looked up and saw, a large opossum amongst the berries that hung upon the boughs. The game was quickly shaken down, and turned out as fat as a well-fed pig, and as heavy as a full-grown rackoon. My attention was now turned to searching for a place in which I could secrete myself for the day, and dress my provisions in quietness.

This day was dear and beautiful until the afternoon, when the air became damp, and the heavens were overhung with clouds. The night that followed was dark as pitch, compelling me to remain in my camp all night. The next day brought with it a terrible storm of rain and wind, that continued with but little intermission, more than twenty- four hours, and the sun was not again visible until the third day; nor was there a clear night for more than a week. During all this time I lay in my camp, and subsisted upon the provisions that I had brought with me to this place. The corn and potatoes looked so tempting, when I saw them in the fields, that I had taken more than I should have consumed, had not the bad weather compelled me to remain at this spot; but it was well for me, for this time, that I had taken more than I could eat in one or two days.

At the end of the cloudy weather, I felt much refreshed and strengthened, and resumed my journey in high spirits, although I now began to feel the want of shoes—those which I wore when I left my mistress having long since been worn out, and my boots were now beginning to fail so much, that I was obliged to wrap straps of hickory bark about my feet, to keep the leather from separating, and falling to pieces. It was now, by my computation, the month of November, and I was yet in the state of South Carolina. I began to consider with myself, whether I had gamed or lost, by attempting to travel on the roads; and, after revolving in my mind all the disasters that had befallen me, determined to abandon the roads altogether, for two reasons:— the first of which was, that on the highways, I was constantly liable to meet persons, or to be overtaken by them; and a second, no less powerful, was, that as I did not know what roads to pursue, I was oftener travelling on the wrong route than on the right one.

Setting my face once more for the north-star, I advanced with a steady, though slow pace, for four or five nights, when I was again delayed by dark weather, and forced to remain in idleness nearly two weeks; and when the weather again became clear, I was arrested, on the second night, by a broad and rapid river, that appeared so formidable, that I did not dare to attempt its passage, until after examining it in daylight. On the succeeding night, however, I crossed it by swimming—resting at some large rocks near the middle. After gaining the north side of this river, which I believed to be the Catawba, I considered myself in North Carolina, and again steered towards the north.

CHAPTER XXIII.

The month of November is, in all years, a season of clouds and vapours; but at the time of which I write the good weather vanished early in the month, and all the clouds of the universe seemed to have collected in North Carolina. From the second night after crossing the Catawba, I did not see the north-star for the space of three weeks; and during all this time, no progress was made in my journey; although I seldom remained two days in the same place, but moved from one position to another, for the purpose of eluding the observation of the people of the country, whose attention might have been attracted by the continual appearance of the smoke of my fires in one place.

There had, as yet, been no hard frost, and the leaves were still on the oak trees, at the close of this cloudy weather; but the northwest wind which dispelled the mist, also brought down nearly all the leaves of the forest, except those of the evergreen trees; and the nights now became clear, and the air keen with frost. Hitherto the oak woods had afforded me the safest shelter, but now I was obliged to seek for groves of young pines to retire to at dawn. Heretofore, I had found a plentiful subsistence in every corn-field and potato-lot, that fell in my way: but now began to find some of the fields in which corn had grown, destitute of the corn, and containing nothing but the stalks. The potatoes had all been taken out of the lots where they grew, except in some few instances where they had been buried in the field; and the means of subsistence became every day more difficult to be obtained; but as I had fine weather, I made the best use of those hours in which I dared to travel, and was constantly moving from a short time after dark until daylight. The toil that I underwent for the first half of the month of December was excessive, and my sufferings for want of food were great. I was obliged to carry with me a stock of corn, sufficient to supply me for two or three days; for it frequently happened that I met with none in the fields for a long time. In the course of this period, I crossed innumerable streams, the greater portion of which were of small size, but some were of considerable magnitude; and in all of them the water had become almost as cold as ice. Sometimes I was fortunate enough to find boats or canoes tied at the side of the streams, and when this happened, I always made free use of that which no one else was using at the time; but this did not occur often, and I believe that in these two weeks I swam over nine rivers, or streams, so deep, that I could not ford them. The number of creeks and rivulets through which I waded, was far greater; but I cannot now fix the number.

In one of these fine nights, passing near the house of a planter, I saw several dry hides hanging on poles, under a shed. One of these hides I appropriated to myself, for the purpose of converting it into moccasins, to supply the place of my boots, which were totally worthless. By beating the dry hide with a stick it was made sufficiently pliable to bear making it into moccasins; of which I made for myself three pair, wearing one, and carrying the others on my back.

One day as I lay in a pine thicket, several pigs, which appeared to be wild, having no marks on their ears, came near me, and one of them approached so close without seeing me, that I knocked it down with a stone, and succeeded in killing it. This pig was very fat, and would have weighed thirty if not forty pounds. Feeling now greatly exhausted with the fatigues that I had lately undergone, and being in a very great forest, far removed from white inhabitants, I resolved to remain a few days in this place, to regale myself with the flesh of the pig, which I preserved by hanging it up in the shade, after cutting it into pieces. Fortune, so adverse to me heretofore, seemed to have been more kind to me at this time, for the very night succeeding the day on which I killed the pig, a storm of hail, snow, and sleet, came on, and continued fifteen or sixteen hours. The snow lay on the ground four inches in depth, and the whole country was covered with a crust almost hard enough to bear a man. In this state of the weather I could not travel, and my stock of pork was invaluable to me. The pork was frozen where it hung on the branches of the trees, and was as well preserved as if it had been buried in snow; but on the fourth day after the snow fell, the atmosphere underwent a great change. The wind blew from the south, the snow melted away, the air became warm, and the sun shone with the brightness, and almost with the warmth of spring. It was manifest that my pork, which was now soft and oily, would not long be in a sound state. If I remained here, my provisions would become putrid on my hands in a short time, and compel me to quit my residence to avoid the atmosphere of the place.

I resolved to pursue my journey, and prepared myself, by roasting before the fire, all my pork that was left, wrapping it up carefully in green pine leaves, and enveloping the whole in a sort of close basket, that I made of small boughs of trees. Equipping myself for my journey with my meat in my knapsack, I again took to the woods, with the stars for my guide, keeping the north-star over my left eye.

The weather had now become exceedingly variable, and I was seldom able to travel more than half of the night. The fields were muddy, the low grounds in the woods were wet, and often covered with water, through which I was obliged to wade—the air was damp and cold by day, the nights were frosty, very often covering the water with ice an inch in thickness. From the great degree of cold that prevailed, I inferred, either that I was pretty far north, or that I had advanced too much to the left, and was approaching the mountain country.

To satisfy myself as far as possible of my situation, one fair day, when the sky was very clear, I climbed to the top of a pine-tree that stood on the summit of a hill, and took a wide survey of the region around me. Eastward, I saw nothing but a continuation of plantations, intervened by forests; on the south, the faint beams of a winter sun shed a soft lustre over the woods, which were dotted at remote distances, with the habitations of men, and the openings that they had made in the green champion of the endless pine-groves, that nature had planted in the direction of the midday sun. On the north, at a great distance, I saw a tract of low and flat country, which, in my opinion, was the vale of some great river, and beyond this, at the farthest stretch of vision, the eye was lost in the blue transparent vault, where the extremity of the arch of the world touches the abode of perpetual winter. Turning westward, the view passed beyond the region of pine-trees, which was followed afar off by naked and leafless oaks, hickories, and walnuts; and still beyond these rose high in air, elevated tracts of country, clad in the white livery of snow, and bearing the impress of mid-winter.

It was now apparent that I had borne too far west and was within a few days travel of the mountains. Descending from my observations, I determined, on the return of night, to shape my course, for the future, nearly due east, until I should at least be out of the mountains.

According to my calendar, it was the day before Christmas that I ascended the pine-tree; and I believe I was at that time in the north-western part of North Carolina, not far from the banks of the Yadkin river. On the following night I travelled from dark until, as I supposed, about three or four o'clock in the morning, when I came to a road which led, as I thought, in an easterly direction. This road I travelled until daylight, and encamped near it in an old field, overgrown with young pines, and holly-trees.

This was Christmas-day, and I celebrated it by breakfasting on fat pork, without salt, and substituted parched corn for bread. In the evening, the weather became cloudy and cold, and when night came, it was so dark, that I found difficulty in keeping in the road, at some points where it made short angles. Before midnight it began to snow, and at break of day the snow lay more than a foot deep. This compelled me to seek winter quarters; and fortunately, at about half a mile from the road, I found, on the side of a steep hill, a shelving rock that formed a dry covert, with a southern prospect.

Under this rock I took refuge, and kindling a fire of dry sticks, considered myself happy to possess a few pounds of my roasted pork, and more than half a gallon of corn that I carried in my pockets. The snow continued falling, until it was full two feet deep around me, and the danger of exposing myself to discovery by my tracks in the snow, compelled me to keep close to my hiding place until the third day, when I ventured to go back to the road, which I found broken by the passage of numerous wagons, sleds, and horses, and so much beaten that I could travel it with ease at night, the snow affording good light.

Accordingly at night I again advanced on my way, which indeed I was obliged to do, for my corn was quite gone, and not more than a pound of my pork remained to me. I travelled hard through the night, and after the morning star rose, came to a river which I think must have been the Yadkin. It appeared to be about two hundred yards wide, and the water ran with great rapidity in it.

Waiting until the eastern horizon was tinged with the first rays of the morning light, I entered the river at the ford, and waded until the water was nearly three feet deep, when it felt as if it was cutting the flesh from the bones of my limbs, and a large cake of ice floating downward, forced me off my balance, and I was near falling. My courage failed me, and I returned to the shore, but found the pain that already tormented me, greatly increased, when I was out of the water, and exposed to the action of the open air. Returning to the river, I plunged into the current to relieve me from the pinching frost, that gnawed every part of my skin that had become wet; and rushing forward as fast as the weight of the water, that pressed me downward, would permit, was soon up to my chin in melted ice, when rising to the surface, I exerted my utmost strength and skill to gain the opposite shore by swimming in the shortest space of time. At every stroke of my arms and legs, they were cut and bruised by cakes of solid ice, or weighed down by floating masses of congealed snow.

It is impossible for human life to be long sustained in such an element as that which encompassed me; and I had not been afloat five minutes before felt chilled in all my members, and in less than the double of that time, my limbs felt numbed, and my hands became stiff, and almost powerless.

When at the distance of thirty feet front the shore, my body was struck by a violent current, produced by a projecting rock above me, and driven with resistless violence down the stream. Wholly unable to contend with the fury of the waves, and penetrated by the coldness of death, in my most vitals. I gave myself up for lost, and was commending my soul to God, whom I expected to be my immediate judge, when I perceived the long hanging branch of a large tree, sweeping to and fro, and undulating backward and forward, as its extremities were washed by the surging current of the river, just below me. In a moment I was in contact with the tree, and making the effort of despair, seized one of its limbs. Bowed down by the weight of my body, the branch yielded to the power of the water, which rushing against my person, swept me round like the quadrant of a circle, and dashed me against the shore, where clinging to some roots that grew near the bank, the limb of the tree left me, and springing with elastic force to its former position, again dipped its slender branches in the mad stream.

Crawling out of the water, and being once more on dry land, I found my circumstances little less desperate, than when I was struggling with the floating ice. The morning was frosty, and icicles hung in long pendant groups from the trees along the shore of the river, and the hoar frost glistened in sparkling radiance upon the polished surface of the smooth snow, as it whitened all the plain before me, and spread its chill but beautiful covering through the woods.

There were three alternatives before me, one of which I knew must quickly be adopted. The one was to obtain a fire, by which I could dry and warm my stiffened limbs; the second was to die, without the fire; the third, to go to the first house, if I could reach one, and surrender myself as a runaway slave.

Staggering, rather than walking forward, until I gained the cover of a wood, at a short distance from the river, I turned into it, and found that a field bordered the wood within less than twenty rods of the road. Within a few yards of this fence I stopped, and taking out my fire apparatus, to my unspeakable joy, found them dry and in perfect safety. With the aid of my spunk, and some dry moss gathered from the fence, a small flame was obtained, to which dry leaves being added from the boughs of a white oak tree, that had fallen before the frost of the last autumn had commenced, I soon had fire of sufficient intensity, to consume dry wood, with which I supplied it, partly from the fence, and partly from the branches of the fallen tree. Having raked away the snow from about the fire, by the time the sun was up, my frozen clothes were smoking before the coals—warming first one side and then the other— I felt the glow of returning life, once more invigorating my blood, and giving animation to my frozen limbs.

The public road was near me on one hand, and an enclosed field was before me on the other, but in my present condition, it was impossible for me to leave this place to-day, without danger of perishing in the woods, or of being arrested on the road.

As evening came on, the air became much colder than it was in the forenoon, and after night the wind rose high, and blew from the northwest, with intense keenness. My limbs were yet stiff from the effects of my morning adventure, and to complete my distress, I was totally without provisions, having left a few ears of corn, that I had in my pocket, on the other side of the river.

Leaving my fire in the night, and advancing into the field near me, I discovered a house at some distance and as there was no light, or sign of fire about it, I determined to reconnoitre the premises, which turned out to be a small barn, standing alone, with no other inhabitants about it than a few cattle and a flock of sheep. After much trouble, I succeeded in entering the barn by starting the nails that confined one of the boards at the corner. Entering the house I found it nearly filled with corn, in the husks, and some from which the husks had been removed, was lying in a heap in one corner.

Into these husks I crawled. and covering myself deeply under them, soon became warm, and fell into a profound sleep, from which I was awakened by the noise of people walking about in the barn, and talking of the cattle and sheep, which it appeared they had come to feed, for they soon commenced working in the corn husks, with which I was covered, and throwing them out to the cattle. I expected at every moment that they would uncover me; but fortunately before they saw me, they ceased their operations, and went to work, some husking corn, and throwing the husks on the pile over me, while others were employed in loading the husked corn into carts, as I learned by their conversation, and hauling it away to the house. The people continued working in the barn all day, and in the evening gave more husks to the cattle and went home.

Waiting two or three hours after my visiters were gone, I rose from the pile of husks, and filling my pockets with ears of corn, issued from the barn, at the same place by which I had entered it, and retired to the woods, where I kindled a fire in a pine thicket, and parched more than half a gallon of corn. Before day I returned to the barn, and again secreted myself in the corn husks. In the morning the people again returned to their work, and husked corn until the evening. At night I again repaired to the woods, and parched more corn. In this manner I passed more than a month, lying in the barn all day, and going to the woods at night; but at length the corn was all husked, and I watched daily the progress that was made in feeding the cattle with the husks, knowing that I must quit my winter retreat, before the husks were exhausted. Before the husked corn was removed from the barn, I had conveyed several bushels of the ears into the husks, near my bed, and concealed them for my winter's stock.

Whilst I lay in this barn, there were frequent and great changes of weather. The snow that covered the earth to the depth of two feet, when I came here, did not remain more than ten days, and was succeeded by more than a week of warm rainy weather which was in turn succeeded by several days of dry weather, with cold high winds from the north. The month of February was cloudy and damp, with several squalls of snow and frequent rains. About the first of March, the atmosphere became clear and dry, and the winds boisterous from the west.

On the third of this month, having filled my little bag and all my pockets with parched corn, I quitted my winter quarters about ten o'clock at night, and again proceeded on my way to the north, leaving a large heap of corn husks still lying in the corner of the barn.

On leaving this place, I again pursued the road that had led me to it, for several nights; crossing many small streams in my way, all of which I was able to pass without swimming, though several of them were so deep, that they wet me as high as my arm-pits. This road led nearly northeast, and was the only road that I had fallen in with since I left Georgia, that had maintained that direction for so great a distance. Nothing extraordinary befell me until the twelfth of March, when venturing to turn out earlier than usual in the evening, and proceeding along the road, I found that my way led me down a hill, along the side of which the road had been cut into the earth ten or twelve feet in depth, having steep banks on each side, which were now so damp and slippery, that it was impossible for a man to ascend either the one or the other.

Whilst in this narrow place, I heard the sound of horses proceeding up the hill to meet me. Stopping to listen, in a moment almost two horsemen were close before me, trotting up the road. To escape on either hand was impossible, and to retreat backwards would have exposed me to certain destruction. Only one means of salvation was left, and I embraced it. Near the place where I stood, was a deep gully cut in one side of the road, by the water which had run down here in time of rains. Into this gully I threw myself, and lying down close to the ground, the horsemen rode almost over me, and passed on. When they were gone I arose, and descending the hill, found a river before me.

In crossing this stream, I was compelled to swim at least two hundred yards; and found the cold so oppressive, after coming out of the water, that I was forced to stop at the first thick woods that I could find and make a fire to city myself. I did not move again until the next night; and on the fourth night after this, came to a great river, which I suppose was the Roanoke. I was obliged to swim this stream, and was carried a great way down by the rapidity of the current. It must have been more than an hour from the time that I entered the water, until I reached the opposite shore, and as the rivers were yet very cold, I suffered greatly at this place.

Judging by the aspect of the country, I believed myself to be at this time in Virginia; and was now reduced to the utmost extremity, for want of provisions. The corn that I had parched at the barn, and brought with me, was nearly exhausted, and no more was to be obtained in the fields, at this season of the year. For three or four days I allowed myself only my two hands full of parched corn per day; after this I travelled three days without tasting food of any kind; but being nearly exhausted with hunger, I one night entered an old stack-yard, hoping that I might fall in with pigs, or poultry of some kind. I found, instead of these, a stack of oats, which had not been threshed. From this stack I took as much oats in the sheaf, as I could carry, and going on a few miles, stopped in a pine forest, made a large fire, and parched at least half a gallon of oats, after rubbing the grain from the straw. After the grain was parched, I again rubbed it in my hands, to separate it from the husks, and spent the night in feasting on parched oats.

The weather was now becoming quite warm, though the water was cold in the rivers; and I perceived the farmers had everywhere ploughed their fields, preparatory to planting corn. Every night I saw people burning brush in the new grounds that they were clearing of the wood and brush; and when the day came, in the morning after I obtained the oats, I perceived people planting corn in a field about half a mile from my fire. According to my computation of time, it was on the night of the last day of March that I obtained the oats; and the appearance of the country satisfied me, that I had not lost many days in my reckoning.

I lay in this pine-wood two days, for the purpose of recruiting my strength, after my long fast; and when I again resumed my journey, determined to seek some large road leading towards the north, and follow it in future; the one that I had been pursuing of late, not appearing to be a principal high-way of the country. For this purpose, striking off across the fields, in an easterly direction, I travelled a few hours, and was fortunate enough to come to a great road, which was manifestly much travelled, leading towards the northeast.

My bag was now replenished with more than a gallon of parched oats, and I had yet one pair of moccasins made of raw hide; but my shirt was totally gone, and my last pair of trousers was now in actual service. A tolerable waistcoat still remained to me, and my great coat, though full of honourable scars, was yet capable of much service.

Having resolved to pursue the road I was now in, it was necessary again to resort to the utmost degree of caution, to prevent surprise. Travelling only after it was dark, and taking care to stop before the appearance of day, my progress was not rapid, but my safety was preserved.

The acquisition of food had now become difficult, and when my oats began to fail, I resorted to the dangerous expedient of attacking the corn-crib of a planter that was near the road. The house was built of round logs, and was covered with boards. One of these boards I succeeded in removing, on the side of the crib opposite from the dwelling, and by thrusting my arm downwards, was able to reach the corn—of which I took as much as filled my bag, the pockets of my great coat, and a large handkerchief, that I had preserved through all the vicissitudes of my journey. This opportune supply of corn furnished me with food more than a week, and before it was consumed, I reached the Appomattox river, which I crossed in a canoe, that I tied at the shore, a few miles above the town of Petersburg. Having approached Petersburg in the night, I was afraid to attempt to pass through it, lest the patrol should fall in with me; and turning to left through the country, reached the river, and crossed in safety.

The great road leading to Richmond is so distinguishingly marked above the other ways in this part of Virginia, that there was no difficulty in following it, and on the third night after passing Petersburg, I obtained a sight of the capitol of Virginia. It was only a little after midnight, when the city presented itself to my sight; but here, as well as at Petersburg, I was afraid to attempt to go through the town, under cover of the darkness, because of the patrol. Turning, therefore, back into a forest, about two miles from the small town on the south-side of the river, I lay there until after twelve o'clock in the day, when loosening the package from my back, and taking it in my hand in the form of a bundle, I advanced into the village, as if I had only come from plantation in the neighbourhood.

This was on Sunday, I believe, though according to my computation, it was Monday; but it must have been Sunday, for the village was quiet, and in passing it, I only saw two or three persons, whom I passed as if I had not seen them. No one spoke to me, and I gained the bridge in safety, and crossed it without attracting the least attention.

Entering the city of Richmond, I kept along the principal street, walking at a slow pace, and turning my head from side to side, as if much attracted by the objects around me. Few persons were in the street and I was careful to appear more attentive to the houses than to the people. At the upper end of the city I saw a great crowd of ladies and gentlemen, who were, I believe, returning from church. Whilst these people were passing me, I stood in the street, on the outside of the foot pavement, with my face turned to the opposite side of the street. They all went by without taking any notice of me; and when they were gone, I again resumed my leisure walk along the pavement, and reached the utmost limit of the town without being accosted by any one. As soon as I was clear of the city I quickened my pace, assumed the air of a man in great haste, sometimes actually ran, and in less than an hour was safely lodged in the thickest part of the woods that lay on the north of Richmond, and full four miles from the river. This was the boldest exploit that I had performed since leaving my mistress, except the visit I paid to the gentleman in Georgia.

My corn was now failing, but as I had once entered a crib secretly, I felt but little apprehension on account of future supplies. After this time I never wanted corn, and did not again suffer by hunger, until I reached the place of my nativity.

After leaving Richmond, I again kept along the great road by which I had travelled on my way south, taking great care not to expose my person unnecessarily. For several nights I saw no white people on the way, but was often met by black ones, whom I avoided by turning out of the road; but one moonlight night, five or six days after I left Richmond, a man stepped out of the woods almost at my side, and accosting me in a familiar manner, asked me which way I was travelling, how long I had been on the road, and made many inquiries concerning the course of my late journey. This man was a mulatto, and carried a heavy cane, or rather club, in his hand. I did not like his appearance, and the idea of a familiar conversation with any one seemed to terrify me. I determined to watch my companion closely, and he appeared equally intent on observing me; but at the same time that he talked with me, he was constantly drawing closer to, and following behind me. This conduct increased my suspicion, and I began to wish to get rid of him, but could not at the moment imagine how I should effect my purpose. To avoid him, I crossed the road several times; but still he followed me closely. The moon, which shone brightly upon our backs, cast his shadow far before me, and enabled me to perceive his motions with the utmost accuracy, without turning my head towards him. He carried his club under his left arm, and at length raised his right hand gently, took the stick by the end, and drawing it slowly over his head, was in the very act of striking a blow at me, when, springing backward, and raising my own staff at the same moment, I brought him to the ground by a stroke on his forehead; and when I had him down, beat him over the back and sides with my weapon, until he roared for mercy, and begged me not to kill him. I left him in no condition to pursue me, and hastened on my way, resolved to get as far from him before day as my legs would carry me.

This man was undoubtedly one of those wretches who are employed by white men to kidnap and betray such unfortunate people of colour as may chance to fall into their hands; but for once the deceiver was deceived, and he who intended to make prey of me, had well nigh fallen a sacrifice himself.

The same night I crossed the Pammunky river, near the village of Hanover by swimming, and secreted myself before day in a dense cedar thicket. The next night, after I had travelled several miles, in ascending a hill, I saw the head of a man rise on the opposite side, without having heard any noise. I instantly ran into the woods, and concealed myself behind a large tree. The traveller was on horseback and the road being sandy, and his horse moving only at a walk, I had not heard his approach until I saw him. He also saw me; for when he came opposite the place where I stood, he stopped his horse in the road, and desired me to tell him how far it was to some place, the name of which I have forgotten. As I made no answer, he again repeated the inquiry; and then said, I need not be afraid to speak, as he did not wish to hurt me; but no answer being given him, he at last said I might as well speak, and rode on.

Before day I reached the Matapony river, and crossed it by wading; but knowing that I was not far from Maryland, I fell into a great indiscretion, and forgot the wariness and caution that had enabled me to overcome obstacles apparently insurmountable. Anxious to get forward, I neglected to conceal myself before day; but travelled until daybreak before I sought a place of concealment, and unfortunately, when I looked for a hiding place, none was at hand. This compelled me to keep on the road, until gray twilight, for the purpose of reaching a wood that was in view before me; but to gain this wood I was obliged to pass a house, that stood at the road side, and when only about fifty yards beyond the house, a white man opened the door, and seeing me in the road, called to me to stop. As his order was not obeyed, he set his dog upon me. The dog was quickly vanquished by my stick, and setting off to run at full speed, I at the same moment heard the report of a gun, and received its contents in my legs, chiefly about, and in my hams. I fell on the road, and was soon surrounded by several persons, who it appeared were a party of patrollers, who had gathered together in this house. They ordered me to cross my hands, which order not being immediately obeyed, they beat me with sticks and stones until I was almost senseless, and entirely unable to make resistance. They then bound me with cords, and dragged me by the feet back to the house, and threw me into the kitchen, like a dead dog. One of my eyes was almost beaten out, and the blood was running from my mouth, nose and ears; but in this condition they refused to wash the blood from my face, or even to give me a drink of water.

In a short time, a justice of the peace arrived, and when he looked at me, ordered me to be unbound, and to have water to wash myself, and also some bread to eat. This man's heart appeared not to be altogether void of sensibility, for he reprimanded, in harsh terms, those who had beaten me; told them that their conduct was brutal, and that it would have been more humane to kill me outright, than to bruise and mangle me in the manner they had done.

He then interrogated me as to my name, place of abode, and place of destination, and afterwards demanded the name of my master. To all these inquiries I made no reply, except that I was going to Maryland, where I lived. The justice told me it was his duty under the law, to send me to jail; and I was immediately put into a cart, and carried to a small village called Bowling Green, which I reached before ten o'clock.

There I was locked up in the jail, and a doctor came to examine my legs, and extract the shot from my wounds. In the course of the operation he took out thirty-four duck shot, and after dressing my legs left me to my own reflections. No fever followed in the train of my disasters, which I attributed to the state of my blood, by long fasting, and the fatigues I had undergone.

In the afternoon, the jailer came to see me, and brought my daily allowance of provisions, and a jug of water. The provisions consisted of more than a pound of corn-bread, and some boiled bacon. As my appetite was good, I immediately devoured more than two-thirds of this food, but reserved the rest for supper.

For several days I was not able to stand, and in this period found great difficulty in performing the ordinary offices of life for myself, no one coming to give me any aid; but I did not suffer for want of food, the daily allowance of the jailer being quite sufficient to appease the cravings of hunger. After I grew better, and was able to walk in the jail, the jailer frequently called to see me, and endeavoured to prevail on me to tell where I had come from; but in this undertaking, he was no more successful than the justice had been in the same business.

I remained in the jail more than a month, and in this time became quite fat and strong but saw no way by which I could escape. The jail was of brick, the floors were of solid oak boards, and the door, of the same material, was secured by iron bolts, let into its posts, and connected together by a strong band of iron, reaching from the one to the other.

Every thing appeared sound and strong, and to add to my security, my feet were chained together, from the time my wounds were healed. This chain I acquired the knowledge of removing from my feet, by working out of its socket a small iron pin that secured the bolt that held the chain round one of my legs.

The jailer came to see me with great regularity, every morning and evening, but remained only a few minutes, when he came, leaving me entirely alone at all other times.

CHAPTER XXIV.

When I had been in prison thirty-nine days, and had quite recovered from the wounds that I had received, the jailer was late in coming to me with my breakfast, and going to the door I began to beat against it with my fist, for the purpose of making a noise. After beating some time against the door I happened, by mere accident, to strike my fist against one of the posts, which, to my surprise, I discovered by its sound, to be a mere hollow shell, encrusted with a thin coat of sound timber, and as I struck it, the rotten wood crumbled to pieces within. On a more careful examination of this post, I became satisfied that I could easily split it to pieces, by the aid of the iron bolt that confined my feet. The jailer came with my breakfast, and reprimanded me for making a noise, This day appeared as long to me, as a week had done heretofore; but night came at length, and as soon as the room in which I was confined, had become quite dark, I disentangled myself from the irons with which I was bound, and with the aid of the long bolt, easily wrenched from its place, the large staple that held one end of the bar, that lay across the door. The hasps that held the lock in its place, were drawn away almost without force, and the door swung open of its own weight.

I now walked out into the jail-yard, and found that all was quiet, and that only a few lights were burning in the village windows. At first I walked slowly along the road, but soon quickened my pace, and ran along the high-way, until I was more than a mile from the jail, then taking to the woods, I travelled all night, in a northern direction. At the approach of day I concealed myself in a cedar thicket, where I lay until the next evening, without any thing to eat.

On the second night after my escape, I crossed the Potomac, at Hoe's ferry, in a small boat that I found tied at the side of the ferry flat; and on the night following crossed the Patuxent, in a canoe, which I found chained at the shore.

About one o'clock in the morning, I came to the door of my wife's cabin, and stood there, I believe, more than five minutes, before I could summon sufficient fortitude to knock. I at length rapped lightly on the door, and was immediately asked, in the well-known voice of my wife, "Who is there?"—I replied "Charles." She then came to the door, and opening it slowly, said, "Who is this that speaks so much like my husband?" I then rushed into the cabin and made myself known to her, but it was some time before I could convince her, that I was really her husband, returned from Georgia. The children were then called up, but they had forgotten me.

When I attempted to take them in my arms, they fled from me, and took refuge under the bed of their mother. My eldest boy, who was four years old when I was carried away, still retained some recollections of once having had a father, but could not believe that I was that father. My wife, who at first was overcome by astonishment at seeing me again in her cabin, and was incapable of giving credit to the fidelity of her own vision, after I had been in the house a few minutes, seemed to awake from a dream; and gathering all three of her children in her arms, thrust them into my lap, as I sat in the corner, clapped her hands, laughed, and cried by turns; and in her ecstasy forgot to give me any supper, until I at length told her that I was hungry. Before I entered the house I felt as if I could eat any thing in the shape of food; but now that I attempted to eat, my appetite had fled, and I sat up all night with my wife and children.

When on my journey I thought of nothing but getting home, and never reflected, that when at home, I might still be in danger; but now that my toils were ended, I began to consider with myself how I could appear in safety in Calvert county, where everybody must know that I was a runaway slave. With my heart thrilling with joy, when I looked upon my wife and children, who had not hoped ever to behold me again; yet fearful of the coming of daylight, which must expose me to be arrested as a fugitive slave, I passed the night, between the happiness of the present and the dread of the future. In all the toils, dangers, and suffering of my long journey, my courage had never forsaken me. The hope of again seeing my wife and little ones, had borne me triumphantly through perils, that even now I reflect upon as upon some extravagant dream; but when I found myself at rest under the roof of my wife, the object of my labour attained, and no motive to arouse my energies, or give them the least impulse, that firmness of resolution which had so long sustained me, suddenly vanished from my bosom; and I passed the night, with my children around me, oppressed by a melancholy foreboding of my future destiny. The idea that I was utterly unable to afford protection and safeguard to my own family, and was myself even more helpless than they, tormented my bosom with alternate throbs of affection and fear, until the dawn broke in the cast, and summoned me to decide upon my future conduct.

When morning came, I went to the great house, and showed myself to my wife's master and mistress who treated me with great kindness, and gave me a good breakfast. Mr. Symmes at first advised me to conceal myself, but soon afterwards told me to go to work in the neighbourhood for wages. I continued to hire myself about among the farmers, until after the war broke out; and until Commodore Barney came into the Patuxent with his flotilla, when I enlisted on board one of his barges, and was employed sometimes in the capacity of a seaman, and sometimes as cook of the barge.

I had been on board, only a few days, when the British fleet entered the Patuxent, and forced our flotilla high up the river. I was present when the flotilla was blown up, and assisted in the performance of that operation upon the barge that I was in. The guns and the principal part of the armament of the flotilla, were sunk in the river and lost.

I marched with the troops of Barney, from Benedict to Bladensburg, and travelled nearly the whole of the distance, through heavy forests of timber, or numerous and dense cedar thickets. It is my opinion, that if General Winder had marched the half of the troops that he had at Bladensburg, down to the lower part of Prince George county, and attacked the British in these woods and cedar thickets, not a man of them would ever have reached Bladensburg.

I feel confident that in the country through which I marched, one hundred Americans would have destroyed a thousand of the enemy, by felling trees across the road, and attacking them in ambush.

When we reached Bladensburg, and the flotilla men were drawn up in line, to work at their cannon, armed with their cutlasses, I volunteered to assist in working the cannon, that occupied the first place, on the left of the Commodore. We had a full and perfect view of the British army, as it advanced along the road, leading to the bridge over the East Branch; and I could not but admire the handsome manner in which the British officers led on their fatigued and worn-out soldiers. I thought then, and think yet, that General Ross was one of the finest looking men that I ever saw on horseback.

I stood at my gun, until the Commodore was shot down, when he ordered us to retreat, as I was told by the officer who commanded our gun. If the militia regiments, that lay upon our right and left, could have been brought to charge the British, in close fight, as they crossed the bridge, we should have killed or taken the whole of them in a short time; but the militia ran like sheep chased by dogs.

My readers will not, perhaps, condemn me if I here make a short digression from my main narrative, to give some account of the part that I took in the war, on the shores of the Chesapeake, and the Patuxent. I did not enlist with Commodore Barney until the month of December, 1813; but as I resided in Calvert county, in the summer of 1813, I had an opportunity of witnessing many of the evils that followed in the train of war, before I assumed the profession of arms myself.

In the spring of the year 1813, the British fleet came into the bay, and from this time, the origin of the troubles and distresses of the people of the Western Shore, may be dated. I had been employed at a fishery, near the mouth of the Patuxent, from early March, until the latter part of May, when a British vessel of war came off the mouth of the river, and sent her boats up to drive us away from our fishing ground. There was but little property at the fishery that could be destroyed; but the enemy cut the seines to pieces, and burned the sheds belonging to the place. They then marched up two miles into the country, burned the house of a planter, and brought away with them several cattle, that were found in his fields. They also carried off more than twenty slaves, which were never again restored to their owner; although, on the following day, he went on board the ship, with a flag of truce, and offered a large ransom for these slaves.

These were the first black people whom I had known to desert to the British, although the practice was afterwards so common. In the course of this summer, and the summer of 1814, several thousand black people deserted from their masters and mistresses, and escaped to the British fleet. None of these people were ever regained by their owners, as the British naval officers treated them as free people, and placed them on the footing of military deserters.

In the fall of this year, a lady by the name of Wilson, who owned more than a hundred slaves, lost them all in one night, except one man, who had a wife and several children on an adjoining estate, and as he could not take his family with him, on account of the rigid guard that was kept over them, he refused to go himself.

The slaves of Mrs. Wilson effected their escape in the following manner. Two or three of the men having agreed amongst themselves, that they would run away and go to the fleet, they stole a canoe one night, and went off to the ship, that lay nearest the shore. When on board, they informed the officer of the ship that their mistress owned more than a hundred other slaves, whom they had left behind them. They were then advised to return home, and remain there until the next night, and then bring with them to the beach, all the slaves on the plantation—the officer promising that he would send a detachment of boats to the shore, to bring them off. This advice was followed, and the fugitives returned before day, to their cabins, on the plantation of their mistress.

On the next night, having communicated their plans to some of their fellow-slaves, they rose about midnight, and partly by persuasion, partly by compulsion, carried off all the slaves on the plantation, with the exception of the man already named.

When they reached the beach, they kindled a fire, as had been concerted with the British officers, and the boats of the fleet came off, and removed this whole party on board. In the morning, when the overseer of Mrs. Wilson arose, and went to call his hands to the field, he found only empty cabins in the quarter, with a single man remaining, to tell what had become of his fellows.

This was the greatest disaster that had befallen any individual in our neighbourhood, in the course of the war; and as the sufferer was a lady, much sympathy was excited in her favour. A large number of gentlemen met together, for the purpose of endeavouring to devise some means of recovering the fugitive slaves. Their consultations ended in sending a deputation of gentlemen, on board the fleet, with a flag of truce, to solicit the restoration of the deserters, either as a matter of favour, or for such ransom, as might be agreed upon. Strong hopes were entertained, that the runaways might be induced voluntarily to return to the service of their mistress, as she had never treated them with great severity.

To accomplish, if possible, this latter end, I was spoken to, to go along with the flag of truce, in the assumed character of the servant of one of the gentlemen who bore it; but in the real character of the advocate of the mistress, for the purpose of inducing her slaves to return to her service.

We went on board the ship in the afternoon, and I observed, that the gentlemen who went with me, were received by the British officers with very little ceremony. The captain did not show himself on deck, nor were the gentlemen invited into his cabin. They were shown into a large square room under the first deck of the ship, which was a 74, and here a great number of officers came to talk to them, and ask them questions concerning the war, and the state of the country.

The whole of the runaways were on board this ship, lounging about on the main deck, or leaning against the sides of the ship's bulwarks. I went amongst them, and talked to them a long time, on the subject of returning home; but found that their heads were full of notions of liberty and happiness in some of the West India islands.

In the afternoon, all the gentlemen, except one, returned home in the boat that they had come off in. The gentleman, who remained on board, was a young man of pleasing manners and lively conversation, who appeared, even before the other gentlemen who had come with the flag had left the ship, to have become quite a favourite with the younger British officers. Permission was obtained of the British captain, for this young gentleman to remain on board a few days, for the purpose, as he alleged, of seeing the curiosities of the ship. He had permission to retain me with him as his servant: and I was instructed to exert myself to the utmost, to prevail on the runaway slaves to return to their mistress. The ship lay at anchor off the shore of Calvert county, until the second night after I came on board, when, from some cause which I was not able to understand, this ship and all the rest of the fleet, got under weigh, and stood down the Bay to the neighbourhood of Tangier Islands; where she again cast anchor, soon after sunrise the next morning, in ten fathoms water. I was now at least seventy or eighty miles from home, in a ship of the public enemies of the country, and liable to be carried off to sea, and to be conveyed to the most distant part of the world. To increase my alarm, about noon of this day, a sloop of war cast anchor under the stern of our ship; and all the black people that were with us, were immediately removed on board the sloop. I was invited, and even urged to go with the others, who, I was told, were bound to the island of Trinidad, in the West Indies, where they would have lands given to them, and where they were to be free. I returned many thanks for their kind offers; but respectfully declined them; telling those who made them, that I was already a freeman, and though I owned no land myself, yet I could have plenty of land of other people to cultivate.

In the evening, the sloop weighed anchor, and stood down the Bay, with more than two hundred and fifty black people on board. I watched her as she sailed away from us, until the darkness of the night shut her out from my sight. In the morning she was not to be seen. What became of the miserable mass of black fugitives, that this vessel took to sea, I never learned.

My mission was now at an end, and I spoke this day to the young gentleman, under whose care I was, to endeavour to procure some means of conveying both him and me back again to Calvert. My protector seemed no less embarrassed than I was, and informed me, that the officers of the ship said they would not land us on the Western Shore, within less than two weeks. I was obliged to content myself the best way I could, in my confinement on shipboard; and I amused myself by talking to the sailors, and giving them an account of the way in which I had passed my life on the tobacco and cotton plantations; in return for which, the seamen gave many long stories of their adventures at sea, and of the battles they had been engaged in.

I lived well whilst on board this ship, as they allowed me to share in a mess. In compensation for their civility, I gave them many useful instructions in the art of taking fish in the Bay.

This great ship lay at anchor like a vast castle, moored by the cable; but there were many small vessels, used as tenders to the fleet, that were continually sailing up and down the Bay, by night, as well as by day, in pursuit of any thing that, they might fall in with, that they could take from the Americans. Whilst I was on board, I saw more than thirty vessels, chiefly Bay craft, brought to our anchorage, and there burned, after being stripped of every thing valuable that could be, taken from them. The people who manned and navigated these vessels, were made prisoners, and dispersed amongst the several ships of the fleet, until they could be removed to Halifax, or the West Indies. One day a small schooner was seen standing out of the mouth of Nanticoke river, and beating up the Bay. Chase was immediately given by several of the light vessels belonging to the fleet, and continued until nightfall, when I could no longer see the sails; but the next day, the British vessels returned, bringing in their company the little schooner, which was manned by her owner, who acted as captain, and two boys. On board the schooner, besides her crew, were several passengers, seven in number, I believe. The people were taken out of this little vessel, which was laden with

Indian corn, and after her cargo had been removed, she was burned in view of her owner, who seemed much affected at the sight, and said that it was all the property he owned in the world, and that his wife and children were now beggars. The passengers and crew of this little vessel, were all retained as prisoners of war, on board the 74, in which I was; and were shut up every night in a room on the lower gun deck. In this room there were several port-holes, which were suffered to remain open for the benefit of the air.

After these people had been on board three or four days, a boat's crew, that had been out somewhere in the evening, when they returned to the ship, tied the boat with a long rope to one of the halyards of the ship, and left the boat floating near the ship's bows. Some time after night the tide turned, moved the boat along the side of the ship, and floated it directly under the port-holes of the prisoners' room. The night was dark and warm, and I had taken a station on the upper deck, and was leaning over the bulwarks, when my attention was drawn towards the water, by hearing something drop into the boat that lay along side. Dark as it was, I could see the forms of men passing out of the port-holes into the boat. In less than two minutes, nine persons had entered the boat; and I then heard a low whisper, which I could not understand; but immediately afterwards, saw the boat drifting with the tide; which convinced me that she was loose, and that the prisoners were in her. I said nothing and in a short time the boat was out of sight. She had, however, not been long gone, when the watch on deck passed near me, and looking over the side of the ship, called to the officer on deck, that the yawl was gone. The officer on deck instantly called to some one below to examine the room of the prisoners; and received for answer, that the prisoners had fled. A gun was immediately fired under me, on one of the lower decks; the ship's bells were tolled; numerous blue lights were made ready, and cast high into the air, which performing a curve in the atmosphere, illuminated the face of the water all the way from the ship to the place where they fell. The other ships in the fleet all answered by firing guns, casting out lights, and ringing their large bells. Three boats put off from our ship, in search of the fugitives, with as little delay as possible; and, after being absent more than an hour, returned without finding those who had escaped.

This affair presented one of the finest night scenes that can well be imagined. The deep thunder of the heavy artillery, as it broke upon the, stillness of the night, and re-echoed from the distant shores; the

283

solemn and mournful tones of the numerous bells, as they answered each other from ship to ship, as the sounds rose in the air, and died away in the distance, on the wide expanse of waters; with the shouts of the seamen, and the pale and ghastly appearance of the blue lights, as they rose into the atmosphere, and then descended and died away in the water—all combined together, to affect both the eye and the ear, in a manner the most impressive.

One of the prisoners remained in the ship: not having courage to undertake, with his companions, the daring and dangerous exploit of escaping from the ship in her own boat. When the morning came, this man explained, to the officers of the ship, the whole plan that had been devised, and pursued by his companions. When they found that the boat had floated under the port-holes of their room, some one of the number proposed to the rest, to attempt to escape, as the oars of the boat had been left in her; but a difficulty suggested itself, at the outset, which was this: the oars could not be worked on the boat without making a great noise, sufficient to alarm the watch on deck. To avoid this, one of the prisoners said he would undertake to pull off his coat, and muffle one of the oars with it, and scull the boat until they should be clear of the fleet; when they could lay both oars on the boat, and row to shore. We lay much nearer to the Western Shore, than we were to the Eastern but this man said, the design of the prisoners was to pull to the Eastern Shore. All the boats that went from our ship pulled for the Western Shore, and by this means the prisoners escaped, without being seen.

The captain of the ship was much enraged at the escape of these prisoners, and swore he would be avenged of the Yankees in a short time. In this he was as good as his word; for the very next day he fitted out an expedition, consisting of eleven long boats, and more than two hundred men, who landed on the Western Shore, and burned three house, with all their furniture, and killed a great number of cattle.

The officer who headed this expedition, brought back with him a large silk handkerchief full of silver spoons, and other articles of silver plate. I saw him exhibit these trophies of his valour amongst his brother officers, on the deck of the ship.

After I had been on board nearly a week, a furious northeast storm came on and blew for three days, accompanied with frequent gusts of rain. In the evening of the second day, we saw two schooners standing down the bay, and sailing close on the wind, so as to pass between the fleet and the Eastern Shore. As it was dangerous for large ships to approach much nearer the Eastern Shore than where we lay, several of the tenders of the fleet, amounting in all, to more than a dozen, were ordered by signal, to to intercept the strange sails, and bring them to the fleet.

The tenders got under weigh and stood before the wind, for the purpose of encountering the schooners, as they came down the Bay. These schooners proved to be two heavy armed American privateers, and when the tenders approached them a furious battle commenced with cannon, which lasted more than an hour, and until the privateers had passed quite below the anchorage of the fleet.

Several of the tenders were much damaged in their hulls and rigging; and it was said that they lost more than twenty men. I could not perceive that the privateers sustained the least injury, as they never shortened sail, nor altered their course, until they had passed to the windward of all the ships of the fleet, when they changed their bearing, and stood for the Capes of Virginia. There were nearly forty vessels in the fleet, great and small; and yet these two privateers braved the whole of them in open daylight, and went to sea in spite of them.

On the ninth day after we came on board, the fleet again moved up the Bay, and when we were off the mouth of the Potomac, the captain sent the young gentleman, in whose service I was, together with myself, on shore in his own gig.

The lieutenant who had command of the gig, after he set us on shore, went up to the house of a farmer, whose estate lay upon to the Bay, and after pilfering the premises of every thing that he could carry away, set fire to the house, and returned to his boat. In the course of the summer and fall of the year 1813, I witnessed many other atrocities, of equal enormity.

I continued with the army after the sack of Washington, and assisted in the defence of Baltimore; but in the fall of 1814, I procured my discharge from the army, and went to work in Baltimore, as a free black man. From this time, until the year 1820, I worked in various places in Maryland, as a free man; sometimes in Baltimore, sometimes in Annapolis, and frequently in Washington. My wife died in the year 1816, and from that time I was not often in Calvert county. I was fortunate in the enjoyment of good health; and by constant economy I found myself in possession, in the year 1820, of three hundred and fifty dollars in money, the proceeds, of my labour.

I now removed to the neighbourhood of Baltimore, and purchased a lot of twelve acres of ground, upon which I erected a small house, and became a farmer on my own account, and upon my own property. I purchased a yoke of oxen and two cows, and became a regular attendant of the Baltimore market, where I sold the products of my own farm and dairy. In the course of two or three years, I had brought my little farm into very good culture, and had increased my stock of cattle to four cows and several younger animals. I now lived very happily, and had an abundance of all the necessaries of life around me. I had married a second wife, who bore me four children, and I now looked forward to an old age of comfort, if not of ease; but I was soon to be awakened from this dream.

CHAPTER XXV.

In the month of June, 1830, as I was ploughing in my lot, three gentlemen rode up to my fence, and alighting from their horses, all came over the fence and approached me, when one of them told me he was the sheriff, and had a writ in his pocket, which commanded him to take me to Baltimore. I was not conscious of having done any thing injurious to any one; but yet felt a distrust of these men, who were all strangers to me. I told them I would go with them, if they would permit me to turn my oxen loose from the plough; but it was my intention to seek an opportunity of escaping to the house of a gentleman, who lived about a mile from me. This purpose I was not able to effect, for whilst I was taking the yoke from the oxen, one of the gentlemen came behind me, and knocked me down, with a heavy whip, that he carried in his hand.

When I recovered from the stunning effects of this blow, I found myself bound with my hands behind me, and strong cords closely wrapped about my arms. In this condition I was forced to set out immediately, for Baltimore, without speaking to my wife, or even entering my door. I expected that, on arriving at Baltimore, I should be taken before a judge for the purpose of being tried, but in this I was deceived. They led me to the city jail, and there shut me up, with several other black people, both men and women, who told me that they had lately been purchased by a trader from Georgia.

I now saw the extent of my misfortune, but could not learn who the persons were, who had seized me. In the evening however, one of the gentlemen, who had brought me from home, came into the jail with the jailer, and asked me if I knew him. On being answered in the negative, he told me that he knew me very well; and asked me if I did not recollect the time when he and his brother had whipped me, before my master's door, in Georgia.

I now recognised the features of the younger of the two brothers of my mistress; but this man was so changed in his appearance, from the time when I had last seen him, that if he had not declared himself, I should never have known him. When I left Georgia, he was not more than twenty-one or two years of age, and had black, bushy hair. His hair was now thin and gray, and all his features were changed.

After lying in jail a little more than two weeks, strongly ironed, my fellow prisoners and I were one day chained together, handcuffed in pairs, and in this way driven about ten miles out of Baltimore, where we remained all night.

On the evening of the second day, we halted at Bladensburg, and were shut up in a small house, within full view of the very ground, where sixteen years before I had fought in the ranks of the army, of the United States, in defence of the liberty and independence of that which I then regarded as my country. It seemed as if it had been but yesterday that I had seen the British columns, advancing across the bridge now before me, directing their fire against me, and my companions in arms.

The thought now struck me, that if I had deserted that day, and gone over to the enemies of the United States, how different would my situation at this moment have been. And this, thought I, is the reward of the part I bore in the dangers and fatigues of that disastrous battle.

On the next morning, we marched through Washington, and as we passed in front of the President's house, I saw an old gentleman walking in the grounds, near the gate. This man I was told was the President of the United States.

Within four weeks after we left Washington, I was in Milledgeville in Georgia, near which the man who had kidnapped me, resided. He took me home with him, and set me to work on his plantation; but I had now enjoyed liberty too long to submit quietly to the endurance of slavery. I had no sooner come here, than I began to devise ways of escaping again from the hands of my tyrants, and of making my way to the northern states.

The month of August was now approaching, which is a favourable season of the year to travel, on account of the abundance of food that is to be found in the corn fields and orchards; but I remembered the dreadful sufferings that I had endured in my former journey from the south, and determined, if possible, to devise some scheme of getting away, that would not subject me to such hardships.

After several weeks of consideration, I resolved to run away, go to some of the seaports, and endeavour to get a passage on board a vessel, bound to a northern city. With this view, I assumed the appearance of resignation and composure, under the new aspect of my fortune; and even went so far as to tell my new master that I lived more comfortably with him, in his cotton fields, than I had formerly done, on my own small farm in Maryland; though I believe my master did me the justice to give no credit to my assertions, on this subject.

From the moment I discovered in Maryland, that I had fallen into the hands of the brother of my former mistress, I gave up all hope of contesting his right to arrest me, with success, at law, as I supposed he had come with authority to reclaim me as the property of his sister; but after I had returned to Georgia, and had been at work some weeks on the plantation of my new master, I learned that he now claimed me as his own slave, and that he had reported he had purchased me in Baltimore. It was now clear to me that this man, having by some means learned the place of my residence, in Maryland, had kidnapped and now held me as his slave, without the colour of legal right; but complaint on my part was useless, and resistance vain.

I was again reduced to the condition of a common field slave, on a cotton plantation in Georgia, and compelled to subsist on the very scanty and coarse food, allowed to the southern slaves. I had been absent from Georgia, almost twenty years, and in that period, great changes had doubtlessly taken place in the face of the country, as well as in the condition of human society.

I had never been in Milledgeville, until I was brought there by the man who had kidnapped me in Maryland; and I was now a slave among entire strangers, and had no friend to give me the consolation of kind words, such as I had formerly received from my master in Morgan county. The plantation on which I was now a slave, had formerly belonged to the father of my mistress; and some of my fellow-slaves had been well acquainted with her, in her youth. From these people I learned, that after the death of my master, and my flight from Georgia, my mistress had become the wife of a second husband, who had removed with her to the state of Louisiana, more than fifteen years ago.

After ascertaining these facts, which proved beyond all doubt that my present master had no right whatsoever to me, in either law or justice, I determined, that before encountering the dangers and sufferings, that must necessarily attend my second flight from Georgia, I would attempt to claim the protection of the laws of the country, and try to get myself discharged from the unjust slavery in which I was now held. For this purpose, I went to Milledgeville, one Sunday, and inquired for a lawyer, of a black man whom I met in the street. This person told me that his master was a lawyer, and went with me to his house.

The lawyer, after talking to me some time, told me that my master was his client, and that he therefore could not undertake my cause; but referred me to a young gentleman, who he said would do my business for me. Accordingly to this young man I went, and after relating my whole story to him, he told me that he believed he could not do any thing for me, as I had no witnesses to prove my freedom.

I rejoined, that it seemed hard that I must be compelled to prove myself a freeman: and that it would appear more consonant to reason, that my master should prove me to be a slave. He, however, assured me that this was not the law of Georgia, where every man of colour was presumed to be a slave, until he could prove that he was free. He then told me that if I expected him to talk to me, I must give him a fee; whereupon I gave him all the money I had been able to procure, since my arrival in the country, which was two dollars and seventy-five cents.

When I offered him this money, the lawyer tossed his head, and said such a trifle was not worth accepting; but nevertheless he took it, and then asked me if I could get some more money before the next Sunday. That if I could get another dollar, he would issue a writ and have me brought before the court; but if he succeeded in getting me set free, I must engage to serve him a year. To these conditions I agreed, and signed a paper which the lawyer wrote and which was signed by two persons as witnesses.

The brother of my pretended master, was yet living in this neighbourhood, and the lawyer advised me to have him brought forward, as a witness, to prove that I was not the slave of my present pretended owner.

On the Wednesday following my visit to Milledgeville, the sheriff came to my master's plantation, and took me from the field to the house, telling me as I walked beside him, that he had a writ which commanded him to take me to Milledgeville. Instead, however, of obeying the command of his writ, when we arrived at the house, he took a bond of my master that he would produce me at the court-house on the next day, Friday, and then rode away, leaving me at the mercy of my kidnapper.

Since I had been on this plantation, I had never been whipped, although all the other slaves, of whom there were more than fifty, were frequently flogged without any apparent cause. I had all along attributed my exemption from the lash to the fears of my master. He knew I had formerly run away from his sister, on account of her cruelty, and his own savage conduct to me; and I believed that he was still apprehensive that a repetition of his former barbarity might produce the same effect that it had done twenty years before.

His evil passions were like fire covered with ashes, concealed, not extinguished. He now found that I was determined to try to regain my liberty at all events, and the sheriff was no sooner gone, than the overseer was sent for, to come from the field, and I was tied up and whipped, with the long lashed negro whip, until I fainted, and was carried in a state of insensibility, to my lodgings in the quarter. It was night when I recovered my understanding, sufficiently to be aware of my true situation. I now found that my wounds had been oiled, and that I was wrapped in a piece of clean linen cloth; but for several days I was unable to leave my bed. When Friday came, I was not taken to Milledgeville, and afterwards learned that my master reported to the court, that I had been taken ill, and was not able to leave the house. The judge asked no questions as to the cause of my illness.

At the end of two weeks, I was taken to Milledgeville, and carried before a judge, who first asked a few questions of my master, as to the length of time that he had owned me, and the place where he had purchased me. He stated in my presence that he had purchased me, with several others, at public auction, in the city of Baltimore, and had paid five hundred and ten dollars for me. I was not permitted to speak to the court, much less to contradict this falsehood in the manner it deserved.

The brother of my master was then called as a witness, by my lawyer; but the witness refused to be sworn or examined, on account of his interest in me, as his slave. In support of his refusal, he produced a bill of sale from my master to himself, for an equal, undivided half part of the slave Charles. This bill of sale was dated several weeks previous to the time of trial, and gave rise to an argument between the opposing lawyers, that continued until the court adjourned in the evening.

On the next morning I was again brought into court, and the judge now delivered his opinion, which was that the witness could not be compelled to give evidence in a cause to which he was really, though not nominally, a party.

The court then proceeded to give judgment in the cause now before it, and declared that the law was well settled in Georgia, that every negro was presumed to be a slave, until he proved his freedom by the clearest evidence. That where a negro was found in the custody or keeping of a white man, the law declared that white man to be his master, without any evidence on the subject. But the case before the court, was exceedingly plain and free from all doubt or difficulty. Here the master has brought this slave into the state of Georgia, as his property, has held him as a slave ever since, and still holds him as a slave. The title of the master in this case, is the best title that a man can have to any property, and the order of the court is that the slave Charles be returned to the custody of his master.

I was immediately ordered to return home, and from this time until I left the plantation, my life was a continual torment to me. The overseer often came up to me in the field, and gave me several lashes with his long whip, over my naked back, through mere wantonness; and I was often compelled, after I had done my day's work in the field, to cut wood, or perform some other labour at the house, until long after dark. My sufferings were too great to be borne long by any human creature; and to a man who had once tasted the sweets of liberty, they were doubly tormenting.

There was nothing in the form of danger that could intimidate me, if the road on which I had to encounter it, led me to freedom. That season of the year, most favourable to my escape from bondage, had at length arrived. The corn in the fields was so far grown, as to be fit for roasting; the peaches were beginning to ripen, and the sweet potatoes were large enough to be eaten; but notwithstanding all this, the difficulties that surrounded me were greater than can easily be imagined by any one who has never been a slave in the lower country of Georgia.

In the first place I was almost naked, having no other clothes than a ragged shirt of tow cloth, and a pair of old trousers of the same material, with an old woollen jacket that I had brought with me from home. In addition to this, I was closely watched every evening, until I had finished the labour assigned me, and then I was locked up in a small cabin by myself for the night.

This cabin was really a prison, and had been built for the purpose of confining such of the slaves of this estate, as were tried in the evening, and sentenced to be whipped in the morning. It was built of strong oak logs, hewn square, and dovetailed together at the corners. It had no window in it; but as the logs did not fit very close together, there was never any want of air in this jail, in which I had been locked up every night since my trial before the court.

On Sundays I was permitted to go to work in the fields, with the other people who worked on that day, if I chose so to do; but at this time I was put under the charge of an old African negro, who was instructed to give immediate information, if I attempted to leave the field. To escape on Sunday was impossible, and there seemed to be no hope of getting out of my sleeping room, the floor of which was made of strong pine plank.

Fortune at length did for me that which I had not been able to accomplish, by the greatest efforts, for myself. The lock that was on the door of my nightly prison, was a large stock lock, and had been clumsily fitted on the door, so that the end of the lock pressed against the door-case, and made it difficult to shut the door even in dry weather. When the weather was damp, and the wood was swollen with moisture, it was not easy to close the door at all.

Late in the month of September, the weather became cloudy, and much rain fell. The clouds continued to obscure the heavens for four or five days. One evening, when I was ordered to my house, as it was called, the overseer followed me without a light, although it was very dark. When I was in the house, he pushed the door after me, with all his strength. The violence of the effort caused the door to pass within the case at the top, for one or two feet, and this held it so fast that he could not again pull it open.

Supposing in the extreme darkness, that the door was shut, he turned the key; and the bolt of the lock passing on the outside of the staple intended to receive it, completely deceived him. He then withdrew the key, and went away. Soon after he was gone, I went to the door, and feeling with my hands, ascertained that it was not shut. An opportunity now presented itself for me to escape from my prisonhouse, with a prospect of being able to be so far from my master's residence before morning, that none could soon overtake me, even should the course of my flight be ascertained. Waiting quietly, until every one about the quarter had ceased to be heard, I applied one of my feet to the door, and giving it a strong push, forced it open.

The world was now all before me, but the darkness was so profound, as to obscure from my vision the largest objects, even a house, at the distance of a few yards. But dark as it was, necessity compelled me to leave the plantation without delay, and knowing only the great road that led to Milledgeville, amongst the various roads of this country, I set off at a brisk walk on this public highway, assured that no one could apprehend me in so dark a night.

It was only about seven miles to Milledgeville, and when I reached that town several lights were burning in the windows of the houses; but keeping on directly through the village, I neither saw nor heard any person in it, and after gaining the open country, my first care was to find some secure place where shelter could be found for the next day; but no appearance of thick woods was to be seen for several miles, and two or three hours must have elapsed before a forest of sufficient magnitude was found to answer my purposes.

It was perhaps three o'clock in the morning, when I took refuge in a thick and dismal swamp that lay on the right hand of the road, intending to remain here until daylight, and then look out for a secret place to conceal myself in, during the day. Hitherto, although the night was so extremely dark, it had not rained any, but soon after my halt in the swamp, the rain began to fall in floods, rather than in showers, which made me as wet as if I had swum a river.

Daylight at length appeared, but brought with it very little mitigation of my suffering, for the swamp, in which my hiding-place was, lay in the midst of a well-peopled country, and was surrounded, on all sides, by cotton and corn fields, so close to me, that the open spaces of the cleared land could be seen from my position. It was dangerous to move, lest some one should see me;

and painful to remain without food, when hunger was consuming me.

My resting place, in the swamp, was within view of the road; and, soon after sunrise, although it continued to rain fast, numerous horsemen were seen passing along the road by the way that had led me to the swamp. There was little doubt on my mind, that these people were in search of me, and the sequel proved that my surmises were well founded. It rained throughout this day, and the fear of being apprehended by those who came in pursuit of me, confined me to the swamp, until after dark the following evening, when I ventured to leave the thicket, and return to the high road, the bearing of which it was impossible for me to ascertain, on account of the dense clouds that obscured the heavens. All that could be done in my situation, was to take care not to follow that end of the road which had led me to the swamp. Turning my back once more upon Milledgeville, and walking at a quick pace, every effort was made to remove myself, as far as possible this night, from the scene of suffering, for which that swamp will be always memorable in my mind.

The rain had ceased to fall at the going down of the sun; and the darkness of this second night, was not so great as that of the first had been. This circumstance was regarded by me, as a happy presage of the final success that awaited my undertaking. Events proved that I was no prophet; for the dim light of this night, was the cause of the dreadful misfortune that awaited me.

In a former part of this volume, the reader is made acquainted with the deep interest that is taken by all the planters, far and wide, around the plantation from which a slave has escaped, by running away. Twenty years had wrought no change in favour of the fugitive; nor had the feuds and dissensions, that agitate and distract the communities of white men, produced any relaxation in the friendship that they profess to feel, and really do feel, for each other, on a question of so much importance to them all.

More than twenty miles of road had been left behind me this night; and it must have been two or three o'clock in the morning, when, as I was passing a part of the road that led through a dense pine grove, where the trees on either side grew close to the wheel tracks, five or six men suddenly rushed upon me, from both sides of the road, and with loud cries of "Kill him! kill him!" accompanied with oaths and opprobrious language, seized me, dragged me to the ground, and bound me fast with a long cord, which was wrapped round my arms and body, so as to confine my hands below my hips.

In this condition, I was driven, or rather dragged, about two miles to a kind of tavern or public house, that stood by the side of the road; where my captors were joined, soon after daylight, by at least twenty of their companions, who had been out all night waiting and watching for me, on the other roads of this part of the country. Those who had taken me were loudly applauded by their fellows; and the whole party passed the morning in drinking, singing songs, and playing cards, at this house. At breakfast time, they gave me a large cake of corn bread, and some sour milk, for breakfast.

About ten o'clock in the morning, my master arrived at the tavern, in company with two or three other gentlemen, all strangers to me. My master, when he came into my presence, looked at me, and said, "Well, Charles, you had bad luck in running away this time;" and immediately asked aloud, what any person would give for me. One man, who was slightly intoxicated, said he would give four hundred dollars for me. Other bids followed, until my price was soon up to five hundred and eighty dollars, for which I was stricken off, by my master himself, to a gentleman, who immediately gave his note for me, and took charge of me as his property.

CHAPTER XXVI.

The name of my new master was Jones, a planter, who was only a visiter in this part of the country his residence being about fifty miles down the country. The next day, my new master set off with me to the place of his residence; permitting me to walk behind him, as he rode on horseback, and leaving me entirely unshackled. I was resolved, that as my owner treated me with so much liberality, the trust he reposed in me should not be broken until after we had reached his home; though the determination of again running away, and attempting to escape from Georgia, never abandoned me for a moment.

The country through which we passed, on our journey, was not rich. The soil was sandy, light, and, in many places, much exhausted by excessive tillage. The timber, in the woods where the ground was high, was almost exclusively pine; but many swamps, and extensive tracts of low ground intervened, in which maple, gum, and all the other trees common to such land in the south, abounded.

No improvement in the condition of the slaves on the plantations, was here perceptible; but it appeared to me, that there was now even a greater want of good clothes, amongst the slaves on the various plantations that we passed, than had existed twenty years before. Everywhere, the overseers still kept up the same custom of walking in the field with the long whip, that has been elsewhere described; and everywhere, the slaves proved, by the husky appearance of their skins, and the dry, sunburnt aspect of their hair, that they were strangers to animal food.

On the second day of our journey, in the evening, we arrived at the residence of my master; about eighty miles from Savannah. The plantation, which had now become the place of my residence, was not large: containing only about three hundred acres of cleared land, and having on it, about thirty working slaves of all classes.

It was now the very midst of the season of picking cotton, and, at the end of twenty years from the time of my first flight, I again had a daily task assigned me, with the promise of half a cent a pound, for all the cotton I should pick, beyond my day's work. Picking cotton, like every other occupation requiring active manipulation, depends more upon sleight, than strength; and I was not now able to pick so much in a day, as I was once able to do.

My master seemed to be a man ardently bent on the acquisition of wealth, and came into the field, where we were at work, almost every day; frequently remonstrating, in strong language, with the overseer, because he did not get more work done.

Our rations, on this place, were a half peck of corn per week; in addition to which, we had rather more than a peck of sweet potatoes allowed to each person.

Our provisions were distributed to us on every Sunday morning by the overseer; but my master was generally present, either to see that justice was done to us, or that injustice was not done to himself.

When I had been here about a week, my master came into the field one day, and, in passing near me, stopped and told me, that I had now fallen into good hands, as it was his practice not to whip his people much. That he, in truth, never whipped them, nor suffered his overseer to whip them, except in flagrant cases. That he had discovered a mode of punishment much more mild, and, at the same time, much more effectual, than flogging; and that he governed his negroes exclusively under this mode of discipline. He then told me, that when I came home in the evening, I must come to the house; and that he would then make me acquainted with the principles upon which he chastised his slaves.

Going to the house in the evening, according to orders, my master showed me a pump, set in a well in which the water rose within ten feet of the surface of the ground. The spout of this pump, was elevated at least thirteen feet above the earth, and when the water was to be drawn from it, the person who worked the handle ascended by a ladder to the proper station. The water in this well, although so near the surface, was very cold; and the pump discharged it in a large stream. One of the women employed in the house, had committed some offence for which she was to be punished; and the opportunity was embraced of exhibiting to me, the effect of this novel mode of torture upon the human frame. The woman was stripped quite naked, and tied to a post that stood just under the stream of water, as it fell from the spout of the pump. A lad was then ordered to ascend the ladder, and pump water upon the head and shoulders of the victim; who had not been under the waterfall more than a minute, before she began to cry and scream in a most lamentable manner. In a short time, she exerted her strength, in the most convulsive throes, in trying to escape from the post; but as the cords were strong, this was impossible. After another minute or a little more, her cries became weaker, and soon afterwards her head fell forward upon her breast; and then the boy was ordered to cease pumping the water. The woman was removed in a state of insensibility; but recovered her faculties in about an hour. The next morning she complained of lightness of head; but was able to go to work.

This punishment of the pump, as it is called, was never inflicted on me; and I am only able to describe it, as it has been described to me, by those who have endured it.

When the water first strikes the head and arm, it is not at all painful; but in a very short time, it produces the sensation that is felt when heavy blows are inflicted with large rods, of the size of a man's finger. This perception becomes more and more painful, until the skull bone and shoulder blades appear to be broken in pieces. Finally, all the faculties become oppressed; breathing becomes more and more difficult; until the eye-sight becomes dim, and animation ceases. This punishment is in fact a temporary murder; as all the pains are endured, that can be felt by a person who is deprived of life by being beaten with bludgeons;—but after the punishment of the pump, the sufferer is restored to existence by being laid in a bed, and covered with warm clothes. A giddiness of the head, and oppression of the breast, follows this operation, for a day or two, and sometimes longer. The object of calling me to be a witness of this new mode of torture, doubtlessly, was was to intimidate me from running away; but like medicines administered by empirics, the spectacle had precisely the opposite effect, from that which it was expected to produce.

After my arrival on this estate, my intention had been to defer my elopement until the next year, before I had seen the torture inflicted on this unfortunate woman; but from that moment my resolution was unalterably fixed, to escape as quickly as possible. Such was my desperation of feeling, at this time, that I deliberated seriously upon the project of endeavouring to make my way southward, for the purpose of joining the Indians in Florida. Fortune reserved a more agreeable fate for me.

On the Saturday night after the woman was punished at the pump, I stole a yard of cotton bagging from the cotton-gin house, and converted it into a bag, by means of a coarse needle and thread that I borrowed of one of the black women. On the next morning, when our weekly rations were distributed to us, my portion was carefully placed in my bag, under pretence of fears that it would be stolen from me, if it was left open in the loft of the kitchen that I lodged in.

This day being Sunday, I did not go to the field to work as usual, on that day, but under pretence of being unwell, remained in the kitchen all day, to be the better prepared for the toils of the following night. After daylight had totally disappeared, taking my bag under my arm, under pretence of going to the mill to grind my corn, I stole softly across the cotton fields to the nearest woods and taking an observation of the stars, directed my course to the eastward, resolved that in no event should any thing induce me to travel a single yard, on the high road, until at least one hundred miles from this plantation. Keeping on steadily through the whole of this night, and meeting with no swamps, or briery thickets in my way, I have no doubt that before daylight, the plantation was more than thirty miles behind me.

Twenty years before this, I had been in Savannah and noted at that time that great numbers of ships were in that port, taking in loading of cotton. My plan now was to reach Savannah, in the best way I could, by some means to be devised after my arrival in the city, to procure a passage to some of the northern cities.

When day appeared before me, I was in a large cotton field, and before the woods could be reached, it was gray dawn; but the forest bordering on the field was large and afforded me good shelter through the day, under the cover of a large thicket of swamp laurel, that lay at the distance of a quarter of a mile from the field. It now became necessary to kindle a fire, for all my stock of provisions, consisting of corn and potatoes, was raw and undressed. Less fortunate now than in my former flight, no fire apparatus was in my possession, and driven at last to the extremity, I determined to endeavour to produce fire by rubbing two sticks together, and spent at least two hours of incessant toil, in this vain operation, without the least prospect of success. Abandoning this project at length, I turned my thoughts to searching for a stone of some kind, with which to endeavour to extract fire from an old jack knife, that had been my companion in Maryland for more than three years. My labours were fruitless. No stone could be found in this swamp; and the day was passed in anxiety and hunger, a few raw potatoes being my only food.

Night at length came, and with it a renewal of my travelling labours. Avoiding with the utmost care, every appearance of a road, and pursuing my way until daylight, I must have travelled at least thirty miles this night. Awhile before day, in crossing a field, I fortunately came upon a bed of large pebbles, on the side of a hill. Several of these were deposited in my bag, which enabled me when day arrived to procure fire, with which I parched corn and roasted potatoes sufficient to subsist me for two or three days. On the fourth night of my journey, fortune directed me to a broad, open highway, that appeared to be much travelled.

Near the side of this road, I established my quarters for the day in a thick pine wood, for the purpose of making observations upon the people who travelled it, and of judging thence of the part of the country to which it led.

Soon after daylight, a wagon passed along, drawn by oxen, and loaded with bales of cotton; then followed by some white men on horseback, and soon after sunrise, a whole train of wagons and carts, all loaded with bales of cotton, passed by, following the wagon first seen by me. In the course of the day, at least one hundred wagons and carts passed along this road, towards the south-east, all laden with cotton bales; and at least an equal number came towards the west, either laden with casks of various dimensions, or entirely empty. Numerous horsemen, many carriages, and great numbers of persons on foot, also passed to and fro on this road, in the course of the day.

All these indications satisfied me, that I must be near some large town, the seat of an extensive cotton market. The next consideration with me was to know how far it was to this town, for which purpose I determined to travel on the road, the succeeding night.

Lying in the woods, until about eleven o'clock, I rose, came to the road, and travelled it until within an hour of daylight, at which time the country around me appeared almost wholly clear of timber; and houses became much more numerous than they had been in the former part of my journey.

Things continued to wear this aspect until daylight, when I stopped, and sat down by the side of a high fence that stood beside the road. After remaining here a short time, a wagon laden with cotton, passed along, drawn by oxen, whose driver, a black man, asked me if I was going towards town. Being answered in the affirmative, he then asked me if I did not wish to ride in his wagon. I told him I had been out of town all night, and should be very thankful to him for a ride; at the same time ascending his wagon and placing myself in a secure and easy position, on the bags of cotton.

In this manner we travelled on for about two hours, when we entered the town of Savannah. In my situation there was no danger of any one suspecting me to be a runaway slave; for no runaway had ever been known to flee from the country, and seek refuge in Savannah.

The man who drove the wagon, passed through several of the principal streets of the city, and stopped his team before a large warehouse, standing on a wharf, looking into the river. Here I assisted my new friend to unload his cotton and when we were done, he invited me to share his breakfast with him, consisting of corn bread, roasted potatoes, and some cold boiled rice.

Whilst we were at our breakfast, a black man came along the street, and asked us if we knew where he could hire a hand, to help him to work a day or two. I at once replied that my master had sent me to town, to hire myself out for a few weeks, and that I was ready to go with him immediately. The joy I felt at finding employment, so overcame me, that all thought of my wages was forgotten. Bidding farewell to the man who had given me my breakfast, and thanking him in my heart for his kindness, I followed my new employer, who informed me that he had engaged to remove a thousand bales of cotton from a large warehouse, to the end of a wharf at which a ship lay, that was taking in the cotton as a load.

This man was a slave, but hired his time of his master at two hundred and fifty dollars a year, which he said he paid in monthly instalments. He did what he called job work, which consisted of undertaking jobs, and hiring men to work under him, if the job was too great to be performed by himself. In the present instance he had seven or eight black men, beside me, all hired to help him to remove the cotton in wheel-barrows, and lay it near the end of the wharf, when it was taken up by sailors and carried on board the ship, that was receiving it.

We continued working hard all day, and amongst the crew of the ship was a black man, with whom I resolved to become acquainted by some means. Accordingly at night, after we had quit our work, I went to the end of the wharf against which the ship lay moored, and stood there a long time, waiting for the black sailor to make his appearance on deck. At length my desires were gratified. He came upon the deck, and sat down near the main-mast, with a pipe in his mouth, which he was smoking with great apparent pleasure. After a few minutes, I spoke to him, for he had not yet seen me, as it appeared, and when he heard my voice, he rose up and came to the side of the ship near where I stood. We entered into conversation together, in the course of which he informed me that his home was in New-York; that he had a wife and several children there, but that he followed the sea for a livelihood, and knew no other mode of life. He also asked me where my master lived, and if Georgia had always been the place of my residence.

I deemed this a favourable opportunity of effecting the object I had in view, in seeking the acquaintance of this man, and told him at once that by law and justice I was a free man; but had been kidnapped near Baltimore, forcibly brought to Georgia, and sold there as a slave. That I was now a fugitive from my master, and in search of some means of getting back to my wife and children.

The man seemed moved by the account of my sufferings, and at the close of my narrative, told me he could not receive me on board the ship, as the captain had given positive orders to him, not to let any of the negroes of Savannah come on board, lest they should steal something belonging to the ship. He further told me that he was on watch, and should continue on deck two hours. That he was forced to take a turn of watching the ship every night, for two hours; but that his turn would not come the next night until after midnight.

I now begged him to enable me to secrete myself on board the ship, previous to the time of her sailing, so that I might be conveyed to Philadelphia, whither the ship was bound with her load of cotton. He at first received my application with great coldness and said he would not do any thing contrary to the orders of the captain; but before we parted, he said he should be glad to assist me if he could, but that the execution of the plan proposed by me, would be attended with great dangers, if not ruin.

In my situation there was nothing too hazardous for me to undertake, and I informed him that if he would let me hide myself in the hold of the ship amongst the bags of cotton, no one should ever know that he had any knowledge of the fact; and that all the danger, and all the disasters that might attend the affair, should fall exclusively on me. He finally told me to go away, and that he would think of the matter until the next day.

It was obvious that his heart was softened in my favour; that his feelings of compassion almost impelled him to do an act in my behalf, that was forbidden by his judgment, and his sense of duty to his employers. As the houses of the city were now closed, and I was a stranger in the place, I went to a wagon that stood in front of the warehouse, and had been unladen of the cotton that had been brought in it, and creeping into it, made my bed with the driver, who permitted me to share his lodgings amongst some corn tops, that he had brought to feed his oxen.

When the morning came, I went again to the ship, and when the people came on deck, asked them for the captain, whom I should not have known by his dress, which was very nearly similar to that of the sailors. On being asked if he did not wish to hire a hand, to help to load his ship, he told me I might go to work amongst the men, if I chose, and he would pay me what I was worth.

My object was to procure employment on board the ship, and not to get wages; and in the course of this day I found means to enter the hold of the ship several times, and examine it minutely. The black sailor promised that he would not betray me, and that if I could find the means of escaping on board the ship he would not disclose it.

At the end of three days, the ship had taken in her loading, and the captain said in my presence, that he intended to sail the day after. No time was now to be lost, and asking the captain what he thought I had earned, he gave me three dollars, which was certainly very liberal pay, considering that during the whole time that I had worked for him, my fare had been the same as that of the sailors, who had as much as they could consume, of excellent food.

The sailors were now busy in trimming the ship, and making ready for sea, and observing, that this work required them to spend much time in the hold of the ship, I went to the captain and told him, that as he had paid me good wages, and treated me well, I would work with his people, the residue of this day, for my victuals and half a gallon of molasses: which he said he would give me. My first object now, was to get into the hold of the ship with those who were adjusting the cargo. The first time the men below called for aid, I went to them, and being there, took care to remain with them. Being placed at one side of the hold, for the purpose of packing the bags close to the ship's timbers, I so managed, as to leave a space between two of the bags, large enough for a man to creep in, and conceal himself. This cavity was near the opening in the centre of the hold, that was left to let men get down, to stow away the last of the bags that were put in. In this small hollow retreat amongst the bags of cotton, I determined to take my passage to Philadelphia, if by any means I could succeed in stealing on board the ship at night.

When the evening came, I went to a store near the wharf, and bought two jugs, one that held half a gallon, and the other, a large stone jug holding more than three gallons. When it was dark, I filled my large jug with water; purchased twenty pounds of pilot bread at a bakery, which I tied in a large handkerchief; and taking my jugs in my hand, went on board the ship to receive my molasses of the captain, for the labour of the day. The captain was not on board, and a boy gave me the molasses; but, under pretence of waiting to see the captain, I sat down between two rows of cotton bales, that were stowed on deck. The night was very dark, and, watching a favourable opportunity, when the man on deck had gone forward, succeeded in placing both my jugs upon the bags of cotton that rose in the hold, almost to the deck. In another moment, I glided down amongst the cargo; and lost no time in placing my jugs in the place provided for them, amongst the bales of cotton, beside the lair provided for myself.

Soon after I had taken my station for the voyage, the captain came on board, and the boy reported to him, that he had paid me off, and dismissed me. In a short time, all was quiet on board the ship, except the occasional tread of the man on watch. I slept none at all this night; the anxiety that oppressed me, preventing me from taking any repose.

Before day the captain was on deck, and gave orders to the seamen, to clear the ship for sailing, and to be ready to descend the river with the ebb tide, which was expected to flow at sunrise. I felt the motion of the ship when she got under weigh, and thought the time long before I heard the breakers of the ocean surging against her sides.

In the place where I lay, when the hatches were closed, total darkness prevailed; and I had no idea of the lapse of time, or of the progress we made, until, having at one period crept out into the open space, between the rows of cotton bags, which I have before described, I heard a man, who appeared from the sound of his voice to be standing on the hatch, call out and say, "That is Cape Hatteras." I had already come out of my covert, several times, into the open space; but the hatches were closed so tightly, as to exclude all light. It appeared to me that we had already been at sea a long time; but as darkness was unbroken with me, I could not make any computation of periods.

Soon after this, the hatch was opened, and the light was let into the hold. A man descended for the purpose of examining the state of the cargo; who returned in a short time. The hatch was again closed and nothing of moment occurred from this time, until I heard and felt the ship strike against some solid body. In a short time I heard much noise, and a multitude of sounds of various kinds. All this satisfied me, that the ship was in some port; for I no longer heard the sound of the waves, nor perceived the least motion in the ship.

At length the hatch was again opened, and the light was let in upon me. My anxiety now was, to escape fromthe ship, without being discovered by any one; to accomplish which I determined to issue from the hold as soon as night came on, if possible. Waiting until sometime after daylight had disappeared, I ventured to creep to the hatchway, and raise my head above deck. Seeing no one on board, I crawled out of the hold, and stepped on board a ship that lay alongside of that in which I had come a passenger. Here a man seized me, and called me a thief, saying I had come to rob his ship; and it was with much difficulty that I prevailed upon him to let me go. He at length permitted me to go on the wharf; and I once more felt myself a freeman.

I did not know what city I was in; but as the sailors had all told me, at Savannah that their ship was bound to Philadelphia, I had no doubt of being in that city. In going along the street, a black man met me, and I asked him if I was in Philadelphia. This question caused the stranger to laugh loudly: and he passed on without giving me any answer. Soon afterwards I met an old gentleman, with drab clothes on, as I could see by the light of the lamps. To him I propounded the same question, that had been addressed a few moment before to the black man. This time, however, I received a civil answer: being told that I was in Philadelphia.

This gentleman seemed concerned for me, either because of my wretched and ragged appearance, or because I was a stranger, and did not know where I was. Whether for the one cause or the other, I know not; but he told me to follow him, and led me to the house of a black man, not far off, whom he directed to take care of me until the morning. In this house I was kindly entertained all night, and when the morning came, the old gentleman in drab clothes returned, and brought with him an entire suit of clothes, not more than half worn, of which he made me a present, and gave me money to buy a hat and some muslin for a couple of shirts. He then turned to go away, and said, "I perceive that thee is a slave, and has run away from thy master. Thee can now go to work for thy living; but take care that they do not catch thee again." I then told him, that I had been a slave, and had twice run away and escaped from the state of Georgia. The gentleman seemed a little incredulous of that which I told him; but when I explained to him the cause of the condition in which he found me, he seemed to become more than ever interested in my fate. This gentleman, whose name I shall not publish, has always been a kind friend to me.

After remaining in Philadelphia a few weeks, I resolved to return to my little farm in Maryland, for the purpose of selling my property for as much as it would produce, and of bringing my wife and children to Pennsylvania.

On arriving in Baltimore, I went to a tavern keeper, whom I had formerly supplied with vegetables from my garden. This man appeared greatly surprised to see me; and asked me how I had managed to escape from my master in Georgia. I told him, that the man who had taken me to Georgia was not my master; but had kidnapped me, and carried me away by violence. The tavern keeper then told me, that I had better leave Baltimore as soon as possible, and showed me a handbill that was stuck up against the wall of his bar-room, in which a hundred and fifty dollars reward was offered for my apprehension. I immediately left this house, and fled from Baltimore that very night.

When I reached my former residence, I found a white man living in it, whom I did not know. This man, on being questioned by me, as to the time he had owned this place, and the manner in which he had obtained possession, informed me, that a black man had formerly lived here; but he was a runaway slave, and his master had come, the summer before, and carried him off. That the wife of the former owner of the house, was also a slave; and that her master had come about six weeks before the present time, and taken her and her children, and sold them in Baltimore to a slave-dealer from the south.

This man also informed me, that he was not in this neighbourhood at the time the woman and her children were carried away; but that he had received his information from a black woman, who lived half a mile off.

This black woman I was well acquainted with; she had been my neighbour, and I knew her to be my friend. She had been set free, some years before by a gentleman of this neighbourhood, and resided under his protection, on a part of his land. I immediately went to the house of this woman, who could scarcely believe the evidence of her own eyes, when she saw me enter her door. The first words she spoke to me were, "Lucy and her children have all been stolen away." At my request, she gave me the following account of the manner in which my wife and children, all of whom had been free from their birth, were seized and driven into southern slavery.

"A few weeks," said she, "after they took you away, and before Lucy had so far recovered from the terror produced by that event, as to remain in her house all night with her children, without some other company, I went one evening to stay all night with her; a kindness that I always rendered her, if no other person came to remain with her.

"It was late when we went to bed, perhaps eleven o'clock; and after we had been asleep some time, we were awakened by a loud rap at the door. At first we said nothing; but upon the rap being several times repeated, Lucy asked who was there. She was then told, in a voice that seemed by its sound to be that of a woman, to get up and open the door; adding, that the person without had something to tell her that she wished to hear. Lucy, supposing the voice to be that of a black woman, the slave of a lady living near, rose and opened the door; but, to our astonishment, instead of a woman coming in, four or five men rushed into the house, and immediately closed the door; at which one of the men stood, with his back against it, until the others made a light in the fire place, and proceeded deliberately to tie Lucy with a rope. Search was then made in the bed for the children; and I was found, and dragged out. This seemed to produce some consternation amongst the captors, whose faces were all black, but whose hair and visages were those of white men. A consultation was held amongst them, the object of which was to determine whether I should also be taken along with Lucy and the children, or be left behind, on account of the interest which my master was supposed to feel for me.

"It was finally agreed, that as it would be very dangerous to carry me off, lest my old master should cause pursuit to be made after them, they would leave me behind, and take only Lucy and the children. One of the number then said it would not do to leave me behind, and at liberty, as I would immediately go and give intelligence of what I had seen; and if the affair should be discovered by the members of the abolition society, before they had time to get out of Maryland, they would certainly be detected and punished for the crimes they were committing.

"It was finally resolved to tie me with cords, to one of the logs of the housegag me by tying a rope in my mouth, and confining it closely at the back of my neck. They immediately confined me, and then took the children from the bed. The oldest boy they tied to his mother, and compelled them to go out of the house together. The three youngest children were then taken out of bed, and carried off in the hands of the men who had tied me to the log. I never saw nor heard any more of Lucy or her children.

"For myself, I remained in the house, the door of which was carefully closed, and fastened after it was shut, until the second night after my confinement, without any thing to eat or drink. On the second night some unknown persons came and cut the cords that bound me, when I returned to my own cabin."

This intelligence almost deprived me of life; it was the most dreadful of all the misfortunes that I had ever suffered. It was now clear that some slave-dealer had come in my absence, and seized my wife and children as slaves, and sold them to such men as I had served in the south. They had now passed into hopeless bondage, and were gone forever beyond my reach. I myself was advertised as a fugitive slave, and was liable to be arrested at each moment, and dragged back to Georgia. I rushed out of my own house in despair and returned to Pennsylvania with a broken heart.

For the last few years, I have resided about fifty miles from Philadelphia, where I expect to pass the evening of my life, in working hard for my subsistence, without the least hope of ever again seeing my wife and children:— fearful, at this day, to let my place of residence be known, lest even yet it may be supposed, that as an article of property, I am of sufficient value to be worth pursuing in my old age.

THE END.